The New Testament in Cross-Cultural Perspective

MATRIX
The Bible in Mediterranean Context

Forthcoming volumes in the series

Douglas E. Oakman
Jesus and the Peasants

Stuart L. Love
Jesus and Marginal Women:
Healing in Matthew's Gospel

The New Testament in Cross-Cultural Perspective

RICHARD L. ROHRBAUGH

Cascade Books
A division of *Wipf & Stock Publishers*
199 West 8th Avenue, Suite 3 • Eugene OR 97401

THE NEW TESTAMENT IN CROSS-CULTURAL PERSPECTIVE
Matrix: The Bible in Mediterranean Context

Cascade Books
A Division of Wipf and Stock Publishers
199 W. 8th Ave., Suite 3
Eugene, OR 97401

ISBN 10: 1-59752-827-7
ISBN 13: 978-1-59752-827-6

Cataloging-in-Publication data:

Rohrbaugh, Richard L.
The New Testament in cross-cultural perspective / Richard L. Rohrbaugh
Matrix: The Bible in Mediterranean Context

xvi + 212 p.; 23 cm.

ISBN 10: 1-59752-827-7
ISBN 13: 978-1-59752-827-6

1. Bible. N. T.—Social scientific criticism. 2. Bible. N. T. Gospels—Criticism, interpretation, etc. 3. Jesus Christ. I Title. II. Series.

BS2545 .S55 R64 2007

Manufactured in the U.S.A.

Table of Contents

Acknowledgments

The following essays are reprinted with permission of the publishers.

1. Chapter one, "Hermeneutics as Cross-Cultural Encounter: Obstacles to Understanding," was first published in *Hervormde Teologiese Studies* 62 (2006) 1–18.

2. Chapter three, "Luke's Jesus: Honor Claimed, Honor Tested" originally appeared under the title "Legitimating Sonship? A Test of Honour: A Social Science Study of Luke 4:1–30," in *Modelling Early Christianity: Social-scientific Studies of the New Testament in Its Context*, edited by Philip F. Esler (London: Routledge, 1995) 183–97.

3. Chapter four, "Semiotic Behavior in Luke and John" was first published in *Hervormde Teologiese Studies* 58 (2002) 746–66.

4. Chapter five, "What Did Jesus Know (About Himself) and When Did He Know It?" was first published as "Ethnocentrism and Historical Questions," in *The Social Setting of Jesus and the Gospels* edited by Wolfgang Stegemann, Bruce J. Malina, and Gerd Theissen (Minneapolis: Fortress, 2003) 27–43. It also appeared in German in 2003 as "Die Frage nach dem messianichen Bewusstsein Jesu: Ethnozentrismus und historische Fragen," in *Jesus im Neuen Kontexten*, Wolfgang Stegemann, Bruce J. Malina, and Gerd Theissen (Stuttgart: Kohlhammer, 2002) 212–23.

5. Chapter six, "Zacchaeus: Defender of the Honor of Jesus," will appear in a volume in honor of Marvin L. Chaney, *To Break Every Yoke*, edited by Robert B. Coote and Norman K. Gottwald (Sheffield: Sheffield Phoenix, forthcoming).

6. Chapter seven, "A Dysfunctional Family and Its Neighbors: Luke 15:11-32," appeared in *Perspectives on the Parables: Images of Jesus in His Contemporary Setting*, edited by V. George Shillington (Edinburgh: T. & T. Clark, 1998) 141–64.

7. Chapter eight, "The Parable of the Talents/Pounds: A Text of Terror?" was first published in *Biblical Theology Bulletin* 23 (1993) 32–39.

8. Chapter nine, "Gossip in the New Testament," was first published in *Social Scientific Models for Interpreting the Bible: Essays by The Context Group in Honor of Bruce J. Malina*, Biblical Interpretation Series 53 (Leiden: Brill, 2001) 239–59.

9. Chapter ten, "The Preindustrial City in Luke-Acts: Urban Social Relations, A Study of Luke 14:15–24," originally appeared in *The Social World of Luke-Acts: Models for Interpretation*, edited by Jerome H. Neyrey (Peabody, MA: Hendrickson, 1991) 125–49.

10. Chapter eleven, "What's the Matter with Nicodemus? A Social Science Perspective on John 3:1–21," first appeared in *Distant Voices Drawing Near: Essays in Honor of Antoinette Clark Wire*, edited by Holly Hearon (Collegeville, MN: Liturgical, 2004) 145–58.

The diagram on p. 112 "Characteristics of Money" is from Michael Taussig, *The Devil and Commodity Fetishism in South America* (Chapel Hill: University of North Carolina Press, 1980). Used by permission of the publisher.

Preface

THE BIBLE is not a Western book. To be sure, it has generated ideas and attitudes that can be found everywhere in Western cultural and religious history. But the plain fact is that it was written by, for, and about people in the ancient Mediterranean world whose culture, worldview, social patterns, and daily expectations differed sharply from those of the modern West. The simple reality is that in spite of our fondest personal hopes, and even our religious aspirations, the Bible was not written for us.

That said, the question immediately arises whether modern Americans can read the Bible in a meaningful way. Is it possible to hear anything close to what it said to its first readers and still come away with something that is relevant to us now? The argument in these pages will be that it is indeed possible, though it is not nearly as simple or straightforward as we have often tried to pretend. Anachronistic and ethnocentric reading of the Bible is so deeply ingrained in contemporary Christianity that much needs to be un-learned or set aside if we are to understand. In fact, we need to learn a new approach to reading. We need to learn all we can about the cultural world in which the Bible was produced and to which it spoke. We need to learn how to minimize our habitual, though normally unconscious, cultural distortions of the Bible. And most importantly, we need to recognize that, for better or worse, we frequently import our contemporary self-understanding into biblical stories unawares. Indeed, we imagine them speaking to problems and needs that never would have occurred to anyone in the ancient Mediterranean world.

Long ago the ancient psalmist, living in exile in Babylon, sang a mournful song: "How can we sing the Lord's song in a foreign land?" (Ps 137:4). While our circumstances may be rather less traumatic than those of the exiled psalmist, nonetheless the Bible is now being subjected (yes, *subjected* is the right word) to readings its authors not only did not anticipate but probably could not have understood had they tried. Reading the Bible in this foreign land—in the USA, in this land to which it was never addressed—turns out to be more difficult than we have heretofore imagined.

Language and Its Social Context

In the pages that follow we shall explore in some detail the full implications of what this means. We shall raise important questions about how the biblical texts might have been understood by those who read them first. We shall suggest that modern, Western interpretation has often had little in common with ancient ways of understanding. We shall describe the ancient social/cultural context of each text we explore in order to understand the connection between what is written and the ancient social realities it encodes. But before doing that a couple of brief comments are necessary about the way language and social system are related.

It should be self-evident that not everything necessary for understanding can be written down, because a text simply cannot say everything that needs to be known about the topic under discussion. To say everything would be tedious in the extreme. A text would be cluttered to the point of unreadability, and the conversation partners (writer and reader) would simply cease to interact. Inevitably then there is much that a text can only sketch in outline and even more that has to be left to the imagination of the reader. Because this is so, an author inescapably depends upon the general cultural knowledge a reader can supply from his or her own resources to "complete" the text. Successful communication can be carried on in no other way.

For example, a writer in contemporary America who refers to "Katrina" for the first time in a story has no need to explain that this was a hurricane, indeed the worst hurricane ever to hit the United States. No explanation is required that it devastated the city of New Orleans. Because that event has now become a part of our cultural history, an American reader can be counted upon to understand the reference to Katrina and to provide the necessary visual imagery.

Such pictures are not only worth a thousand words; they can save that many and more if supplied by the reader rather than the writer. In other words, written texts always have a kind of "indeterminacy" that requires the reader to participate actively in their completion. Without this a reader would remain largely unengaged and probably bored as well. Written texts provide what is necessary, but they cannot provide everything.

The primary reason all this works is that reading, writing, speaking, and listening are in a very fundamental way *social* acts. Meaning in language is embedded in a social system that ideally is shared and understood by all participants in any communication process. While meanings not rooted in a shared social system can sometimes be communicated, such communication is inevitably fraught with difficulty and often requires extended explanation because a writer cannot depend upon the reader to conjure up the proper sets of related images or concepts needed to complete the text.

Thinking about modern American readers reading ancient Mediterranean texts requires us to clarify the situation one step further. Each time a text is read by a new reader, the fields of reference tend to shift and multiply because each new reader fills in the text in a unique way. Among some literary theorists this latter phenomenon is called "recontextualization." The term refers to the multiple ways different readers may "complete" a text as a result of reading it over against their different social contexts (texts may also be "decontextualized" when read a ahistorically for their aesthetic or formal characteristics).

Such recontextualization is of course familiar to students of the Synoptic Gospels. It is nicely illustrated in the work of redaction critics who have shown us how shifts in the settings of the parables of Jesus in the various Gospels have altered their emphasis and/or meaning (e.g., the parable of the lost sheep in Matthew 18:12–13; Luke 15:4–6; *Gospel of Thomas* 98:22–27). In whatever measure each of these new recontextualizations of the Jesus story "completes" the text differently than an original hearer of Jesus might have done, an interpretative step of significant proportions has been taken.

The same is true for recontextualizations into the world of the modern reader. It cannot be stressed enough that when you move language, you change its meaning. The English word *hot*, for example, means one thing on the desert but something quite different on a basketball court. *Cool* means something different in the context of a teenage conversation than it does in a television weather report. In the chapter that follows this relation of language to context will be explored in greater detail because the matter is complex and requires considerable analysis. But for now we can say that whenever language is moved, whether socially, culturally, historically, or even physically, the meaning is inevitably altered.

Of course moving the biblical text from the ancient Mediterranean cultural context in which it was written to a new setting in the Western industrialized societies of the modern era is a very far-reaching recontextualization indeed. No New Testament writer could have anticipated an American reader. No New Testament writer shared most of the experiences, expectations, knowledge, or even values we bring to our reading of his work. The objection that religious texts such as the Bible transcend culture, and that such texts thus speak to universal human needs, unfortunately obscures the fact that the *means* by which religious texts speak are intrinsic to the ancient culture to which they first spoke. Thus, attempts to abstract the meaning of a biblical text from its original social and cultural context inevitably distort what it says.

Of critical importance for us therefore is honest recognition that this particular recontextualization, this peculiar modernization of the text that takes place when we Americans read it, is truly profound. Having been socialized in the modern industrial world we simply lack the resources to complete *any* piece of the New Testament in ways its ancient authors could have imagined.

In sum, we insist that meanings drawn from reading the Bible inevitably derive from some social system—either from the ancient one in which it was written or from the modern one in which it is read. That is because reading is *always* a social act. If both reader and writer share the same social system, the same experience, the same resources for filling in the unwritten part of the text, adequate communication is highly probable. But if writer and reader come from mutually alien social systems, as do ancient Israelites and modern Americans, then as a rule, non-understanding, or at best misunderstanding, will be the case. We simply will not assume the same social context in which to place what is being said and thus will not complete the text in the same manner.

Our claim then is that understanding the range of meanings that would have been plausible to a first-century reader of the New Testament requires the contemporary reader to seek access to the social system(s) available to the original audience. We need to re-attach text and original context. There is no other way to read responsibly. Moreover, to recover these social systems, in whatever measure that is possible, we assert that it is essential to employ adequate, explicit, social science models that have been drawn especially from circum-Mediterranean social and cultural studies. That approach will be seen in all of the studies that follow. Our claim is that whatever limitations such models might have, the world they describe is closer to the world of the Bible by several orders of magnitude than are *any* of the scenes we are likely to conjure up from contemporary experience. Only with the aid of such models can we read and complete with genuine understanding the written texts which, for better or worse, we have imported into an alien world.

The Essays

Most of the essays that follow have appeared in widely scattered journals or collections and are here brought together for the first time. The purpose of this collection is to demonstrate the nature and implications of reading a Mediterranean Bible in an American world. All are studies of texts in the Gospels—which have been the focus of much of my research over the years.

All presume an original audience socialized in the first century Mediterranean world and thus all set the texts being studied in that particular social context.

No claim is made here that we can re-create the ancient Mediterranean world completely or even in the measure we would like. We lack the evidence necessary to do so along with the local informants who might correct our work. The use of social science models drawn from ethnographic studies of the Mediterranean world offers the closest approximation of the ancient agrarian we can now produce, though readers will always need to remember that they are just that: approximations. Yet we trust that the heuristic utility of these approximations will be self-evident as the reading proceeds.

The initial essay is theoretical in nature rather than a study of a particular New Testament text. It will suggest some of the difficulties we face when reading cross-culturally (modern Americans reading an ancient Mediterranean Bible) and will further develop the arguments offered above about the relation of language and culture.

Chapter two is a previously unpublished essay locating Jesus in the social matrix of the ancient world. Since much of what follows in this book is an attempt to understand Jesus in the ancient agrarian context, it is perhaps appropriate at the outset to offer brief comment about the place of Jesus in the social matrix of his time. In spite of Western attempts to turn him into a middle-class image of ourselves (there was no middle class in antiquity), he was not. He came from the lowest strata of the agrarian society and thereby presented the Gospel writers with a considerable challenge as they sought to gain a hearing for him. Subsequent chapters will make that clear.

Chapter three acknowledges that Luke had the challenge of presenting Jesus as a person of high honor in order to gain a hearing for him in Greco-Roman world. Given Jesus's origins as a low-status village trade worker, that was a challenge of considerable proportions. Claiming Jesus was no less than the Son of God, Luke meets the challenge in a way guaranteed to catch the attention of any ancient reader.

Chapter four presses this issue a bit further in the Gospel of Luke but then contrasts Luke's strategy with that in the Gospel of John. It acknowledges that reading audiences have expectations derived from conventions in society. When authors follow convention, communication flows naturally. When they violate it, they draw attention to what they are doing: audiences are surprised or challenged. Both Luke and John are faced with the challenge of commending Jesus to a reading audience. In commending Jesus to readers, Luke follows convention, providing what his audience would expect. John, however, defies expectations, drawing special attention to his way of presenting Jesus.

The next chapter takes on one of the key questions in all of New Testament study: What did Jesus know and when did he know it? Was he born with a sense that he was the Messiah? Or did he acquire it somewhere along the way? The study focuses on a central text in the Gospel of Mark (8:27–30) that Western scholars have always taken as the climactic moment when the disciples finally recognize who Jesus is. Using the collectivist understanding of identity common in the ancient Mediterranean world, we will suggest exactly the opposite: it is a moment of recognition for Jesus.

For a century and a half scholars have argued over the statement of Zacchaeus in Luke 19:8. Is it that of a repentant sinner resolved to reform his wicked ways? Or is it a defiant self-defense of Zacchaeus's customary behavior in the face of the crowd's hostility? Chapter six will argue that both views fail to take account of the Mediterranean codes of honor and hospitality. Thereby both miss the way Zacchaeus (and thus Luke) defends the honor of Jesus.

Few stories of Jesus are better known than the parable of the so-called prodigal son. To Western readers it is the story of a loving father (an analog for God) welcoming home a long lost son. For us it is all about repentance and forgiveness. Chapter seven will suggest something quite different: that Jesus uses the story to describe what happens when greed tears a family apart and destroys its place in the village.

The parable of the talents is another all-time American favorite. To us it sounds like nothing less than homespun capitalism on the lips of Jesus; indeed it seems like the very kind of self-confirmation we love to recite. In the peasant world of Jesus, however, the story more likely read as a resounding critique of greed and those who exploit the poor.

While gossip and gossipers have been much maligned throughout human history, in oral societies gossip played a very important role in enabling the community to function. It served a wide variety of purposes and played an important role as an informal social means of controlling behavior. Moreover, as the Gospel writers frequently observe, it was a primary means by which listeners evaluated and reported on the teachings of Jesus.

Chapter ten offers a study of yet another parable of Jesus, the one about a dinner invitation gone awry in Luke 14. It makes use of an important model of the preindustrial city, together with the peculiar characteristics of dinner invitations in Mediterranean culture, to describe Luke's critique of rich Christians refusing table fellowship with the poor. Set in the ancient context, the apparently hokey excuses of the original invitees to the dinner will all of a sudden make sense.

The story of Nicodemus in John 3 is usually taken as an example of Johannine conversations filled with double entendre and irony, offering Jesus the opportunity for extended, explanatory theological discourse. Chapter eleven will suggest something far different: The conversation with Nicodemus portrays the experience of outsiders first encountering the strange anti-language of the Johannine Jesus. This is a language designed to obscure, not to reveal, and Nicodemus falls victim in classic fashion.

Finally, a brief epilogue offers a few additional reflections on the hermeneutical problem. The remarks are in the form of a brief personal statement on what motivated the kind of study this volume represents. While it is true that placing the texts in their original social context has the effect of distancing them from us and our world, seemingly making them alien to our hopes and experience, the intent of our study is not to imply that we must leave the matter there. Rather it is to argue that it is only if we can hear the texts on their own terms and avoid (at least some of) the cultural distortions introduced by our contemporary social location, that we can begin to ask whether they can be transposed into something relevant to our world.

Jumping in without this kind of preliminary study risks making the texts mere platforms for declarations of our own creation. We claim to be reading, but are in fact projecting ourselves through the medium of the Bible. As the epilogue will make clear, that remains a besetting ill of much contemporary exegesis. And that in turn points to a wonderful irony that every American reading or studying the Bible must ultimately face: an illiterate peasant living today in one of the remote villages of the Middle East can in many ways understand the Bible more readily than any American. That is because he or she still lives the way of life out of which the Bible came. Of course that way of life is rapidly disappearing and even today is not exactly like the world of Jesus. But it is a whole lot closer than anything in North America has ever been, for even one day in its history. Our only choice, therefore, is to make up with research and education what we lack in native socialization. Our claim is that to the degree that we can do that, closing that cultural gap with hard-earned cross-cultural learning and understanding, it will be possible to open up the writings of the New Testament in a whole new way. And it is with that intent that the studies that follow have been collected in this volume.

CHAPTER I

Hermeneutics as Cross-Cultural Encounter: Obstacles to Understanding

Traffic signs in the American city assume that drivers need directions on how to get to certain destinations. For instance, in Washington, D.C. drivers can pick up directional signs miles distant from the destination. Directions are given by signs placed where drivers must make a choice between two or more alternative routes and again where they will inform drivers that they have made the correct choice. The principle of giving directions to an airport seems clear enough, but consider the situation in a Japanese city where signs are posted according to a different principle. In Tokyo, drivers on their way to the international airport find that the road is marked for the airport only after the last point of choice is behind and the only possible destination up front is the airport.[1]

BAFFLING. THERE must be something wrong with the Japanese—or so it would seem to most Westerners. But of course such cross-cultural disconnects have become the stuff of legend and nearly every traveler who has spent sufficient time in another culture has a stock of similar stories to tell. Cross-cultural communication is fraught with so many difficulties that in recent years a cottage industry has emerged aimed at sensitizing western diplomats, business people, exchange students, and the like to the problems of intercultural communication.[2]

A curiosity here is that while there is widespread recognition of the problem of intercultural communication in face-to-face cross-cultural encounters, it is less often recognized especially by Westerners that intercultural problems

---

[1] Stewart and Bennett, *American Cultural Patterns*, 38.

[2] Literature, training courses, and Web sites abound. Note especially the *Journal of Intercultural Communication*, the *European Journal of Intercultural Communication*, and the many publications of Intercultural Press.

exist in written communication as well. On reflection it should seem obvious that cultural disconnects in writing would be as likely as those in oral speech, but the Western (and especially American) tendency to trust the transparency of written words has a long history in our culture.[3]

That said, the claim that Westerners, like all other people, read the Bible with culturally conditioned eyes is probably news to no one—even if we do not always get the full import of that insight. At one level we know that the Bible is not in fact a Western book, that it was not written by, for, or about Americans; and yet, recent biblical scholarship remains filled with examples of what happens when Western scholars tread this ground unawares.

To understand fully what is happening, we need also to ask about the other end of the conversation: what goes on in Western minds that blocks or confuses the messages being articulated by biblical authors? What accounts for our persistent projection of ourselves and thus for our inability to read as ancient Mediterranean people did? And even more pointedly, what accounts for the near total inability in American churches to understand that the Bible is not a justification for American cultural values? In other words, why is this so intractable a problem?[4]

The Scope of this Study

It would be far beyond the scope of this chapter to list all of the possible obstacles to cross-cultural communication.[5] The matter is simply too complex and the variations on every obstacle too numerous to try to recount them all. So instead, what we propose is to sample various types of roadblocks that plague cross-cultural communication in order to make the case for thinking more carefully than we have about the *persistence* of ethnocentric interpre-

---

[3] Stewart and Bennett, *American Cultural Patterns*, 45–60.

[4] It is unfortunately true that the capitalist obsession with wealth that dominates American culture is regularly legitimated by the use of the Bible in American churches. Witness the recent popularity of the *Prayer of Jabez*. Individualistic achievement, personal problem-solving, affirmations of self-esteem, an entrepreneurial style, and a host of other peculiarly American ways of thinking and doing find ready justification in American preaching, all with the solemn assurance that we are practicing a biblical way of life. The fact is that it still has not dawned on many American preachers or readers of the Bible that the Bible was not written about "us." And in spite of our fondest hopes, it is not a warrant for the baptism of American cultural values.

[5] Obviously the most important obstacle to cross-cultural communication is simple cultural ignorance. In fact we could argue that trying to understand the "other" in cultural and social terms is simply the *sine qua non* of responsible hermeneutics. But there is much more to this story.

tation and therefore the way the peculiar Western style of communication contributes to the intractability of the problem.

A humorous example can be found in a recent publication of the Jesus Seminar, *The Five Gospels: The Search for the Authentic Words of Jesus*, written by Robert Funk and Roy Hoover. They use the following translation (from their "Scholars Version" of the five Gospels) of Jesus's statement in Matthew 6:22–23:

> The eye is the body's lamp. It follows that if your eye is clear, your whole body will be flooded with light. If your eye is clouded, your whole body will be shrouded in darkness. If, then, the light within you is darkness, how dark that can be!

The commentary then states the following:

> It was a common view in the ancient world that the eye admits light into the body (a commonsense notion). A clear eye permits the light to enter the body and penetrate the darkness. Light symbolizes good; darkness evil.[6]

That both this translation and the attendant commentary are misguided is not at all difficult to demonstrate. The notion that light comes into the eye from the outside was not in fact a common view in the ancient world; indeed Plutarch tells us exactly the opposite:

> For odor, voice, and breathing are all emanations of some kind, streams of particles from living bodies, that produce sensation whenever our organs of sense are stimulated by their impact. . . . In all probability the most active stream of such emanations is that which passes through the eye. For vision, being of enormous swiftness and carried by an essence that gives off a flame-like brilliance, diffuses wondrous influence. *(Quaest. Conv.* 680-F)

Or again, when commenting on the ancient belief in the evil eye, Plutarch says:

> Envy, which naturally roots itself more deeply in the mind than any other passion, contaminates the body too with evil. . . .When those possessed by envy to this degree let their glance fall upon a person, their eyes, which are close to the mind and draw from it the evil influence of the passion, then assail that person as if with poisoned arrows; hence, I conclude, it is not paradoxical or incredible that they should have an effect on the persons who encounter their gaze. *(Quaest. Conv.* 681D-E*)*

---

[6] Funk and Hoover, *The Five Gospels*, 151.

The point is that the ancients understood light to issue *out from the eye* and not penetrate into it. As Jesus says, "The eye is the lamp of the body." Lamps do not receive light; they emit light. Sirach reminds us that this is even true of the eyes of God: "the eyes of the Lord are ten thousand times brighter than the sun" (23:19). Thus the idea of light entering the eye was anything but a "common sense notion" in the ancient world.

In addition, lack of "clarity" of the eye (as the translation above would have it) is not really the issue in the Jesus saying at all (the Greek reads: ἐὰν δέ ὁ ὀφθαλμός σου πονηρὸς ᾖ). Rather it is the eye's capacity as an active agent to cause injury to others. As Plutarch indicates, that kind of injury is the result of envy in the heart that is projected outward through the eyes and onto its victim like a stream of poisoned particles. Such a glance can damage whatever it hits.

Of course one could claim that perhaps Funk and Hoover did not know about the evil eye and thus their statement in the Jesus Seminar translation/commentary was the result of cultural ignorance. However that is not quite the whole story. An extensive article on the evil eye and the way it functioned in antiquity was published by John H. Elliott in *Foundations and Facets Forum*.[7] It offered a clear and full explanation of evil eye belief and provided ample documentation, both ancient and modern, from around the world. Elliott's article, which appeared well before the Funk–Hoover volume, was edited by none other than Robert Funk himself. As Jesus put it: "Do you have eyes, and fail to see? Do you have ears, and fail to hear? And do you not remember?" (Mark 8:18).

The point is that it is nearly impossible for modern Americans to believe that light coming into the eye is anything but a common sense notion held by all people everywhere. Like most people, we are prone to what Laray Barna has called the "assumption of similarities"—an unwarranted belief in the universality of things.[8] Thus we cannot conceive of an intelligent person holding Plutarch's view. Yet cross-cultural studies have identified sixty-seven contemporary cultures in which belief in the evil eye persists.[9] It is anything but rare or odd. In fact it persists yet today in cultures throughout the Middle East.

Embedded in this example, therefore, is a clue that opens up the focus of the current inquiry. Cultural awareness of the "other" is only half of the equation when it comes to cross-cultural communication. Cultural *self*-awareness is equally essential if we are to understand why Americans (like all other peoples) so persistently project themselves onto the language and thinking

[7] Elliott, "The Fear of the Leer," 42–71.

[8] Barna, "Stumbling Blocks," 337.

[9] Elliott, "The Fear of the Leer," 45.

of others. Unless we know what is peculiarly American about the way we think and speak, and how our way differs from the cognitive habits and communicative style of other cultures, we are not likely to understand why we cannot accurately hear what they say (or write) even when cultural knowledge of the "other" is readily available to us. In spite of our fondness for our own culture and its way of thinking and doing, the fact is that our way is peculiar. It is not shared by the vast majority of those around the world and was never envisioned by those who wrote the Bible. Like it or not, the biblical writers did not speak American.

Our main task then is to explain why cross-cultural miscommunication persists in spite of our growing knowledge of the cultural world of the Bible. What obstacles are in the way, obstacles that we cannot seem to get around?

Obstacles to Understanding

At a rather simple and basic level, studies of cross-cultural communication indicate that when the familiar guideposts that allow people to proceed without conscious thought are missing, as they are in many cross-cultural situations, people tend to rather quickly substitute markers from their own culture. They assume that their own ways are normal, natural, and right and therefore project their own sense of things onto the situation as a simple means of finding their way.[10]

No doubt something like that is probably at work in the example from *The Five Gospels*. The familiar, the "commonsensical" (in an American mind), has replaced the unfamiliar—the belief in the evil eye—in order to make the text intelligible to American readers.

But the problem really goes much deeper than that. There are in fact a whole series of characteristically American perceptions, values, cognitive habits, and styles of communication that are getting in the way. Each in its own way contributes to the persistence of cross-cultural misunderstanding, and each filters what Americans hear when they read the Bible.

Obviously a full list of the various obstacles to cross-cultural understanding is beyond the scope of this chapter. Linguists recognize that the matter is exceedingly complex. Nonetheless a brief look at six of the more important factors that contribute to the intractability of the problem will perhaps be an adequate base from which to make the point.

---

[10] Stewart and Bennett, *American Cultural Patterns*, 3.

1. Language Availability

Language itself is a factor in the persistence of our cultural self-projection. Studies of intercultural communication have demonstrated that sensory data that cannot be named are not noticed. Moreover, it is only availability of language than enables distinctions. For example, Trukese (a Micronesian language) and Tarahumara (a Uto-Aztecan tongue) do not possess separate words for green and blue. One word covers both (*ocean color*). As a result speakers of those languages typically cannot distinguish the two colors as precisely as the typical speaker of English.[11]

In the same way, a number of Asian languages, including Japanese, have highly elaborated designations for the second-person singular that signal status distinctions between speaker and listener. To speak Japanese with someone requires a decision about which form of the personal pronoun to use. Forced with constantly making this language choice, speakers of Japanese are thus tuned in to status distinctions in ways non-Japanese speakers are not.[12]

Also well known is the fact that German offers speakers two forms of the second-person pronoun (*Sie* and *Du*). The appropriate choice depends on the social distance between persons in a dialogue. Thus Americans who prefer informality in all forms of speech, and who are not forced by their language constantly to choose between *Sie* and *Du*, lack German sensitivity to social distance.

As far back as 1956 Benjamin Whorf argued for what he called the "linguistic relativity" principle, in which users of different grammars are directed to different observations and end up with different views of the world.[13] English, for example, does not distinguish between second- person-singular and second-person-plural pronouns. The term *you* stands for both. Thus English speakers have difficulty seeing that 1 Corinthians 3:16–17 ("Do you not know that you [ὑμῖν] are God's temple?") refers not to individuals but to the Corinthian congregation as a whole. The natural tendency in an individualistic society that lacks language to make the distinction between second-person-singular and second-person-plural pronouns is to assume that the translated English pronoun *you* refers to individual believers. The lack of available language is therefore a significant factor in what listeners notice and understand in the speech of others.

---

[11] Ibid., 27, 47.

[12] Ibid., 49.

[13] Whorf, *Thought and Reality*, 221. For a review of the controversy over the Whorf hypothesis see Gudykunst, *Cross-Cultural and Intercultural Communication*, 55–56. Research indicates that Whorf's view operates more clearly on the grammatical level than on the lexical level.

2. Identity Maintenance and Identity Threats

Cultural, group, and personal identity are always involved in any kind of significant communication.[14] That is because speech creates, specifies, and projects identity. Positive and negative evaluations of the "other" and the fear of positive or negative reinforcement of one's own identity thus have a strong impact on the way people understand what is being said. Identity threats, if recognized or even suspected, often lead to either (1) the rejection of the other, (2) the projection of stereotypes onto the other or even (3) the projection of characteristics of one's own identity that are imagined to be universal.

William Gudykunst notes that the "more important the group identity the stronger the tendency to treat the outgroup as having uniform characteristics."[15] Thus to Israelites, "Cretans are always liars, vicious brutes, lazy gluttons" (Titus 1:12). Strong ingroup identification also leads to the view that outgroups are not like "us" and therefore represent a threat. Should dissimilarity be detected in the way others speak, such negative views are easily reinforced.

For our purposes it is most important to recognize that perceiving an outgroup as dissimilar creates a tendency to dislike them. Since modern Christians almost by definition should "like" the original followers of Jesus, we cannot risk imagining they were strange or too unlike ourselves. We sense intuitively that should they turn out to be quite different, Christianity and American identity would be in fundamental conflict. It therefore becomes psychologically (and theologically) necessary to see early Christians as proto-Americans. In this light it is not difficult at all to see that the incentive in American churches to view Christian faith as a baptism of American cultural values is incredibly powerful. American Christians simply cannot risk a Christianity that would threaten to disconfirm American identity and create a dislike for the actual people who followed Jesus.

Put simply, we project ourselves onto New Testament characters, including Jesus, in order to find them compatible. We feel affirmed and acceptable to God if the followers of Jesus were like us. Witness the delight with which Western capitalists "find" homespun capitalism on the lips of Jesus in the parable of the talents.[16] Never mind that capitalism did not exist in the aristocratic empires of antiquity. Never mind that investment is a modern invention or that ancient markets were anything but "free." We need it, so

---

[14] Collier, "Cultural Identity," 39; Ting-Toomey, *Communicating Across Cultures*, 267.

[15] Gudykunst, *Cross-Cultural and Intercultural Communication*, 116.

[16] For the evidence that this is a misunderstanding of the story see chapter 8 on the Parable of the Talents.

we find it. And if we can find it in the teachings of Jesus, so much the better. That is theological self-confirmation par excellence.

3. High- and Low-Context Communication: Field-Independence and Field-Dependence

A critically important contrast in styles of communication is that between high and low context societies. Edward T. Hall describes the two this way:

> A high context communication or message is one in which most of the information is either in the physical context or internalized in the person, while very little is in the coded, explicit, transmitted part of the message. A low context communication is just the opposite; i.e., the mass of the information is vested in the explicit code.[17]

Using Hall's work, Bruce Malina has demonstrated that the New Testament is in fact a high context document. [18] That is, it presumes a high knowledge of the context on the part of the reader and explains very little. By contrast, the typical low context documents of American culture explain whatever context is needed for understanding and do not presume it is known by the reader ahead of time. Note that the difference between these two types of societies is not in the importance of context, but rather in whether the speaker can presume that the listener knows the context ahead of time and does not need it spelled out.

On reflection it should be obvious that small-scale, homogeneous, face-to-face societies in which there is very little social or technological change over time would be high context societies. In such places contextual knowledge is widely shared and rarely changes. Spelling it out would be tedious and redundant. Large-scale societies, however, in which there are innumerable subcultures, pervasive specialization, rapid social and technological change and anonymous social relations inevitably require speakers and writers to explain the context or background for whatever they mean.

Richard Porter and Larry Samovar list four major differences in the communication expectations of high and low context societies (23).[19] First, low context societies take verbal messages to be the heart of the matter and do not learn how to discern information from the environment. Second, high-context people suspect the credibility of low context speakers. Third, nonverbal clues are critically important in high context cultures. And finally,

---

[17] Hall, *Beyond Culture*, 79.

[18] New Testament scholars were first introduced to the work of Edward T. Hall on "high" and "low" context societies in Malina, "Reading Theory," 3–23.

[19] Porter and Samovar, *Intercultural Communication*, 23.

in high context cultures speech is minimized. The multiplication of words draws suspicion. Note the comment of Jesus: "When you are praying, do not heap up empty phrases as the Gentiles do; for they think that they will be heard because of their many words" (Matt 6:7). The main problem here for readers of the Bible, then, is that we do not know what we do not know. The spare descriptions of context in the Bible often leave us without the essential ingredient for understanding the message.[20]

Closely related to this notion of high and low context communication is what Devorah Lieberman calls "field-dependent/field-independent" communication.[21] If high context societies expect listeners to know the context and low context societies expect to have to spell it out, nonetheless in neither type of society is context always given the same level of importance.

Field-dependent speakers assume that words, messages, context, emotional factors, and the relations between speakers are all inextricably intertwined. Abstraction is not their style. Instead they stick with context as the key to meaning. Research shows that it is collectivist cultures that are predominantly field-dependent in their style of communication. That is because speech, like identity, is understood to be a collective phenomenon. It is completely dependent on the color and character of the social relations in a given situation.

It is individualist cultures that are field-independent in their style of communication. Field-independent persons tend to abstract ideas from contextual messages and arrange them in linear, cause-effect sequences. They deemphasize the emotional or relational aspects of the communication and thereby see context as of lesser importance.

In other words, cultures differ markedly in the relative importance of context in their style of communication.[22] A story reported by Stewart and Bennett illustrates the matter:

> An American student listens with growing impatience to a Nigerian
> student, who is responding to a simple question about his religion

[20] Nowhere is this truer than in our understanding of parables. The current consensus view of parables is that they are something like open-ended, extended metaphors that force readers to arrive at their own conclusions. That may or may not be accurate, but of course the missing piece is knowledge of the context. If we knew all about the setting in which these stories were first told, perhaps we could get the point in the fashion a high context person would expect. But lacking it and, more important, lacking the sense that context is (to use Hall's term) "mutually non-detachable" from the meaning of a parable, we arrive at conclusions that often bear no relation to an ancient context whatsoever. That this "consensus" is often little more than a means of freeing ourselves from the constraints of context in order to import congenial messages of our own creation is not hard to see.

[21] Lieberman, "Ethnocognitivism," 179.

[22] Hall, *Beyond Culture*, 79.

with several long stories about his childhood. Finally, the American breaks in and makes her own point clearly and logically. The American evaluates the Nigerian negatively as being stupid or devious (for talking "in circles"). The Nigerian evaluates the American as being childish or unsophisticated (for being unable to understand subtlety). The American urges the Nigerian to state his point more clearly, and in response the Nigerian intensifies his efforts to provide more context.[23]

Nigerians assume that the conclusion, the "point," will be obvious if enough is known about the context. Since the American lacks knowledge of the Nigerian context, the Nigerian seeks to provide information about that context. Of course, had the Nigerian been speaking with someone from his own high-context culture, the stories about context would have been unnecessary. But that is not the point here. The point is that what the American student wanted from the Nigerian were the ideas abstracted from the context in typical field-independent style.

Where we get into trouble is when field-independent persons try to abstract the meaning from field-dependent communication. Abstracting information from field-dependent communication inevitably changes the meaning of that communication, even though listeners accustomed to field-independent communication have no intention of misunderstanding what has been said. Since abstraction is a common habit in the individualistic cultures of the West, and especially in Christian theology, we are often completely unaware how we change the meaning of biblical texts in the very process of deriving our theology from them.

4. Individualism and Collectivism

The differences between collectivist and individualist societies are also well known to New Testament scholars.[24] Collectivist cultures produce a dependent sense of the self as if the group *is* the self. Individualist cultures produce an independent sense of the self that remains detached. Collectivist cultures focus on community, collaboration, tradition, group values, group loyalty, and group honor. Individualistic cultures focus on individual rights, personal privacy, opinion, responsibility and autonomy, freedom, self-worth, and self-expression.

The result is that persons from these two types of cultures often have great difficulty understanding each other. In fact specialists in intercultural communication usually see the individualist–collectivist divide as the pri-

---

[23] Stewart and Bennett, *American Cultural Patterns*, 165–66.

[24] See Malina and Neyrey, "First-Century Personality," 67–96. For the use of the individualist-collectivist concept in interpreting a biblical text see chapter 5.

mary dimension of intercultural communication difficulties.[25] Recognizing that American culture is probably the most individualistic culture that has ever existed, and that the culture out of which the New Testament came was at the collectivist end of the spectrum, we should not be surprised to find miscommunication between these two cultures.

Not only do persons in these two kinds of cultures communicate differently, they also hold different expectations of what is important in the communications of others. Individualists notice what pertains to self-independency or, if they cannot find it, individualists adapt what they do find to fit that value. The widespread expectation in American Christianity that Jesus is the solution to *personal* problems, and theologies about Jesus as "personal" savior are examples of individualist Christians' adapting biblical material to fit their overriding value.

Collectivists by contrast would be more likely to assume that Jesus articulates the characteristics of a group-dependent self and offers membership in his group on the basis of loyalty, conformity, and the suppression of independent thinking. Should American Christians discover that this is what Jesus was really like, it would be hard not to imagine a growing dislike for New Testament followers of Jesus and a perceived threat to the American value of the individual.

A closely related aspect of individualist expectations is the American approval of merit rather than status. We celebrate character and identity by pointing to achievements, assuming these to be unique to each individual. Collectivist cultures, however, celebrate status rather than achievement. As a result, they are attuned to status indicators in ways Americans are not and use ascriptive language when describing persons.

Just as individualists approve of merit more than status, so also individualist cultures often fall into what Cookie and Walter Stephan call the "fundamental attribution error," that is, the western "tendency to attribute the behavior of others to internal traits."[26] Psychology becomes the explanation for human behavior and the focus of Western descriptions of persons. Psychology is imagined to explain nearly every behavior Westerners observe. Collectivist cultures, however, attribute behavior to external causes and situations. Psychology is irrelevant. For them it is context that explains the motivations for human behavior.

The extensive psychologizing of Western biblical interpretation provides an example of ethnocentric confusion on this point. The following title of

---

[25] Ting-Toomey, *Communicating Across Cultures*, 66; Anderson et al., *Nonverbal Communication*, 77.

[26] Stephan and Stephan, "Cognition and Affect," 151.

Jack Dominian's book, for example, says it all: *One Like Us: a Psychological Interpretation of Jesus.* Other recent examples of psychologizing in biblical interpretation include

- Anthony Bash, "A Psychodynamic Approach to the Interpretation of 2 Corinthians 10–13," *JNTS* 83 (2001) 51–67.

- Michael Reichardt, *Psychologische Erklärung der paulinischen Damaskusvision? Ein Beitrag zum interdisziplinären Gespräch zwischen Exegese und Psychologie seit dem 18. Jahrhundert* (Stuttgart: Katholisches Bibelwerk, 1999).

- Martin Leiner, *Psychologie und Exegese: Grundlagen einer textpsychologischen Exegese des Neuen Testaments.* (Gutersloh: Kaiser, 1995).

- John A. Sanford, *Mystical Christianity: A Psychological Commentary on the Gospel of John* (New York: Crossroad, 1993).

- Gerd Theissen, *Psychological Aspects of Pauline Theology*, trans. John P. Galvin (Philadelphia: Fortress, 1987).

5. Unwarranted Assumptions of Human Similarity

A common assumption is that there is sufficient similarity among all people everywhere so that communication should not be difficult. This assumption fails to recognize self-projection or to believe that communication difficulties are real.

A simple gesture such as a smile can be an example. Americans assume a smile to be a universal gesture of friendliness. It is not. In a number of Asian cultures a smile at a stranger is either rude or an indication of sexual deviance. Tears, especially public tears on the part of a male, have a very different connotation in Middle Eastern culture than they do in the West.

Many Westerners assume that basic biological similarities or perhaps the universal need for food, shelter, and the like, provide a basis for common patterns of communication. The problem with such an assumption is of course that the cultural expressions of these fundamental human needs are so varied that even communication about the basics is fraught with difficulty. Laray Barna has argued, for example, that "there seem to be no universals or 'human nature' that can be used as the basis for automatic understanding." He argues we must "treat each encounter as an individual case, searching for whatever perceptions and communication means are held in common and proceed from there." Barna's conclusion is that seeking out the "cultural modifiers" in expressions of basic need is a strategy that offers hope, whereas unwarranted assumptions of human similarity only confuse the matter.[27]

Of course Westerners often assume not only that such universals exist, but also that they can be abstracted from the biblical writings in the form of theological or ethical ideas.

6. Cognitive Style

Cognitive style, or what Devorah Lieberman has called "ethnocognitivism," is another factor that has a major impact on the communication styles of different cultures.[28] The term simply refers to the thought patterns or habits of mind that dominate a given culture. The subject is enormously complex and it is beyond our scope to recount it fully, but the impact can be illustrated with a few important examples.

In their study of the peculiar ways of thinking that have emerged in Western culture since the industrial revolution, Peter and Brigitte Berger and Hansfried Kellner have demonstrated that certain ways of living become "carriers," to use their term, for certain cognitive styles. By this they mean that institutionalized processes or groups can create the conditions for, transmit, nurture, and reinforce particular habits of mind. If, for example, the technological mode of production and a problem-solving habit of mind tend to go together (and they do), we could speak of the technological mode of production as the "carrier" of that particular cognitive style.[29] In the same way, bureaucracy is the carrier of a taxonomic mentality. The mode of living and the cognitive style it carries thus form what Berger, et al. call a "package." If you get the one you tend to get the other.

Of course not all carriers have exactly the same force. Some are simply more potent than others. But the point is that some carriers—the technologi-

---

[27] Barna, "Stumbling Blocks," 337.

[28] Lieberman, "Ethnocognitivism," 178–93.

[29] Berger, et al., *Homeless Mind*, 26. The style of work that characterizes the technological mode of production is heavily rationalized and is structured in ways that differ sharply from those of earlier eras. Most striking is its *mechanisticity*, a term Berger, et al. borrow from Thorstein Veblen. The work process itself has machine-like qualities that render actions in it reproducible and measurable, and indeed mechanomorphic metaphors used in all areas of modern life derive directly from it. It thus serves as a social location for habits of thinking that follow machine-like patterns. In the words of Elizabeth Sewell, the method of the machine "constructs the mind at the same time that it constructs the constructions of the mind." Or to put it somewhat more cautiously, the technological mode of production provides the occasion for habits of mind to develop that are closely correlated with the production process itself.

cal mode of production and bureaucracy being the most important—are so fundamental that the cognitive styles they nurture cannot be "thought away." Try as we might, the problem-solving mentality cannot simply be "thought away" from the technological mode of production. It is inherent, and therefore has become one of those persistent perceptions Westerners invariably project into cross-cultural dialogue.

In addition, Berger, et al. have shown that such habits of mind tend to "carry over" into all areas of life. By this they mean that a particular element of cognitive style tends to diffuse from its original context into other areas of life. The diffusion of the problem-solving mentality is easily illustrated by ubiquitous how-to manuals in American life. They address not only the mechanical and technical problems of modern living but also everything from marriage enrichment to sexual compatibility and beyond. The way this pragmatic bent of mind affects the American communication style we shall return to in a moment.[30]

As Stewart and Bennett point out, American habits of mind frequently lie at one end of a spectrum with much of the non-Western world at the other. It is a situation ready-made for miscommunication. Americans, for example, are "fact-oriented," considering empirical data to be observable, measurable, located in time and space, objective and reliable. Quantification bears the ring of truth, a notion almost absent in the non-Western world. Unlike much of the world, Americans are also prone to counter-factual speculation, to trial and error, to trying on hypotheses and collecting data to substantiate them as a means of gaining clarity and certainty. Yet many Europeans and Asians strongly resist counterfactual thinking as evidence of confusion or a source of manipulation.[31] The Japanese, for example, rarely consider alternatives or perform feasibility studies.

Because "doing" (as opposed to "being") is a core American value, operational procedures ("How to . . .") are often the center of American attention. We prefer what Berger, et al. call "functional" rationality rather than abstract rationality. Stewart and Bennett describe this as an American preference for "procedural knowledge" that focuses on how to get things done. They contrast it with the German preference for "declarative knowledge" that offers descriptions of the world.[32] Procedural knowledge goes hand in hand

---

[30] Of course there is occasionally substantial motivation to prevent this from happening. In some areas we are successful in putting on the brakes to prevent carryover from happening. Berger, et al. call that phenomenon "stoppage." The struggle to maintain touch with the "natural" world as relief from excessively mechanistic ways of doing things in most areas of modern life is a prime example of stoppage. For this discussion see *Homeless Mind*, 23–40.

[31] Stewart and Bennett, *American Cultural Patterns*, 32.

[32] Ibid., 32.

with the problem-solving mentality that results in the well-known American pragmatism and obsession with technique. By contrast, Germans and Arabs prefer description and see functional rationality as lacking theoretical clarity. The Japanese style is different yet, emphasizing intuition.

It is well known that a future orientation dominates the American perception of time. Much of the non-Western world, however, is oriented toward the past or present. In American procedural thinking, this future orientation takes the form of "anticipated consequences," a habit of mind that undergirds much of our capitalist economic activity. It stands in stark contrast to the present-time orientation of Mediterranean peasants (and much of the non-Western world) who are more likely to "take no thought for tomorrow, for tomorrow will take thought for itself" (Matt 6:34).

Another key habit of American thinking is what Stewart and Bennett call a "preoccupation with causation." As they say, we are obsessed with "'how' questions."[33] We want to know how things work or how they came to be as they are. Berger, et al. speak of "componential" thinking, by which they mean an analytical tendency to break things down into their constituent parts in order to display (and therefore reproduce) the sequential causation that makes them tick. By contrast, description-oriented cultures prefer layered and cumulative attention to details. Chinese, Japanese, and Brazilians resist analysis and prefer a more holistic type of thought.[34]

The analytical thinking that characterizes American technicism can be contrasted with the thinking patterns of other cultures in another way. Americans are *inductive* thinkers, deriving principles from multiple examples or amassed data. Many Europeans are *deductive* thinkers, giving priority to theory and concepts for which illustrative examples can then be sought. Even more important for biblical scholars is the fact that much of the non-Western world, including the Mediterranean area, prefers *relational* thinking. What matters there are not data and derived principles but context, status, relationships, and the ascriptive qualities of persons. Only from factors of this sort can conclusions be drawn.

While there are many more characteristics of the American cognitive style that could be cited, enough has been said to indicate that a communication style built on American habits of mind will not resonate with much of the world. Nor will the reverse be true. The inability to understand differences in cognitive style is another major cause in the communication disconnect between Americans and the Bible.

---

[33] Ibid., 39.

[34] Berger, et al., *Homeless Mind*, 23–40; Stewart and Bennett, *American Cultural Patterns*, 41.

Conclusion

By now it is obvious that wishing communication failures away, ignoring them, or pretending they are transcended by the commonalities of human nature will only exacerbate the problem. The fact is that the intractability of the problem has a solid basis in the cultural peculiarities of communication style.

Moreover, a host of additional obstacles to cross-cultural communication could easily be cited. For example, much more could be said about cultural values or the culture-specific character of gender expectations in communication. The way language functions (as opposed to what it means) in different cultural situations is equally important. Additional aspects of cognitive style such as anonymous social relations, moralized anonymity, segmented jurisdictions, expectations of distributive justice, and the tendency to progressivity (newer, bigger, better) could also be taken into account. Code preference (verbal or nonverbal), speech sequencing (linear, spiral, dialectical) and a wide variety of other factors also differ from culture to culture. All affect communication.

Nonetheless the list of obstacles cited above should be sufficient to make at least two important points. First, the intractability of the problem of projecting ourselves onto the pages of the Bible goes far beyond simple cultural ignorance on our part, important as that factor may be. The intractability of cultural differences has very deep roots in the styles of communication that are peculiar to Western and non-Western cultures. Knowledge of the biblical culture therefore is only a part—albeit a critically important part—of the hermeneutical problem. Self-knowledge, especially knowledge of what the non-Western world does *not* share in our Western style of communication, is every bit as much a factor in reading biblical texts.

Second, when Americans read the Bible using (and assuming the universality of) the American style of communication, they make misunderstanding inevitable. We think we understand when in fact we do not. We are simply projecting our own cultural perceptions onto the texts we claim we are reading, to see what they might say to us. We often remain oblivious to the distortions we introduce simply because of who we are and the way we speak.

In sum, what has come into view here is an explanation for the near total inability of American Bible readers to distinguish between canon and culture. We often claim the canon to be the rule for faith and practice in the Christian community, and yet we demonstrate by the way we read the Bible that our commitment to culture has been far more profound than we have been willing to admit. Culture, not canon, has too often shaped the life of the church

Finally, the point is simple: Without clarity about the peculiarities of the cognitive world we Westerners inhabit, communication with the biblical writers is not possible. As has often been said, exegesis becomes a soliloquy. In short, without this kind of cultural clarity we would have to raise serious questions about whether we are actually hearing the biblical writers speak rather than imagining congenial messages of our own creation.

CHAPTER 2

Jesus: Village Artisan

WHILE OUR evidence for Jesus is at least as good as for any other character from antiquity, nonetheless the evidence we have is extremely limited and difficult to sort out from the theologically motivated stories in which it is embedded. Add to that the fact that is nearly impossible to avoid reading the evidence selectively, and the result is that producing a portrait of the historical Jesus has proven an elusive scholarly task.

In recent decades the vast majority of attempts to describe the historical Jesus have tried to locate him on the map of key religious characters or types in the first century. Was Jesus a rabbi? A Cynic philosopher? A political revolutionary? A religious reformer? A messiah? A spirit-person? This particular attempt is something New Testament scholars have been at for a very long time.

By contrast, the task of locating Jesus in the *social* matrix of antiquity has a less celebrated history. It is not that there have been no attempts to do this in the past; indeed there have. In fact, in the late nineteenth and early twentieth centuries it was common to romanticize Jesus as a warm and gentle rustic whose down-home peasant wisdom could be counterposed against the cold and sterile winds of modern technocracy. More recently a number of attempts, which unfortunately describe Israelite society without the use of macrosociological models, have produced such absurdities as a literate, trilingual, theater-going, Hellenistic, individualistic, self-aware, middle class Jesus. Only a few sustained attempts have been made by New Testament scholars to study Mediterranean societies in sufficient depth to begin to offer a culturally sensitive, social characterization of Jesus.[1] What follows is one such attempt to locate Jesus in the social matrix of the first century.

---

[1] The most sustained attempt to date is Crossan, *Historical Jesus*. While the conclusions in that study seem curiously disconnected from the social analysis with which it begins, nonetheless the social analysis is extremely valuable in its own right. The attempt that follows here to

Social Stratification

We begin with a brief note about social class stratification. It is extremely difficult for modern Americans to understand the feel that social stratification gave to ancient social relations, though such stratification is approximated in some third-world countries today. Much of it we Americans find offensive because it violates our Enlightenment ideal of an egalitarian society. But social class conflict was simply a pervasive fact of life in the first century and its corrosive effects are present throughout the Gospel stories of Jesus. Let us look briefly at two simple but relevant illustrations.

The first has to do with land. The Israelite elite of Jesus's day had come to see land as capital to be exploited. In violation of the Torah, they bought and sold it with regularity. By contrast, peasants retained the older view that all the land was owned by God who had given it to Israelite families as inalienable plots meant to ensure family subsistence.[2] In large measure, this class conflict over land manifested itself as hostility between the city and the rural areas, as increasing portions of the arable land came under the control of the city elites.[3] In Jesus's day, for example, there is widespread evidence for latifundialization in all areas of the country, including the Galilee.[4]

This social class conflict over land also became deadly serious. The eventual war that broke out between the Jews and the Romans in the mid-first century was as much a class war of Israelite peasants against their own Israelite nobility as it was a conflict against their Roman oppressors.[5] In fact, many of the Zealot fighters in that war were originally peasant farmers who had lost their land to elite urban creditors and who then resorted to increasingly bitter, violent social banditry in an attempt to get it back.[6]

In light of this conflict over land, it is worth reminding ourselves that Jesus, at least as he is presented in the Gospels, was himself a landless villager. In fact, if Jesus's family was originally from Bethlehem (and this is by no means certain as historical fact), and if his Judean family was trying to make a living as artisans in the tiny Galilean village of Nazareth, it means that they

---

locate Jesus in the social matrix of ancient Mediterranean society is a macrosociological view for which Crossan's work will frequently provide microsociological detail. In the argument below, however, we shall suggest that the term *peasant* is best applied to those smallholders actually farming the land and not to those landless types whose social status was below even that of peasants.

[2] Fiensy, *Social History of Palestine*, 1–20; Oakman, *Jesus and the Economic Questions*, 38.

[3] Fiensy, *Social History of Palestine*, 144.

[4] Ibid., 21–73.

[5] Horsley and Hanson, *Bandits*, 220–26.

[6] Horsley, *Sociology*, 220–26.

were basically landless, displaced economic refugees who carried with them daily the burden of this social class conflict over land.[7]

A second example of ancient social class conflict that is relevant to our consideration of Jesus has to do with the much-disputed matter of literacy. Just how widespread was literacy in ancient, rural Syria-Palestine? Are we to imagine the recipients of the Gospels, for example, reading privately to themselves as any modern American might do? Should we picture a literate audience, perhaps even a scholastic one, in which the Gospels were studied and debated?

Perhaps. But there is now general agreement among social historians that only 2 to 4 percent of the population in agrarian societies could read, or read *and* write (they did not always go together), and that the vast majority of those lived in the cities. Recent studies show that neither literacy nor schooling was as extensive as many New Testament scholars have usually assumed.[8] In fact, claims of near-universal access to at least elementary education simply do not stand up to scrutiny.[9]

Especially important for understanding Jesus and his audience is the lack of evidence that significant schooling existed at the village level.[10] Literacy rates (of at least a minimal sort) among upper-class males were indeed very high. They were even a distinguishing mark of such status. But to generalize from that group to about 90 percent of the population who left no written record that we can analyze is simply nonsense. As the studies of William Harris show, access to elementary education was sharply limited, and access to the rhetorical education that was the mark of the elite was extremely limited.[11] The fact is that very few village people could read or write, and many could not use numbers either.[12] That Jesus was any exception is extremely doubtful.

Two observations are relevant here. One is that writing was a primary tool in the control of the lower classes. Debt records are an obvious example and were of course the first thing destroyed by the Zealots when war broke out in the 66 CE. Fear of writing and of those who could write was widespread among peasants, who often resisted it as a tool of elitist deception. If I write the contract and you cannot read it, obviously you are at a serious disadvantage. As Harris has demonstrated, literacy creates a very special kind of

---

[7] Recent historical Jesus studies have questioned whether the tradition about Jesus's birth in Bethlehem represents historical fact or was rather an early Christian creation that historicizes prophecy. See Crossan, *Jesus*, 18–20.

[8] Harris, *Ancient Literacy*, 244. See J. H. Humphrey, editor. *Literacy in the Roman World*.

[9] Harris, *Ancient Literacy*, 241, 349.

[10] Ibid., 241.

[11] Ibid., 334.

[12] Hanson, "Ancient Illiteracy," 183–89.

exploitation in class-stratified societies with a high degree of literacy among the elite and the servants of the elite and a low degree of literacy in the rest of the population.[13] Such, of course, was exactly the situation in Syria-Palestine in the first century.

Second, though the teaching of Jesus was entirely oral, and though the environment in which he was first received was equally oral, the records we have of him are entirely written. What happened when oral recitation of the Jesus tradition was replaced by reading of written records is a fascinating study in its own right, which we cannot deal with here. But the point is that by the time we get to the written Gospels, we have already migrated a considerable social distance from the world of Jesus. We have crossed a divide that the ancient world thought uncrossable: from the nonliterate, oral world of peasant farmers and landless village artisans to the sophisticated, literate, elite world of writers like Matthew and Luke.

Social Class Stratification in First-Century Palestine

Given the fundamental importance of social stratification in agrarian societies, an attempt to locate Jesus in the social matrix requires us to describe key social groups that would have either been present in or had an impact on life in the villages and small towns of Galilee, southern Syria, or Transjordan, that is, on the world of Jesus. To structure our comments we shall refer to the diagrammatic description of social relationships in the Herodian period in Figure 1 below:

Social Stratification in the Herodian Period

Urban Elite 1–2% of the population	Roman emperor (prefect/procurator) Client king, tetrarch or ethnarch Herodians High priests Lay aristocracy
Retainers 5% of the population	Bailiffs Tax farmers Bureaucrats
Urban Nonelite 3-7% of the population	Merchants Artisans Day Laborers

---

[13] Harris, *Ancient Literacy*, 333.

Rural Peasants and Other Villagers 75% of the population	Freeholders (15-50 acres) Small Freeholders (4-15 acres) Tenant Farmers Village Artisans Day Laborers Slaves
Unclean and Degraded 5% of the population	Prostitutes Porters, Dung Carriers Sailors Tanners Etc.
Expendables 5% of the population	Lame Blind Deformed Diseased Etc.

Fig. 1 (Adapted from Duling)

We shall look at each group on the chart in turn and then try to locate Jesus on this social map in a way that will give perspective to any discussion of the Jesus of history.

URBAN ELITE

As the chart shows, the first group, the urban elite, made up about 2 percent of the total population. At its upper levels this elite included the highest-ranking military officers, ranking priestly families, the Herodians, and other ranking aristocratic families. They lived in the heavily fortified central areas of the cities, usually enclosed in separate walls, hence they were physically and socially isolated from the rest of the society. Since this elite was the only group with disposable income, they constituted the only real "market" in the ancient economy. The literacy rate among these people was high in some areas, even among women, and, along with their retainers, they maintained control of writing, coinage, taxation, and the military and judicial systems. The elite's control was legitimated by the religious and educational bureau-cracy that typically became the keeper of the so-called Great Tradition, that is, the "official" version of the religious tradition that only the elite could afford to practice. Although birthrates were high in all segments of the society, survival rates meant that large extended families were characteristic only of this urban elite. In fact socially, culturally, and politically this elite had little in common with the lower classes of the society. Since they maintained their own mannerisms, vocabulary, speech patterns, and dress, they could easily be spotted on sight.

The wealth of the elite was based primarily on land ownership and taxation that effectively drained the resources of the rural areas. As in most agrarian societies, between 1 and 3 percent of the population owned the majority of the arable land. David Fiensy describes large Galilean estates varying from roughly 50 acres to the very large one at Qawarat Bene-Hassan that covered 2500 acres.[14] Especially important was the land controlled by the Herodian family that included tens of thousands of acres. By contrast, Fiensy estimates the average peasant plot was six acres or less.[15] Our first group, then, the elite, stands at the apex of the social pyramid.

RETAINERS

In a continuum from the lower echelons of this elite and ranging downward toward nonelite levels is our second group, those whom anthropologists call "retainers." They constitute another 5 percent of the population and include lower-level military officers, officials and bureaucrats such as clerks and bailiffs, personal retainers, household servants, scholars, legal experts, and the lower-level lay aristocracy. They worked primarily in the service of the elite and served to mediate both governmental and religious functions to the lower classes and to village areas. The Tebtunis papyri, for example, report the appointment of village scribes by city aristocrats in order to extend elite control to the rural areas.[16] Retainers, of course, did not wield much power independently, but depended for their position on close relationships with the urban elite.

Such retainers play key roles in the Jesus story. Significantly we see more people here who are followers of Jesus (the people from Jairus's house, Levi, chief tax collectors, centurions) than we found in the elite group. But of course the majority here are opponents of Jesus, especially the lay aristocracy that included the Pharisees.

Before leaving these two dominant groups, it is worth noting the sheer number of references to them in the Jesus story. There are 113 references to them in Mark's Gospel alone. This is not because much of the story takes place in an urban environment where these groups lived, because it does not. In Mark, Jesus enters no city other than Jerusalem. It is because elite control extended into the rural areas in a pervasive way. In fact, conflict between the

---

[14] Fiensy, *Social History of Palestine*, 60.

[15] Ibid., 94.

[16] Hunt and Edgar, *Select Papyri II: Non-Literary Papyri*, no. 339 (p. 393).

elite or their retainers and the rural populations was a constant reality of village life.

URBAN NONELITE

A third group playing a role in the Jesus story is the nonelite of the cities. In most agrarian societies this group represents the vast bulk of the city population and between 3 and 7 percent of the total population. It included merchants, artisans, day laborers and service workers of various kinds. Given the extremely high death rates among the urban poor, cities were able to absorb a constant stream of such persons from the rural areas with little or no gain in city population. Their economic situation could vary from extreme poverty among day laborers and certain artisan groups to considerable wealth among successful merchants. Yet even the rich among them bore little social or cultural influence.

Most of the urban poor lived in segregated areas at the outer edges of the cities and banded together into neighborhood or craft associations as a means of survival. These urban neighborhoods often had internal walls that could be used to separate elite and nonelite populations as well as occupational or ethnic groups. Both internal and external gates were locked at night and guards were posted on the walls. Among the urban poor, health and nutrition were often worse than in the villages, and life expectancies were shorter. A child born among the lower classes in the city of Rome during the first century had a life expectancy of only twenty years.[17]

It is not surprising, of course, that this group plays a very small role in the Jesus story, simply because, aside from the passion narrative, so little of the story takes place in an urban environment. Mark mentions the urban nonelite only thirteen times. These people are central in the story of the Pauline churches of the Greco-Roman world, but are relatively absent from the stories of Jesus.

DEGRADED, UNCLEAN, AND EXPENDABLES

Outside the walls of every preindustrial city lived a fourth group—the degraded, unclean and expendables: beggars, prostitutes, the poorest day laborers, tanners (forced to live outside the cities because they smelled), peddlers, bandits, sailors, gamblers, ass drivers, usurers, dung collectors, and even some merchants. They were present around both villages and cities, although they were more numerous around the cities. All such persons were forced out of the cities at night when gates were locked but frequented the cities during

---

[17] Lenski and Lenski, *Human Societies*, 249.

the daytime to beg or find work. The poorest lived just outside the city walls or along the hedgerows of adjacent fields. While not a large portion of the total population, most of these people faced appalling living conditions and life chances.

Given the fact that they were a relatively small percentage of the population (perhaps about 10 percent of the total), the striking thing about this group is the sheer number of references to them in the Jesus story. In Mark there are twenty-two such references, and eight different times Mark gives us a kind of summary of Jesus's interaction with them (1:28; 1:32–34; 1:45; 3:7–10; 6:31–34; 6:54–56; 7:36–37). Mark wants us to know very early in his story that Jesus's healing activity among this particular group of people was a major reason for the reputation he developed (1:28).

RURAL PEASANTS AND OTHER VILLAGERS

Up to this point we have looked at four distinct groups: the elite, the retainers, the urban poor, and the degraded. Lastly, we must describe what was by far the largest group: rural peasants. The cities of antiquity dominated life culturally, economically, and politically. Yet 90 percent of the population lived in villages and engaged in what social scientists call "primary" industries: farming and the extracting of raw materials. We must look briefly here at several rural groups who play a role in the Jesus story, including freeholding peasants, tenant farmers, day laborers, slaves, and the various landless groups that included fishermen, artisans, and other craftsmen.

Freeholders

First there were the freeholders, that is, peasants who owned and worked their own land. Farming provided the bulk of their living, though for many about one-fourth of their income had to be derived from nonagricultural work in the off-season. Estimating standards of living for freeholding peasants has proven a difficult task, but taking into account (1) seed saved for the next year's crop, (2) fodder for animals, (3) grain to trade for what a family did not produce, and (4) the crushing burden of taxation to support the temple, the priesthood, the Herodian regime, and Roman tribute, it is not difficult to see that peasant economic viability was in crisis. Peasant debt leading to loss of land was epidemic in Jesus's time, and indeed his own family may well have been one of the victims.

Tenants, Day Laborers, and Slaves

A second group were the landless tenant farmers whose numbers were increasing at an alarming rate in Jesus's lifetime. Tenancy contracts were usually written rather than oral, which led to no end of conflict, and contracts could cover one year, five years (the most frequent), seven years, or even a lifetime. Some tenants paid fixed rents in kind, others in money, and still others paid a percentage of the crop. Rents for tenants could go as high as two-thirds of a crop, though rabbinic sources more commonly mention figures ranging from one-fourth to one-half. Many tenants, particularly those with fragmented extended families, fell hopelessly in debt and abandoned their ancestral lands altogether. In some extreme cases, such as Qawarat Bene-Hassan for example, an entire village worked as tenants of a single landlord.[18]

In addition to freeholding and tenant farmers, there were both day laborers and slaves. Many did seasonal work during harvests, though they were often employed as barbers, bathhouse attendants, cooks, messengers, scribes, manure gatherers, thorn gatherers, or construction workers. While day laborers were not necessarily landless people (small freeholders often worked out to supplement farming income), those who were indeed without land were near the bottom of the socioeconomic scale. Commonly they were either peasants who had lost land through indebtedness or they were non-inheriting sons whom small peasant plots could not support. Our sources indicate that they worked by the hour, by the day, by the month, by the year, or for three- or seven- year periods.[19] Many such landless people drifted to the cities and towns, which were in frequent need of new labor not because of expanding economic opportunity but because of extremely high death rates among the urban nonelite.

Other Rural Groups

Finally, we must note that most village and rural areas contained at least several other groups. Lower-level retainers and lay aristocrats often provided village leadership, and most villages of any size had a council to govern local affairs. Fishermen and herders were common as well and, though we cannot take time to say much about these groups, both fishing and herding were despised occupations. And of course there were village artisans or craftsmen: potters, weavers, blacksmiths, shoemakers, carpenters, and the like. In the rural areas they were never present in large numbers, and indeed few artisans could make a living in the smaller villages like Nazareth. Village artisans usually had to travel around to get work in several locations, and since people who traveled around were considered by all villagers to be socially deviant, itinerant artisans were very low on the social scale. With the exceptions of the degraded and expendables, perhaps, they were at the very bottom.

[18] Fiensy, *Social History of Palestine*, 84.
[19] Ibid., 85.

And that, finally, brings us to Jesus. The Gospels call Jesus a *tekton* in Greek. We have translated it "carpenter," but it may refer equally well to any kind of worker in metal or wood. Legend has it that the family of Jesus made yokes for oxen; if this is true, that work would have placed them among the poorest of the poor.

Peasant Health

Before leaving these comments about artisans and other rural peasants, we should make a few comments about peasant health. We make these comments partly to recognize the prominent role of Jesus in the Gospels as a healer of the sick and partly to explode the nineteenth-century myth that romanticized the peasant way of life. Peasant life was nothing like what is often pictured on our Sunday school walls.

Birthrates in the first century were approximately forty per thousand per year, twice that in the U.S. today, though death rates were even higher still; hence in the modern world we have the curious phenomenon of far fewer births and a rapidly rising population. Infant mortality rates have been estimated at 30 percent in many peasant societies today, and that may well have been the case in first-century Palestine. Of the children who made it past infancy, a third were dead before the age of six. By age sixteen, 60 percent had died. By age twenty-six, 75 percent were gone and by age forty-five, 90 percent were dead. Only 3 percent made it to age sixty.[20] The fact is that Jesus was not a young man when he died. Eighty percent of his audience was younger than he and looking at less than a decade of life remaining.

Obviously, disease and death rates were not evenly spread across all elements of the population but fell disproportionately upon the lower classes of both city and village. Among most lower-class people who did make it to adulthood, health would have been atrocious. By age thirty, the majority of them suffered from internal parasites, tooth decay, and bad eyesight. Most had lived with the debilitating results of protein deficiency since childhood. Parasites were especially prevalent, carried to humans by sheep, goats, and dogs. Fifty percent of the hair combs from Qumran, Masada, and Murabbat were infected with lice and lice eggs, probably reflecting conditions elsewhere.[21] If infant mortality rates, the age structure of the population, and pathological evidence from skeletal remains can be taken as indicators, malnutrition was a constant threat as well.[22]

---

[20] Carney, *Shape of the Past*, 88.

[21] Zias, "Death and Disease," 148.

[22] Fiensy, *Ancient History of Palestine*, 98.

Infectious disease was the most serious threat to life and undoubtedly accounted for much of the high mortality rate among children.[23] Few peasants could afford professional physicians, and so most frequented folk healers of various kinds, one of whom was Jesus. As in virtually every known society economically dependent on animal husbandry (especially on large domestic animals such as camels, sheep, and goats), there was widespread belief in spirit aggression as an important cause of physical illness.

Finally, as Douglas Oakman has shown in his study of Luke, violence was a regular part of village experience.[24] Fraud, robbery, forced imprisonment or labor, beatings, inheritance disputes, and forcible removal of rents are all reflected in the village life of the Jesus story. There are fifteen reports or stories about such violent incidents in the Gospel of Mark alone (1:14; 1:45; 3:6; 3:27; 5:3; 6:16–28; 10:33–34; 12:1–8; 12:40; 12:41–44; 13:9–13; 14:1; 14:43–48; 15:7; 15:15–20). Widows, aged parents without children or parents of children with disabilities, the very young, the very old, those with diseases, deformities, or disabilities, and those without land were the most common victims of violence. Suspicion of outsiders, fear and distrust of officials (especially of those officials who could read and write), and hatred of anyone who threatened subsistence, were the social constants of ancient village life. In sum, given poor housing, nonexistent sanitation, constant violence, economically inaccessible medical care, and bad dietary habits (as much as one-fourth of a male Palestinian peasant's calorie intake came from alcohol) one quickly abandons any temptation to romanticize the world of ancient peasants.[25] One only need ask whether Jesus was in any way exempt from all this to realize that the answer is clearly no.

Jesus the Village Artisan

Finally, we need add only a additional few comments about Jesus the village artisan. The Gospels report considerable conflict between Jesus on the one hand and the temple authorities and their representatives on the other. It is well known, of course, that Jesus is constantly criticized by the authorities— read: by the urban elite—because he breaks nearly all the purity rules of the Great Tradition. In Mark's Gospel, Jesus repeatedly violates the purity rules regarding persons (1:41; 2:13–14; 4:35–42; 5:24–28; 5:41; 7:24–30; 7:31) by coming in contact with the diseased, the dead, those with physical defects, and the demon-possessed. He violates rules about the body (7:33; 8:23), about meal practice (6:37–44; 8:1–10), about sacred times (2:24; 3:1–6),

[23] Zias, "Death and Disease," 149.

[24] Oakman, "Countryside," 158.

[25] Broshi, "Diet of Palestine," 41–56.

and about sacred places (11:15–16; 12:33). We are not surprised that in the controversy about the source of Jesus's power in the Gospels, his opponents claim that his rule breaking has its origin in Satan.

Important as these familiar comments about breaking purity rules are, however, they tend to miss a critical fact of peasant life. Jesus's lifestyle may have been seen as unholy and unwashed by the religious elite, and his behavior may have seemed to them iconoclastic or even perverse. But to a peasant, his behavior would have been nothing out of the ordinary at all. Very few peasants could maintain the Great Tradition even if they wanted to. Jesus touched dead bodies? So did they. Peasants came in constant contact with bodily secretions, dead animals, and unwashed food. Jesus didn't follow Sabbath rules? Neither did they. In dry-land farming with marginal or uneven rainfall, peasants could not always afford to keep the Sabbaths and holy days, because each day that passed between first rains and plowing reduced the final yields. Like Jesus, peasants could not always afford the prescribed sacrifices. And they could guarantee neither their own cleanliness nor the cleanliness of their meal companions.

Jesus, the iconoclast, is thus the creation of an elite outlook on life. We pick it up from the literate stage of the Jesus tradition: the written Gospels. If one identifies with the viewpoint of the elite, Jesus is indeed a rule-breaker. But if the reader of the Gospels identifies with the peasant way of life, then Jesus is simply an ordinary person. The rules he breaks having to do with dietary laws, washing, Sabbath observance, and temple sacrifice are precisely those rules that peasants had the most difficulty keeping. Jesus's lifestyle would thus have been familiar to peasants in every respect. His defense of an internal holiness before God that could be maintained without heavy expense or without the disruption of necessary peasant farming practices would have surprised Jesus's peasant hearers indeed. But his lifestyle as such would not.

Thus it seems probable that what is really being provided in the Gospel stories is a statement that holiness before God is possible within the limits of a peasant way of life. And of that we may take Jesus himself to be the primary example. Any portrait of Jesus, of whatever stripe, must begin with this astonishing but consistent testimony in the gospel tradition. Moreover, Jesus's ability to operate across all the rigid lines that his stratified society offered (and we note that he ate with anyone: rich, poor, elite, outcast, anyone at all), together with his call to be a community of God's people that also crossed every one of these boundaries (boundaries that people in the ancient world thought uncrossable) is surely central to the impact that Jesus had upon the group that followed him first.

CHAPTER 3

Luke's Jesus: Honor Claimed, Honor Tested

L UKE 4:1–30 presents two remarkable scenes in which the birthright of Jesus is seriously challenged: first at the cosmic level, where no secrets of the heart can ever be concealed, and then at the most uncompromising level of all, where unwarranted honor claims would quickly be cut to ribbons, in Jesus's own hometown. The tension in Luke 4 rises sharply as claims and counterclaims, challenges and counterchallenges are played out in a drama where the honor (credibility, in our terms) of both Jesus and Luke is on the line. In order to understand the nature of these challenges and their import for Luke's story, however, it will be necessary to see them (as far as we are able) through the eyes of the honor–shame society to which the story was originally addressed.

Honor and Shame

The working assumption in what follows is that Luke 4, like every other text in the New Testament, emerged from a Mediterranean society in which honor was the core social value. Since the basic concepts of honor and shame are by now well known to most New Testament scholars. however, it will be necessary only to summarize a few of the more salient points.[1]

Of first importance is to recognize that concern for honor permeated every aspect of public life in the Mediterranean world. Honor was the fundamental value, the core, the heart, the soul. Aristotle thought honor the "greatest of all external goods." He identified it with "happiness," and considered it "akin to being loved" (*Nic. Eth.*, I). Xenophon claimed that love of honor was

---

[1] For a more complete review of the concepts of honor and shame in the New Testament see Malina, "Hospitality," 104–107; and Malina and Neyrey, "Honor and Shame," 25–65.

what distinguished human beings from animals (*Hiero*, 7.3) . Philo speaks of "wealth, fame, official posts, honors and everything of that sort with which the majority of mankind are busy" (*Det.*122). He complains that "fame and honor are a most precarious possession, tossed about on the reckless tempers and flighty words of careless men" (*Abr.* 264). We should not be surprised, then, to find it an overriding concern in the New Testament as well.[2]

Simply stated, honor is public reputation. It is name or place. It is one's status or standing in the village *together with the public recognition of it*. Public recognition is all-important: "Honor is the value of a person in his own eyes, but also in the eyes of his society."[3] To claim honor that is not publicly recognized is to play the fool. To grasp more honor than the public will allow is to be a greedy thief. To hang on to what honor one has is essential to life itself.

Moreover, as Paul Friedrich points out in his study of the *Iliad*, honor is at the center of a wide network of related values: "power, wealth, magnanimity, personal loyalty, 'precedence,' sense of shame, fame or 'reputation,' courage, and excellence."[4] It is a claim to excel over others, to be superior, to demand *rights* on the basis of social precedence.[5] Honor is likewise a limited good—related to control of scarce resources including land, crops, livestock, political clout, and female sexuality.[6] Thus honor gained is always honor taken from another.

---

[2] Malina and Neyrey, "Honor and Shame," 26. Plutarch makes a modest attempt at exploring the semantic field of *honor* by commenting on Greek equivalents for the Latin term *honor*. He suggests δόξα and τιμή as appropriate substitutes for his Greek readers (*Moralia* 4.266). Josephus speaks of honors bestowed by Caesar, Vespasian, David, Saul, Jonathan, Augustus, Claudius, and the city of Athens (*J.W.* 1.194; 1.199; 1.358; 1.396; 1.607; 3.408; *Life* 423; *Ant.* 7.117, 6.168, 6.251, 13.102, 14.152, 19.292). He tells of the honor that belongs to consuls, governors, priests, village judges, and prophets (*J.W.* 4.149, 7.82; *Ant.* 4.215, 10.92, 11.309, 15.217). Philo speaks often of honor, glory, fame, high reputations, being adorned with honors and public offices, noble birth, the desire for glory, honor in the present and a good name for the future (*Migr.* 172; *Leg.* 3.87; *Det.* 33, 157; *Post.* 112; *Abr.* 185, 263).

In the same way, the OT speaks often of honor: הדר (1 Chr 16:27; Ps 8:5; Dan 4:37), כבד (Job 14:21, Nah 3:10), הוד (1 Sam 9:6; Isa 23:9), אדר (Isa 42:21), יקר (Ps 49:12; Dan 2:6). It speaks of being "lifted up of face": ונשא פנים (2 Kgs 5:1; Isa 3:3; 9:15). Equivalent terms are common in the NT as well: τιμή (John 4:44; Rom 2:7; 2:10; 9:21; 12:10; 1 Cor 12:23; 1 Thess 4:4; 1 Tim 1:17; 5:17; 6:1; 2 Tim 2:20; Heb 2:7; 3:3; 1 Pet 1:7; 2 Pet 1:17; Rev 4:9; 4:11; 5:12; 19:1; 21:26), τιμάω (Matt 15:8; John 5:23; Acts 28:10), ἔντιμος (Luke 14:8), δόξα (John 5:41; 2 Cor 6:8; Rev 19:7), δόξαζω (John 8:54; 1 Cor 12:26), ἔνδοξος (1 Cor 4:10), τίμιος (Heb 13:4); and for dishonor: ἄτιμος (Matt 13:57; 1 Cor 12:23).

[3] Pitt-Rivers, *Fate of Shechem*, 21

[4] Friedrich, "Sanity," 290.

[5] Pitt-Rivers, *Fate of Shechem*, 21–23.

[6] Brandes, "Reflections," 121–22.

The result is that honor and shame are forms of social evaluation in which people are constantly compelled to assess "their own conduct and that of their fellows" in relation to each other.[7] The vocabulary of praise (καλός) and blame (αἰσχρός) functions as a means of sanctioning social and moral behavior, and thereby a network of evaluation—the gossip network—creates an informal but effective mechanism of social control.

It is important here to recall how honor is obtained. Honor may either be *ascribed* or *acquired*. *Ascribed* honor, the honor derived from birth, comes from the standing one's family has—and has always had—in the village. All members of the family, whether male or female, have the same general honor rating, though differences could also occur within families as well (birth order is an obvious example).

Honor could also be gained or lost. Thus *acquired* honor could be won in the pursuit of virtue. It might be bestowed as the result of favors done for a beneficent patron or granted to those with skill in the never-ending game of challenge and response. Significant gains could also result from great exploits of one family member and all would benefit. Of course major loss could occur from some public shame and every member of the family would suffer grief.

But most gains and losses of honor in ancient village life were small and came on a daily basis. They were the result of the never-ending game of challenge and response that goes on among Mediterranean males in every waking, public moment. In virtually every public interaction of whatever kind, honor is subject to challenge. Honor can be challenged positively by means of a gift or compliment, sometimes so subtly that it is hard for non-Mediterraneans to catch the drift. Or honor can be challenged negatively with some small slander or insult, with some gift not given in an appropriate way or time, or even with a public question.

In every case an honor challenge must be met, and that too can be done in a variety of ways. An equal gift or compliment can be returned and a relationship has regained its equilibrium. Or a comparable insult can be offered and the playing field is level once again. Sometimes a challenge is met by a greater challenge, a slightly more expensive gift, or deeper insult, and a game of one-upmanship ensues. Challenges may be answered, brushed aside with the scorn allowed a superior, or responded to in kind, but they are never, ever, under any circumstances, to be run from or ignored. To ignore a challenge is to have no shame. To run from a challenge is a coward's disgrace.

At its best, the game of challenge and riposte is primarily a game of wits. Sometimes things could go too far, however, and result in excessive

---

[7] Péristiany, *Honour and Shame*, 9.

public damage to the honor of another. Because uncontrolled challenge and response could result in violence (feuding) that would disrupt the stability of the village, a family or group would normally "restrain its own obstreperous members in order to keep them from getting into a feud unnecessarily."[8] In a sense, then, the overquick resort to violence was frequently an unintended public admission of failure in the game of wits.

Of key importance in all this is that one's honor status determined who talked and who listened. Inferiors did not initiate conversations, nor were they accorded a public audience. They had no "authority" to speak. Thus Jesus's opponents offer him a challenge: "Tell us, by what authority are you doing these things?" (Luke 20:2). His interrogators assume that Jesus had no *ascribed* honor justifying the public initiative he was taking, so they press the proper question: "Who is it that *gave* you this authority?" Since the birth status of Jesus warranted nothing like the behavior he exhibited, the challengers naturally assumed that Jesus's honor must have been *acquired*, i.e., bestowed on Jesus by someone with the right to confer it.

This is exactly the problem with which Luke's drama confronts readers. In antiquity people were expected to act in accordance with birth status, and anyone who did not conform represented a troublesome social anomaly. Thus when someone such as Jesus, who lacked significant ascribed honor, spoke in public or played a public role, a satisfactory explanation was required in order to avoid a dysfunctional social compass.

Luke's Rhetorical Strategy

These basic characteristics of honor–shame social interaction are sufficient background for us now to assert a thesis regarding the rhetorical strategy Luke uses to persuade or influence his readers. Luke intends to tell the story of Jesus to an audience skeptical of his authority to speak and act. They know (or assume they know) that his ascribed honor status is of no account. Ascribed honor neither justifies nor legitimates the initiative Jesus takes, and thus makes problematic for Luke any appeal on behalf of Jesus. Based on his lack of ascribed honor, Jesus is the kind of person who should be listening, not speaking. Therefore, early in his story, if he wants to be taken seriously, Luke must resort to one or more of the available strategies for explaining to his audience Jesus, the social anomaly.[9] Moreover, if he expects his explanation of Jesus the anomaly to hold up under fire, Luke must subject his story

---

[8] Boehm, *Blood Revenge*, 97.

[9] For an excellent discussion of the trouble caused by social anomalies and the strategies for dealing with them, see Malina, *New Testament World*, 165–70.

to harsh scrutiny before his reading public. It is our thesis in what follows that this scrutiny is exactly what Luke displays for his readers in 4:1–30.

The Honor Claim

First, of course, we must be clear that an honor claim is being made (Luke 3:23–38). It is therefore striking to note that Luke offers the genealogy of Jesus immediately before we get to the honor tests of Luke 4. A number of commentators have seen Luke's genealogy as awkwardly placed; some have even argued that it has only minimal relation to what follows.[10] Yet when one considers the social function of genealogies in antiquity, that judgment must be revised.

Anthropological studies indicate a wide variety of social purposes for genealogies, social purposes that in turn affect the form and character of genealogies. Genealogies are used to preserve tribal homogeneity or cohesion, to interrelate diverse traditions, to acknowledge marriage contracts between extended families, to legitimate fictive kinship, to maintain ethnic identity, and so on. But above all else, *genealogies are honor claims.* They seek to establish social status (ascribed honor) and thereby provide the all-important map for proper social interaction.[11]

In a neglected but excellent study of genealogies in antiquity, Rodney Hood points out that lineage was not only a source of pride but also a device for self-aggrandizement.[12] It was a claim to authority, to place, to political or civil rights, to various social roles, or to the right to speak. The best-known case is that of Josephus, who begins his autobiography with a lengthy and somewhat convoluted (probably concocted) claim to come from Jerusalem's finest royal and priestly stock (*Life*, 1.1–6). As Hood notes, "With this dazzling pedigree, which he gives in detail to the fifth generation, he [Josephus] feels that his would-be slanderers are effectively silenced."[13]

By providing his genealogy, Josephus conforms to social convention: he offers readers the justifying evidence for his right to speak.[14] To further solidify his claim, Josephus asserts that his father was not only born a man of honor (ascribed honor, honor as precedence) but was also a man of righteous reputation in Jerusalem (acquired honor, honor as virtue) (*Life*, 1.7). Thus,

---

[10] Fitzmyer, *Luke,* 1:98.

[11] Hanson, "Herodians, Part I," 75–84.

[12] Much of the following discussion is taken from Hood's "Genealogies of Jesus," including a number of the primary sources he cites. He describes six important functions of genealogical lists in antiquity.

[13] Hood, "Genealogies of Jesus," 4.

[14] Ibid., 6–8. See also Mason, *Josephus,* 37.

being who he claims to be, Josephus asserts a right to the attention and sympathy of readers. We note with some amusement, of course, that Josephus defensively insists that the Jerusalem archives provide the necessary public record confirming his status claims. Naturally, he knows all too well that his Roman readers would have no access to these archives to confirm his story (*Life*, 1.7).

Since genealogies justified privilege, they also were subject to considerable manipulation. Plutarch tells of a group of writers ingratiating themselves with noble Roman families by producing fictitious genealogies for the families showing descent from Numa Pompilius. To have a written pedigree, and especially a long one, was a mark of honor. However, most ancient people did not have written genealogies because they could not read them. Peasant genealogies usually consisted of only the three generations in living memory, sometimes attached to a short list of eponymous ancestors (e.g., Abraham, Isaac and Jacob). [15]

By publicly acknowledging a boy to be his son, a father not only accepted responsibility for him and made him his heir, but the father also determined his son's status (honor) in the community. Genealogies thus documented what rituals of naming and circumcision acknowledged. It is significant, therefore, that the genealogy in Luke immediately follows the baptism scene, where God acknowledges in regard to Jesus both paternity ("my beloved son"—*ascribed* honor, honor as precedence) and pleasure ("in whom I am well pleased"—*acquired* honor, honor as virtue).

Equally important is the form of the Lukan genealogy, a form that gives special stress to the notion "son of" (τοῦ). The form of Luke's genealogy suggests one of the important social functions of genealogies, what Hood terms "characterization." So Hood cites the example of Theophrastus, who claims that backbiters tell the character of a person "the way a genealogist does."[16] What he means is that ancestry both signifies *and determines* character. Thus, "Cretans are always liars, vicious brutes, lazy gluttons" (Titus 1:12); nothing good can "come out of Nazareth" (John 1:46). Such stereotyping worked because people in antiquity believed the dictum: "Like father like son." "Son of" thus tells us not only *who* the genealogical subject is, but *what kind of person* we should expect him to be. In this way honor as precedence is connected with honor as virtue.

---

[15] As Rodney Hood points out in "Genealogies of Jesus," an incipient genealogy (e.g., "Joshua, son of Nun" or "Simon, son of Jonah") could serve as a personal name.

[16] Hood, "Genealogies of Jesus," 5.

In sum, the genealogy of Jesus is a stunning claim to honor, all out of keeping with the actual circumstances of his birth.[17] Jesus's genealogy declares him to be no less than the son of Adam, son of God.

A Claim Challenged, A Heart Revealed: Luke 4:1–13

Of course an honor claim this outrageous must be challenged. After all, claiming that one born in the lowliest of peasant circumstances has been raised to nothing less than Son of God traverses virtually the entire social spectrum. Luke's Jesus is thus a classic social anomaly: one who acts all out of keeping with his birth status and social authority. This means that Luke must explain himself quickly or risk losing his reading audience. To do that, the outrageous claim must be tested. In fact, it must be tested by an adversary that no ordinary village carpenter (if indeed that is what Jesus really was) could be expected to match. Luke therefore goes immediately from the honor claim (genealogy) to a test of Jesus's honor at the level of the cosmic powers (4:1–13).

In looking at 4:1–13, it is important at the outset to be clear on the term πειράζω (4:2,13). The word's focus is testing, not "temptation" or seduction. It is used in the LXX both of God testing humans (Gen 22:1–19; Exod 16:4; 20:20; Deut 8:2; 13:2ff.) and of humans testing God (Exod 17:2). As Birger Gerhardsson has shown, πειράζω frequently refers to the testing of the partner in a covenant "to see whether he is keeping his side of the agreement."[18] "Remember the long way that YHWH your God has led you these forty years in the wilderness, in order to humble you, testing you to know what was in your heart" (Deut 8:2). What is offered here, then, is a test of Jesus's true heart.

We come now to the crux of the matter: a challenge–riposte drama occurs in which the very foundation of Luke's honor claim for Jesus is put to the test. It occurs at the cosmic level where false hearts are inexorably exposed and no secrets can be hidden. Note carefully how the devil frames the chal-

---

[17] A fact that may provide sufficient explanation for the curious phrase in 3:23: ὡς ἐνομίζετο. The usual explanation is that Luke edited the comment into the text when the infancy narratives were added, in order to harmonize the genealogy with his story of virgin birth (So Danker 1972:53; Marshall 1978:162). But the verb νομίζω can refer to something habitual or customary, hence Hood (1961:12) speculates that it might be translated, "as his genealogy was ordinarily reckoned." If Hood's translation is appropriate, and if the clause modifies only "the son of Joseph," as has recently been argued (Fitzmyer, *Luke*, 1:499), it could be understood as a reference to the stereotyping of Jesus commonly prevailing among those who knew his father.

[18] Gerhardsson, *Testing of God's Son*, 26, 31.

lenge. "*If* you are the son of God . . ." Precisely that has been the claim and precisely that is what is what is being tested.

It is common among commentators, of course, to suggest that what is being tested here is Jesus's misuse of his miraculous powers or perhaps the character of his messianic mission. But Gerhardsson has correctly noted that such comment reads into the text what simply is not there. This is first of all a test of kinship in which "*Son of God* is *the key term* in the narrative" (emphasis original).[19] However, what neither Gerhardsson nor any other commentator to date has noticed is that in the series of challenges the devil puts to Jesus, the issues of kinship are very cleverly intertwined with issues of patronage. The result is subtlety that is truly astonishing. We shall see this as we look at the text in more detail, but anticipating it we must not lose sight of the overall point. Whatever this story may have meant in Q or elsewhere, Luke uses it to test a claim of status. He signals this strategy clearly by placing the testing story immediately following the genealogy.

So note how carefully Jesus answers, when his lineage is questioned. He does *not* answer in his own words, as if his honor derives from what he is in himself. To do that would be to grasp honor above that of his own Father and turn honor into dishonor. So he answers as a loyal Middle Eastern son would always answer—with something from his family tradition. He offers the words of his true Father in Deuteronomy 8:3: "A human being shall not live by bread alone." By such laudable behavior, Jesus gains honor as virtue. Jesus wins that round hands down.

The second challenge asks Jesus to *worship*—the term should be translated *honor*—the devil rather than God. Here, terms from the semantic field of honor–shame abound: *authority* (ἐξουσία), *glory* (δόξα), *to worship* (προσκυνέω). The term προσκυνέω is especially important. It is widely used in antiquity to describe the gesture of falling down before a person and kissing the person's feet, the hem of a garment, or the ground on which the person walked. Herodotus explains:

> When they meet each other in the streets, you may know if the persons meeting are of equal rank by the following token: if they are, instead of speaking, they kiss each other on the lips. In the case where one is a little inferior to the other, the kiss is given on the cheek; where the difference of rank is great, the inferior prostrates himself upon the ground. (Herodotus, *Hist.*)

---

[19] Ibid., 19. See also Fitzmyer, *Luke*, 1:512.

Falling down in front of someone was thus a recognition of the honor superiority of the other. It was especially common as the proper gesture before a patron (or before his broker) to whom a client owed his well-being. [20]

The use of precisely this terminology in the devil's second test makes it clear that this time, kinship is not the issue, patronage is. The devil makes the audacious claim to be God's broker; the devil claims that both the kingdoms of the world and the right to dispose of their resources in whatever manner he wishes (i.e., to act as God's broker) have been given to him (ἐμοὶ παραδέ δοται καὶ ἐὰν θέλω δίδωμι αὐτήν). The devil thereby introduces a brazen counterclaim against the claim Luke makes for Jesus. In Luke's Gospel, Jesus is the broker of God.

Both the devil's offer and the request he makes of Jesus are important. In return for offering to broker dazzling resources from God to Jesus, the devil asks Jesus to give two of the most important responses a client owes a patron or broker: worship (praise, honor) and the proper gesture to indicate inferiority (falling down before a superior—προσκυνήσῃς ἐνώπιον). In return, the devil offers to make Jesus a client-broker in the patronage chain running from God to the devil to Jesus to whatever clients Jesus may subsequently garner. The devil even throws into the deal the honor status that goes with the client-broker role (τὴν δόξαν αὐτῶν).

Here Jesus's client loyalty to his patron (God) is being fundamentally challenged. Since this test involves a counterclaim in which the devil asserts his own priority over Jesus in the patronage chain, if Jesus acquiesces to the devil's request, Luke's claim that Jesus acts by the power of God's Spirit (Luke 4:1) would be effectively refuted. But a true and honorable client would never switch patrons in this way or try to serve two masters at the same time (Luke 16:13).[21] So the loyalty challenge is thrust aside once again with the words of God, the true Patron of all. In this regard the rejected reading in some Byzantine and Caesarean texts (ὕπαγε ὀπίσω μου, Σατανα—almost certainly imported from Matthew) is somewhat amusing. In this reading, Jesus rather forcefully commands the devil to move down the patronage chain one notch and to take a place behind him!

Finally, in the third test—the best challenge stories must have three tests (cf. Wis 2:17–18)—the adversary again presses the matter of lineage: "*If* you are the son of God . . ." A challenge over the roles of patron, broker, and client

---

[20] Arndt and Gingrich, *Greek–English Lexicon*, 716–17. Here, Arndt and Gingrich have collected the evidence from the tragedians, Philo, Herodotus, Josephus, et al.

[21] For a discussion of competition for clients among patrons in the provinces and the revulsion against such perfidy among elite Romans, see Malina and Rohrbaugh, *Synoptic Gospels*, 388–90.

has not worked in favor of the devil, so kinship again becomes the issue. But the challenge here takes a subtle new form not seen in test number one.

The devil quotes Scripture himself (Ps 91:11–12). The particular quotation is carefully chosen, demonstrating that the devil too is adept at calling upon the tradition of the Father. What the content of that quotation offers is the kind of protection a father offers a son: "[God] will command his angels concerning you, to protect you" and "on their hands they will bear you up, lest you strike your foot against a stone" (Luke 4:10–11). Implied is a subtle counterclaim that Western commentators have either missed or misconstrued. Who has the right to speak the words of the Father? Only a son. By thus adopting the strategy that Jesus (the honorable son) had used in test number one, the devil here poses the possibility that he, rather than Jesus, is the one with the right to quote the Father. It is a claim that the devil is the Father's true son. Thus lineage claim and lineage counterclaim are juxtaposed, so that all of a sudden Jesus's final reply makes perfect sense: "You shall not test the Lord your God" (4:12). Challenging the lineage of God is simply not acceptable.

Thus in reasserting his own right to quote the Father, Jesus once again passes a test of loyalty and shows himself to be worthy of an outrageous honor claim. In a classic Middle Eastern game of challenge and riposte, Jesus has bested an adversary who would frighten any mortal man. His honor has been vindicated in a frightening contest of wits.[22] So with a final note of satisfaction and relief, Luke tells us that the devil slinks off to await an opportune moment to strike again (4:13).

A Public Notice: 4:14–15

By now any Middle Eastern reader of Luke 4 would be awestruck. Jesus has demolished a challenge of superhuman proportions. Nonetheless Luke's readers also might have been a bit nervous. Jesus might be reaching for too much honor and thus violating the notion of limited good. Therefore Luke wants the reader to understand that what Jesus will do in Galilee is possible only because the power of the Spirit has been given to him (4:14).

Luke also provides a public notice. This short text in 4:14–15 is almost universally labeled a "summary" by Western scholars (by Fitzmyer, Marshall, Tannehill, et al.), but the label is not a good one. Luke 4:14–15 is actually in the form of a public notice that provides the necessary rationale for what will

[22] I. Howard Marshall, *Luke*, 166, complains that reducing the testing story "to the level of a *Streitgespräch*" wrongly places the emphasis on Jesus's "dialectical skill." Admittedly there is more to this story than winning a debate. Nonetheless debating skill was much prized in the agonistic world of the first century and would have been properly appreciated by Luke's Greco-Roman readers.

follow (4:16–30). The public notice reports two pieces of critical information.

One is that the gossip network has been functioning properly.[23] Luke tells us that the report about Jesus has spread through all the surrounding country. Among nonliterate people, communication is basically by word-of-mouth, so where reputation (honor status) is concerned, gossip informed the community about (and validated) ongoing gains and losses. In that way, gossip provided an updated guide to proper social interaction. This is especially important information because it allows readers to assume that (1) the news would have spread to Jesus's hometown and (2) that people there would thus be in a position to test what the notice indicates is going on.

Of course the other item Luke reports is that the gossip network is in the process of validating a new honor status for Jesus (δοξαζόμενος ὑπὸ πάντων) throughout Galilee. As noted above, honor claimed must be validated in the court of public opinion because honor claimed is only of value if recognized by the public. For Jesus, validation is happening among "all."

So far, then, Jesus has passed a frightening cosmic challenge, and the honor gained has been recognized in all the surrounding territory. But a challenge on the cosmic level alone is perhaps not sufficient to convince Lukan readers that this low-born village trade worker is worthy of the claims being made. So perhaps a more solid test, one down-to-earth and plausible enough for even the most suspicious reader to appreciate, would simply be to check with the people who know Jesus best: his hometown folks. They know his origin, they know his family, they know his proper honor level. Outrageous honor claims can be refuted there, if anywhere. So, being a good Mediterranean type, Luke takes us next to Jesus's hometown.

Honor Challenged, Honor Vindicated: 4:16–30

The story of the ruckus at Nazareth is well known, and all its details need not be cited here. Our interest is primarily the way in which the story displays the honor of Jesus. Jesus reads from the book of Isaiah, and all are amazed. That is what the notice in Luke 4:15 said he had been doing elsewhere, so that is what needs to be tested here.

Note that Luke begins by carefully reminding his readers that Nazareth is where Jesus grew up. Some have seen this information as unnecessary, given the preceding chapters, but it is very much to the point. It clarifies the fact that this second test of Jesus's honor status is going to take place where the most knowledgeable and critical audience possible is located. Luke wants us

---

[23] Malina and Rohrbaugh, *Synoptic Gospels*, 242–46. See also chapter 9 below.

to know that harsh scrutiny is being given to the claim made in the genealogy of chapter 3.

At first the crowd in Nazareth appears ready to grant Jesus the honor that his way both with words and the tradition might properly warrant. But then notice what someone asks: "Is this not Joseph's son?" (4:22). Is this not the son of that menial family we all know so well? That is the way you get to someone in the Middle East. That is how you deflate overblown egos. That is how you cut down to size those who make claims all out of keeping with their proper place in the honor system. You remind them of where they were born.

Coming to v. 22 we pause to note the astonishing volume of ink poured out in the attempt to explain what Western interpreters see as a break here in the chain of logic (e.g., Bultmann, O'Fearghail, Fitzmyer, Hill, Jeremias, Marshall, Tannehill, and many, many others). As John Kilgallen puts it, the sentiments in v. 22 "do not justify Jesus' words in v. 23."[24] It has seemed to Westerners that the positive and appreciative reaction to Jesus in v. 22 is illogically followed by an angry outburst from Jesus in vv 23–27. Moreover, the angry congregation in v. 28 also appears to have switched its opinion rather quickly and sharply.

We cannot take the time here to review all the proposed solutions to this problem because they are diverse. But Feargus O'Fearghail has perhaps come closest to a solution in recognizing that Jesus's identity is the real issue. Yet he sees Jesus's identity primarily as a theological matter. He suggests that a failure on the part of the hometown audience to recognize the wider salvific import of Jesus triggers the impatient reaction from Jesus in v. 23.[25]

Our argument is that O'Fearghail is on the right track: identity is indeed the issue. But it is *social* identity first of all.[26] The social implications of the question put to Jesus are crystal clear: Asking if Jesus is Joseph's son, the synagogue participants are pondering Jesus, the social anomaly. They want to know how such honorable teaching could come from one born to a lowly village artisan. And, as always, the *public* question is a challenge that anyone sensitive to his own precarious honor status must pick up. Thus Jesus knows immediately that he has been insulted, and that a failure to respond will belie every claim he might later try to make. He is on the spot. As Luke points out, "the eyes of all in the synagogue were fixed on him" (4:21).

---

[24] Kilgallen, "Provocation," 514. For an excellent review of the many positions taken to explain the apparent break in logic, see O'Fearghail, "Rejection at Nazareth," 60–72.

[25] O'Fearghail, "Rejection at Nazareth," 70.

[26] On social identity see Malina, "Circum-Mediterranean Person?" 66–87.

It has shocked most Western interpreters that Luke's Jesus responds to the to the question in v. 22 by insulting the entire audience. He dumps all over them. His attitude does not seem to accord with the apparently positive reaction of the crowd. What has been completely missed, however, is the magnitude of the insult in the public question asked about Jesus's lineage. Obviously some in the crowed react positively. O'Fearghail is correct that no other connotation is really possible for the term μαρτυρέω or for the words οἱ λόγοι τῆς χάριτος, notwithstanding Jeremias's contrived attempts to claim otherwise. But the person in the crowd who asked the insulting question about Jesus's lineage does not respond positively at all. We must recall that aspersions cast on lineage are the most extreme insults Mediterranean cultures have to offer.

Corroborating evidence has been there all along even if Western commentators have not understood what to do with it. Long ago Cyril of Alexandria (4–5 CE) recognized the question as a serious insult. He comments that the ones who first marveled at the gracious words coming from the mouth of Jesus later "wished to disparage him [κατευτελίζειν], for they were asserting: 'Is this not Joseph's son?'" (*Explanatio in Lucae Evangelium*, PG 72: 541d). Theophylactus, a Byzantine exegete flourishing around 1070 CE, writes similarly: "Hearing the things being said by Christ, the crowds were marveling at the gracious words. But at the same time, they were 'ridiculing him [διεκωῴδουν],' saying, 'Is this not the son of the carpenter?'" (*Enarratio in Evangelium Lucae,* PG 123: 752 bc). To both writers it is clear that the question is a public attempt to belittle Jesus's birth status. Theophylactus pointedly notes that it is Joseph's vocation (low-status village artisan) that is the cause of the ridicule.

Of course, once the insulting character of the question is understood, Jesus's negative reaction is perfectly clear. There is no "break" at all in the chain of logic. Jesus offers a stinging riposte (4:24) that he illustrates from Scripture (4:25–27). He implies with two examples that God's favor extends far beyond the native sons of Israel (4:23–24; 4:25–27), and that Israelite genealogy has been overrated. Now Israelite honor has been insulted and the game turns deadly serious.

The crowd knows immediately and unmistakably that it has been insulted in return. In fact the ante has just gone way up. Jesus had been challenged with the question about his ascribed honor status. But his response to that challenge questions whether the very lineage of which those in the audience are so proud has the exclusive value they imagine it to have. Note that he does not question their lineage as Israelites, he simply questions its value.

It is important to recognize that an insult like the one that Jesus offers in response to the crowd is directly confrontational. Even the proverb he quotes

(4:25) is especially insulting since it implies that the crowd in Nazareth has no shame (has no ability to understand what is honorable and what is not). Obviously a negative challenge of this magnitude from Jesus could not go unanswered. So the outraged crowd takes Jesus to the edge of town to throw him off a cliff.

But ironically at that very moment the crowd loses the exchange. The death of a challenger is sometimes a worthy response to public dishonor, though as we noted earlier, in the Middle East, an overquick resort to violence is an inadvertent admission that one has lost control of the challenge situation. Wits have failed and bully tactics have taken over. As the crowd gives in to violence, therefore, Jesus wins the exchange. Lukan readers have been allowed to see once again that Jesus is capable of upholding the outrageous honor claim of the genealogy, this time in front of the most critical audience Luke could conjure up.

Conclusion

Had we time to follow the narrative strategy of Luke's Gospel, all the way to its conclusion, we would discover that Luke plays out the nuances of claim and counterclaim, challenge and counterchallenge, all the way to the end of the Gospel. But Mediterranean readers would already know that this Jesus is capable of far more than his birth status would suggest. Is he the Son of God? Perhaps it is too early to acknowledge that. But there is clearly more to him than meets the eye; of that we are already convinced. By claiming for Jesus an exalted honor status, successfully tested and defended, Luke has drawn us into a Mediterranean melodrama that would have had every Middle Eastern reader clinging to the edge of the seat.

CHAPTER 4

Semiotic Behavior in Luke and John

G IVEN THE individualistic sensibilities of Western culture it is rather easy to think about authors and texts as if one is simply the product of the other. But *semiosis*—the process of producing and exchanging meaning—is in fact extremely interactive behavior and therefore inescapably social. Thus questions about the nature of this social process immediately come to the fore.

In what way is meaning actually created and acknowledged? What are the rules for its production? Who determines the rules? How are rules maintained, modified, or subverted? How do particular styles, genres, narrative choices, or other literary strategies reflect or maintain dominant social interests? Such questions focus our attention on who is producing and receiving what types of meaning and whose interests are being served by the way the process itself is constructed. As a case in point we shall compare the semiotic process in the Lukan and Johannine presentations of Jesus in order to ask what these processes imply for social relations in the communities that produced them.

The Logonomic System

As sociolinguists have effectively demonstrated, communication is a behavior that follows socially generated and commonly understood rules for how messages are to be produced and received. Moreover, this complex of rules, often called a "logonomic system" by sociolinguists, constitutes a complex and pervasive mechanism of social control—even if it is not often recognized as such. The rules can be neither obscure nor confusing if communication is to work. Nor can they be arbitrarily or whimsically altered without causing confusion or conflict, though of course precisely that may be the intent of a speaker or writer.

This logonomic system is part of the socialization process for children and is taught by educators, parents, public figures, and peers. The rules are policed by these same social agents, often by coercion, and are reinforced in all sorts of public discourse, including something as formal as the discourse taught in the rhetorical schools or as informal as discourse heard in the gossip network. Because such rules are part of an ongoing and continuously negotiated social contract, they are always part of an ideological complex that both expresses and reflects specific social relations.

Equally important for our purposes is the fact that logonomic systems can be challenged or resisted by subordinate persons or groups. Anti-languages are an obvious example. So also are off-color jokes in inappropriate settings, or talking during an operatic aria, or calling newly introduced dignitaries by their first names. Semiotic challenges in the form of unexpected speech behaviors are often very subtle but at the same time can carry heavy freight in terms of meaning.

A simple example is afforded by the way greetings are exchanged in American culture. A handshake and "How are you?" is expected to be followed rather quickly with the response, "Fine, how are you?" But suppose the handshake and initial question are followed by a significant pause. The belated "Fine, how are you?" raises immediate suspicion. Is the respondent distracted? Caught off guard? Or does the pause indicate hostility? Perhaps the respondent is Algonquin and so from a culture in which rapid response is deemed impolite. Such "marked speech," as Muriel Saville-Troike calls it, speech in which the logonomic indicators are unusual or unexpected, is difficult for outsiders in any society to catch and understand.

A corollary of all this is that when systems of domination are being challenged, logonomic systems are likely to be challenged as well. Since such systems are the result of long and continuous negotiation between elite and nonelite, and since in large measure logonomic systems reflect the elite view of the world, accommodation to the logonomic system by subordinate groups often mirrors accommodation to the larger social contract. And where structures of domination are undergoing challenge, logonomic systems are often a key point at which social conflict first emerges. An obvious case in point: it is anti-societies that produce anti-languages (for an explanation of anti-language see chapter 11 below).

It is important here to recognize that rules for the production and reception of meaning, even informal ones, are the result of an ongoing process of negotiation and social change—often over long periods of time. They are a social product, a group product, and often represent group interests in the ongoing life of the social contract. Moreover, since they seek to prescribe and control behavior, they are forms of power. As Antonio Gramsci has shown in his discussion of the way hegemonic structures are produced in a society, there is an ongoing struggle between intellectuals who represent various social groups in a society, including even peasants, over the proper way to represent the world. Gramsci sees every communication, every exchange of meaning, as an event, however tiny, in an ongoing struggle that involves a subtle negotiation of power.

Of course a logonomic system is effective only insofar as some group is able to articulate and enforce it—whether through informal persuasion, educational processes, peer sanction, class envy, or whatever. It becomes part of an ideological complex that the dominant think is the way things should be and that the dominated think is the way things are. Speech rules, both formal and informal, are thus examples of group enforcement of hegemonic patterns of behavior.

First- and Second-Level Meanings

Sociolinguists have long recognized that analysis of the rules for the production of meaning requires acknowledging two levels of meaning in every message. Thus first-level meaning (i.e. content) is always accompanied by additional levels of meaning that are conveyed by style, genre, tone, gesture, facial expressions, touching, and the like. Second-level meanings provide indicators for how first-level meanings are to be taken or understood. A joke, for example, should not be taken seriously. Readers have to know the clues that indicate when an author is joking, being sarcastic, using irony or whatever. As Sirach 20:20 puts it: "A proverb from a fool's lips will be rejected, for he does not tell it at the proper time."

Such second-level meanings are deeply embedded in social processes that shape the way authors and speakers make choices about *how* they wish to say what it is they wish to say. Anger, for example, may be expressed in a cold, controlled, impersonal style, or in a loud, aggressive, and emotional manner. The medium is part of the message. Such first- and second-level meanings often coincide, but of course they can also contradict each other. Pounding the table while shouting that one is not angry is an obvious case of contradiction. Jokes may hide nervousness, and excessive bravado may actually signal weakness. As Proverbs 27:6 says, "Well meant are the wounds a friend inflicts, but profuse are the kisses of an enemy."

In sum, in examining the strategies of Luke and John for presenting Jesus, we shall look at their use of the logonomic system—the rules for the production of meaning. We shall observe whose rules are being followed, and what social relations are thereby implied. Part of that analysis will involve second-level meanings. Thus it is not just *what* these writers say, but *how* they choose to say it, that will be the focus of our investigation.

Limitations

Before jumping into this look at semiotic process in Luke and John, however, we must acknowledge that this approach has serious limitations. For example, it is obvious that many of the second-level meanings in New Testament discourse are forever lost to the modern world. It is not just that we lack evidence for things like tone of voice, facial expressions, rapidity of speech, and the like. It is also that being cultural outsiders we have no access to many of the complex indicators that could be used to "mark" speech for an ancient reader. For example, were Jesus's answers to the many questions from antagonists given in rapid-fire fashion? Or were they slow and deliberate? And even more important, what would it mean in first-century Palestine to offer rapid-fire as over against deliberate answers? Analysis of logonomics at that level is simply not possible for us today.

Similarly, even when authors do offer second-level clues they are often ambiguous or unclear. As Sirach 20:6 puts it: "Some people keep silent because they have nothing to say, while others keep silent because they know when to speak." A good example of ambiguous second-level markers can be found in Luke 7:38, where a woman weeps and kisses the feet of Jesus. Both the tears and the kisses are second-level indicators. They are meant to inform the reader how to understand the dynamics of the story. But both actions can be read in a variety of ways.

It turns out there is a lot of kissing in the Bible (57 incidents). But its meaning can vary. It can indicate romance (Song 1:2; 7:9; 8:1), seduction (Prov 7:13), deference (Sir 29:5), kinship ties (Gen 27:27; 29:11; 29:13), fictive kinship ties (Rom 16:16; 1 Cor 16:20; 2 Cor 13:12; 1 Thess 5:26), loyalty (1Kgs 19:18; Hos 13:12), friendship (1 Sam 20:41), peace (Ps 85:10), or love (1 Pet 5:14). It can be used to deceive (Prov 27:6), to ingratiate in the hope of gaining a loan (Sir 29:5), or even to betray (Mark 14:44).

Kissing can also involve contact with a number of different body parts. One can kiss the lips (Prov 24:26), the feet (Ps 2:12; Luke 7:38), or the soles of the feet (Add Esth 13:13). Herodotus says that among some people, kissing certain body parts is a clue to honor relations:

> When they meet each other in the streets, you may know if the persons meeting are of equal rank by the following token: if they are, instead of speaking, they kiss each other on the lips. In the case where one is a little inferior to the other, the kiss is given on the cheek; where

the difference of rank is great, the inferior prostrates himself upon the ground. (*History,* 1.134).

In other words, kissing used as a second-level indicator can imply certain kinds of social relations that are important to the dynamics of ancient stories, but for us today the meaning of the kissing is not always clear.

Tears can be equally ambiguous. They can indicate grief (Ps. 6:6; Isa 22:4), joy (Gen 34:4; 45:14–15), sincerity (2 Kgs 20:5; Isa 38:5; Heb 5:7; 12:17), insincerity (Sir 12:16), mourning (Ps 102:9; Sir 38:16; John 11:35), complaint (Mal 3:13), humility (Acts 20:19), anguish (2 Cor 2:4), affection (Gen. 43:30) or empathy (Job 30:25). They can also provide support for a plea or supplication (Ps 39:12).

When kisses and tears are combined, this same ambiguity appears. Kissing and weeping can indicate joy (Gen 29:11; 33:4; 45:15), sorrow (Ruth 1:14), or mourning (Gen 50:1). The woman in Luke 7:38 both weeps and kisses the feet of Jesus. Are these tears of joy or of sorrow and repentance? Commentators cannot decide.[1] And what about the fact that she kisses Jesus's feet? Should we assume this is status recognition, indicating the woman's humility and Jesus's honor? Or is it a plea for forgiveness? (cf. Add Esth 8:3). Perhaps it is worship? (cf. Matt 4:9; Acts 10:25). These second-level indicators are not all that clear to us now even when we know that the story is contrasting the woman's behavior with that of the man hosting the dinner.

Narrative Choices

If rules for the production and reception of meaning (including those that rules that employ second-level indicators) are often obscure to cultural outsiders, nonetheless some of those rules in the New Testament remain transparent yet today. One good example can be seen in the choices an author makes about the narrative elements or rhetorical strategy to be employed in addressing a particular audience.

One such choice frequently recognized by sociolinguists is an author's choice of genre. Genres are, after all, rules for the production of meaning. As Robert Hodge and Gunther Kress put it, genres are "socially prescribed classifications of semiotic form."[2] Because they are socially prescribed, genres control the behavior of those who produce texts as well as the expectations of those who receive them. Moreover, the rules for the production of a specific genre not only structure its form, thereby accommodating to audience expectations; the rules also structure or imply certain social relations among

---

[1] Fitzmyer, *Luke,* 1:686–89.

[2] Hodges and Kress, *Social Semiotics,* 7.

various participants in the semiotic process. The business-letter form, for example, implies one type of social relationship between author and recipient; a personal-letter format suggests quite another. Court records, textbooks, nursery rhymes, jokes, gossip, and a host of other forms all imply, indeed depend upon, specific social relations between producer and receiver for the production and reception of meaning.

Other narrative elements might equally well be understood as responses to rules in a production or reception regime. In honor–shame societies, for example, a response is expected whenever any kind of challenge is offered. A missing response speaks volumes, as does one that is inappropriate or ill timed. In addition, since honor that goes unrecognized is of no value whatsoever, readers of an ancient narrative would probably expect an author to provide notice of story-audience approval whenever a character in a story had been given a grant of honor. Ancient audiences would surely notice if these kinds of second-level indicators were missing. Thus narrative elements, chosen by an author as part of a rhetorical strategy, are good indicators of semiotic behavior and how the rules are or are not being followed.

Semiotic Behavior in Luke and John

In order to illustrate what we have been talking about, we shall look briefly at the presentation of Jesus in two of the Gospels: Luke and John. Our argument will be that Luke accepts the logonomic system of elite Greco-Roman society and assumes his readers will do the same. Certain social relations are thereby implied. By contrast, the Johannine community rejects the dominant society, and therefore it is not surprising that one of the places this conflict emerges is in the community's response to the socially prescribed semiotic behaviors that dictate how a story's hero is presented.

Luke: Moving Jesus Up the Honor Scale

The degree to which Luke has bought into the semiotic process of elite Greco-Roman society is quite astonishing. It can be clearly seen in the choices Luke makes about how to commend Jesus to his reading audience. Among the literate elite of the Roman world, honor was a core social value. Thus for Luke, the village artisan Jesus of the Gospel of Mark, who lacked significant standing on the scale of honor (Mark 6:3), was hardly suitable for his version of the story. Luke needed to take dramatic action. By any measure, the lengths to which Luke goes to move Jesus up the honor scale, and thereby to make him acceptable to elite readers, are truly extraordinary.

In attempting to do this, Luke had two basic options. One would be to address the *ascribed* honor status of Jesus—the honor gained from his position at birth. The other option would be to address Jesus's *acquired* honor status—the honor he gained in the course of his public career. Elite audiences would of course expect ascribed and acquired honor to go hand in hand; hence, in order to leave no doubt about the matter of Jesus's honor status, Luke makes bold use of both options. While we cannot describe Luke's strategy comprehensively, a survey of key data will make clear that Luke knows how to make and exchange meaning in the elite world of Roman society.

ASCRIBED HONOR

We begin with *ascribed* honor and Luke's use of a socially prescribed semiotic form: the encomium. There is no better example of a logonomic system at work than the well-known instructions offered in the ancient Greek rhetorical schools for writing an encomium, a piece in praise of someone. Since these instructions from the *progymnasmata* for writing an encomium are well known, a brief summary of their provisions will suffice.

Hermogenes instructs his students to begin with the subject's origin and birth. They are to speak of "race, as the Greek, a city, as Athens, a family as the Alcmaeonidae" (*Rhetores Graeci*, II.14.8–15.5).

This is, of course, exactly what Luke does in his story of Jesus's origins. First, he provides a royal genealogy tracing Jesus's origins back to God (3:23–38). In antiquity, lineage was not only a source of pride but also a device for self-aggrandizement.[3] A genealogy was a claim to authority, to place, to political or civil rights, to various social roles, and even the right to speak. To have a written pedigree, and especially a long one, was a mark of honor. Luke provides the longest genealogy possible.

Menander Rhetor joins the chorus by saying that one of the first things to be done in an encomium is to praise the city from which the subject comes, because honor is ascribed to those born in an honorable city (*Treatise II*, 369.17–370.10). Luke does this too. He reports Jesus's birth in a "royal" city, the city of David (2:4; 2:11). While Bethlehem hardly qualifies as a "city" in any real sense, neither Luke nor his readers seem to know that. Thus Luke offers it as a place that can produce the likes of David and, by implication, a Jesus whose ascribed honor is of a similar kind to David's.

Hermogenes adds that the encomium writer should then describe "what marvelous things befell at birth, as dreams or signs or the like" (*Rhetores Graeci* II.14.8–15.5). Luke once again follows the instructions, reporting on angelic appearances and heavenly songs (2:9–14). Quintilian instructs an encomium writer to note things that happened prior to the birth, such as prophecies

---

[3] Hood, "Genealogies of Jesus," 3–8.

"foretelling future greatness" (*Inst. Orat.* 3.7.10–18). Luke provides these as well. One message comes from heaven, from an angel (1:26–38); the other message comes from Zechariah, who spoke when filled with the Holy Spirit (1:67–73). The angel declares Jesus's royalty (1:32), whereas Zechariah asserts that Jesus is of the house of David and will be nothing less than the "prophet of the Most High" (1:76). For the Jesus who started as a village artisan in Mark, the entire social spectrum has just been traversed. His ascribed honor is thus secure.

ACQUIRED HONOR

Luke's claims about Jesus's *acquired* honor are equally pretentious. While there are a number of means by which Luke seeks to demonstrate the acquired honor of Jesus (e.g., titles, skill at repartee, ability to confound questioners), we shall concentrate on the matter of public reputation since it is reputation that is the necessary public validation of an acquired honor status. No doubt the frequency with which Luke reports public acknowledgment of Jesus's growing reputation seems unnecessary to modern readers, who usually pass over such notices without a second glance. Our logonomic system creates no such expectation for such reports of acknowledgement. But these reports would have been exactly what ancient readers expected. As Aristotle puts it: "A good reputation consists in being considered a man of worth by *all . . .*"

The number of times Luke reports public praise of Jesus is truly amazing. Simeon praises the child in the temple (2:25–35). Anna does the same, before all who will listen (2:38). His parents are amazed at his understanding (2:47). Luke tells us that Jesus increased in divine and human favor (2:52). John the Baptist publicly places Jesus higher than himself on the honor scale (3:16). A divine voice praises Jesus and acknowledges his genealogy (3:22). The gossip network spreads Jesus's fame in the surrounding country, and he is praised by everyone (4:14–15). All are amazed at him in the synagogue of Nazareth (4:22). In Capernaum, listeners are astounded at his teaching (4:32) and at his power over demons (4:36). Reports of Jesus reach every place in the region (4:37). Word of his healing spreads abroad (5:15). He amazes onlookers by healing a paralytic, and everyone is filled with awe (5:26). His reputation even reaches a high-ranking Roman officer (7:3). After raising the son of the widow of Nain, Jesus is praised as a prophet (7:16), and his fame spreads throughout the region (7:17).

In Luke 7:18, the reputation of Jesus reaches John the Baptist, who sends disciples to inquire. Jesus tells these followers to report what they have seen and heard while they are with him (7:22). After Jesus forgives a woman of the city, those at the table with him are taken aback by what they have witnessed (7:49). Jesus's disciples acknowledge that he commands even the wind and water (8:25). When Jesus heals a demoniac in the country of the Gerasenes, the swineherds tell everyone, and the report spreads fear in the area (8:37). Jairus, a member of the elite, falls at Jesus's feet (in a gesture of inferiority) to beg for his daughter's life. When she is healed, he is "astounded" (8:56).

Luke reports that the reputation of Jesus even reaches the royal court (9:9). The crowds near Bethsaida also hear of him (9:11). Divine approval in the hearing of his disciples is again given to Jesus on the mountain (9:35). A great crowd is astounded at the healing of an epileptic boy, and indeed at everything Jesus was doing (9:43). In Luke 10:17 even demons submit to his name (i.e., to his honor, reputation). Later, when Jesus is casting a demon out of a mute person, the crowd is again amazed (11:14), though opponents look for an alternate explanation for what is happening (11:15). In Luke 11: 27 a woman publicly praises Jesus's mother (hence Jesus by implication) by calling her "honored."

Luke's hyperbole in 12:1 ("when the crowd gathered in thousands, so that they trampled one another") implies a growing reputation for Jesus as well. Later, in 13:17, we are told that Jesus's enemies have been "put to shame," while the entire crowd rejoices at what he does. "All" the people praise him when he heals a beggar in 18:43. When Jesus rides into Jerusalem to the praise of a multitude of disciples, Pharisees ask Jesus to quiet them. But Jesus replies that even the stones would cry out if the crowd did not (19:40). Later, when he teaches in the temple, we are told that the people are "spell-bound" by what they hear (19:48). After Jesus has decisively confounded those who publicly challenge him over payment of taxes, Luke reports that even Jesus's opponents are amazed (20:26). And finally, in Luke 21:38 we are told that people will even get up early in the morning just to listen to Jesus in the temple.

Given the fact that *all* these notices are *constructed by the narrator of Luke's Gospel*, it is safe to say that concern for acquired honor, for *public* reputation, is critical to Luke's rhetorical strategy. Of the thirty-seven examples of public honor cited above, Luke has added twenty-two to Mark's story of Jesus. Would a modern writer write this way? It is unlikely. Would an ancient Mediterranean writer? Yes indeed, especially if writing for those who know the rules and therefore expect acknowledgement of public reputation as the justification for any claims the story makes.

John: Leaving the Earthly Jesus Right Where He Is

When we come to the Gospel of John we enter a different world. That is true not only in terms of the Gospel's content but also in terms of its second-level indicators for meaning. This Gospel does not emerge from the peasant world of Mark. Nor is it from the sophisticated urban worlds of Matthew and Luke. This Gospel's Jesus displays neither special identification with the poor nor the high level of honor expected by elite urban readers. As we shall see, something else drives John's unique portrait of Jesus.

Raymond Brown asserts that John is almost certainly a Galilean Gospel recounting the Jesus story for a mixed (Galilean, Samaritan, and Gentile) community of followers.[4] Moreover, this community was likely what socio-linguist M. A. K. Halliday calls an "anti-society," that is, a group that exists within a dominant society but as a "conscious alternative to it."[5] It was an alienated group that had been pushed (or withdrawn) to the social margins, where it stood as a protest to the values of the larger society.[6]

The scope and depth of this alienation is evident in the language of the Gospel itself. John's Jesus says to his disciples: "If the dominant society [κόσμος] hates you, be aware that it hated me before it hated you. If you belonged to the society, the society would love you as its own. Because you do not belong to the society, but I have chosen you out of the society – therefore the society hates you" (15:18–19; my translation).

This is tough talk. Yet it accurately conveys the temper of the group's relations with outsiders. As the story makes clear, the hostility of the Johannine group was especially aimed at Judeans. Members of John's group saw the larger Judean society as hostile to Jesus and therefore hostile to themselves. John's Jesus calls Judeans "children of the devil" (8:44), and they respond by claiming that Jesus is either a Samaritan or possessed by demons (8:48). Obviously this is a group whose relations with the dominant society have gone rather sour.

It is in the midst of this social conflict that John locates the earthly Jesus. We argued earlier that, where systems of domination are being challenged, logonomic systems are often a key point at which social conflict first emerges. In his presentation of Jesus, John has this on full display. Like Luke, John defends Jesus vigorously (attacking Jesus's opponents with equal vigor), but in defending Jesus, the writer of the Fourth Gospel makes no claim for the honor of the earthly Jesus. There is no attempt here to push Jesus up the

---

[4] Brown, *Community*.

[5] Halliday, "Anti-languages," 570.

[6] For a discussion of the Johannine group as an anti-society, see Malina and Rohrbaugh, *Gospel of John*.

scale. Unashamedly, almost defiantly, John admits that the earthly Jesus is nothing.

A key issue in John's Gospel is where Jesus is "from." We have already seen the importance of birth or origin in Mediterranean society because it determined ascribed honor, public legitimacy, and authority. In the instructions of the *progynasmata* (see above) we were told to pay great attention to birthplace because great people are born in great places. Obviously obscure Galilean villages like Nazareth would not qualify as great places (John has no Bethlehem tradition). As Nathanael puts it in the Gospel of John: "Can anything good come out of Nazareth?" (1:46; see also 7:52). Jesus cannot be counted as honorific on the basis of his place of origin.

John is aware of this. In John 7, while Jesus is at the Feast of Tabernacles in Jerusalem, in the midst of a tense and potentially dangerous situation, a dispute arises in the crowd about whether Jesus might be the Messiah. Then someone in the crowd shouts, "We know where this man is *from* . . ." (7:27). The implication of this anonymous statement is that Jesus comes from a place of no account; hence, he could not be the Messiah. Another speaker puts it squarely: "Surely the Messiah does not come from Galilee, does he?" (7:41). A third speaker reminds everyone that the Scripture foretells a Messiah from Bethlehem, from the house of David the king (7:42). The result is chaos and a near arrest.

It is right in the midst of all this that John's Jesus *openly* admits that his origin qualifies him for nothing: "You know me, and you know where I am *from*" (7:28). But he then makes one of the central claims in all of the Gospel of John: "I have not come on my own . . . but the one who sent me is true." Granted Jesus's biological origins are nothing, that he has no ascribed honor, yet in John's eyes that is irrelevant because Jesus does not come in his own name.

Note that *forty-three times* in John we are told that Jesus was "sent" by God. This is language that appears only twice in Matthew (10:40, 15:24), once in Mark (9:37), four times in Luke (4:18, 4:43, 9:48, 10:16), and once in Paul (Rom 8:3). But for John this assertion that Jesus has been sent by someone higher (God) is the entire basis for his claim on people's attention. Jesus's place of origin is irrelevant because *he claims absolutely nothing on his own.* The relevant authority is that of the one who sent him.

The importance of this language about being "sent" can be seen in another way. In antiquity the "sent" messenger was one who came from a patron, a person of unquestioned stature and authority. As broker, the messenger's only claim to fame was access to the patron, nothing more. The messenger simply acted as an intermediary between the patron and those for whom the patron's message or largesse was intended. This broker role is the one Jesus plays throughout John's Gospel. Note that eight times we are reminded that Jesus will return to his Patron, suggesting that the broker has ready access to and from the Patron who sent him (7:33; 13:1; 14:12; 14:28; 16:5; 16:10; 16:17; 16:28).

Readers of John's Gospel will not find it difficult to sense the defensive tone in all this. The sheer repetition of the claim that Jesus was "sent" is part of it. But so also are statements such as: "The Father who has sent me has himself testified on my behalf. You have never heard his voice or seen his form, and you do not have his word abiding in you, because you do not believe him whom he has sent" (5:37–38). John's claim that Jesus is "sent" from God is intended as a defensive strategy meant to counteract the prevailing wisdom that one "from" Nazareth could claim no public standing on his own. John agrees that Jesus has no standing, but he claims that, as broker for God, Jesus bears the authority of his Patron.

One additional charge asserted by Jesus's Judean enemies may be added to all this. The typical instructions in the *progynasmata* remind an encomium writer that after matters of origin and birth, the next conventional topic to be addressed when praising someone is the matter of nurture and education:

> Next comes "nurture." Was he reared in a palace? Were his swaddling clothes robes of purple? Was he from his first growth brought up in the lap of royalty? . . . If he does not have any distinguished nurture . . . discuss his education, . . . the quality of his mind. . . . [S]peak of his love of learning, his quickness, his enthusiasm for study, his easy grasp of what is taught him . . . (Menander Rhetor, *Treatise II*, 371.17–372.2).

John's Jesus would not qualify on this score either. Luke had provided at least a glimpse of Jesus's quickness and enthusiasm for study in the temple incident at twelve years of age (2:41–52). But nothing like this appears in John. In fact, in John 7:15, in the midst of a heated dispute in the temple, someone in the crowd raises an early challenge: "How does this man have such learning, when he has never been taught?" But once again Jesus's reply is typical of the strategy throughout the Gospel of John: "My teaching is not mine but his who sent me" (7:16). It is as if the writer knows he can make no claims for Jesus that will stand up before either his Judean opponents or potential readers of the account. Jesus had neither the proper origin, nor the proper nurture, nor the proper education. The Gospel writer's only recourse is thus to claim that Jesus was sent by God, speaks for God, speaks the words of God, and makes no claim of his own for either his origin or his education.

In sum, unlike Luke, who feels it necessary to move Jesus up the scale of honor to appeal to elite audiences, John employs a unique strategy. He makes no claim for Jesus whatsoever. Everything ultimately comes from God; Jesus is simply the broker whom God has sent to speak on God's behalf.

Implied Social Relations

This brief review of data from Luke and John reveals marked differences in rhetorical strategy. Luke buys into the logonomic system wholeheartedly. His behavior is constrained by the logonomic rules of elite Greco-Roman society, and he apparently assumes his audience's expectations will correspond. In Luke, the author, the implied audience, and no doubt the real audience share a set of common assumptions and an obviously harmonious set of social relations as well.

The case of John is somewhat more interesting. It is obvious that there are two audiences for Jesus in the story-world of the Gospel: opponents of Jesus's group and those who are in the process of becoming members of that group. In the same way, there are parallel audiences among the potential readers of the Gospel: those with standard expectations, who look for typical signs of the honor of Jesus, and those who, like key characters inside the story, are in the process of becoming members of the Johannine community. For each of these groups (for opponents and friends, for folks both inside the story and outside among readers), John's narrative functions in a unique way.

For those open to Jesus, the Gospel offers many indications of the emerging glorification of Jesus. The Prologue and the final chapters of the story anticipate and finally demonstrate how the heavenly honor of the less-than-honorable earthly Jesus is being secured by the power of God. Since the Gospel is primarily meant to reassure new insiders that, in spite of all indications to the contrary, trust in Jesus is fully warranted, the many markers and portents of the heavenly glorification of Jesus are critically important. Of similar importance are key characters in the story-world who see the honor of Jesus before the hour of glorification actually comes (Nicodemus, the Samaritan woman, Mary, Thomas after the resurrection). As they come to believe in him, they model the experience that individual sympathetic readers must themselves go through in joining the Johannine group.

But characters in the story-world who do not have this special insight or who are not really open to believing in Jesus interact with him according to the usual norms of the honor–shame society. They look for the expected indicators of honor and find they are not there. Moreover, the same is true for those outside who read the Gospel expecting a strategy like Luke's. They too will see a Jesus who lacks the honor necessary to make him a significant figure.

It is clear that at the outsider level, John assumes some in his audience will affirm the system and expect to be accommodated. Therefore both the opponents in the audience of Jesus inside the story world, and the implied readers on the outside that John imagines for his Gospel, share the expectation that he will have to present Jesus as honorific. John does not ignore these expectations, nor does he argue against their validity. He simply provides a rather strange way of meeting them. Since he cannot claim much for the earthly Jesus, he shifts the honor claim to God and makes Jesus the bearer of a delegated authority. Jesus is non-authoritative in his own right but becomes a broker who was "sent."

Two things are interesting here. One is that John does not challenge the system in a fundamental way. Just as much as Luke, he still needs to demonstrate an honorific basis for the authority of his message. If he cannot find it in Jesus, he finds it in God. At one level, therefore, John's behavior remains constrained by the same system of rules that energized Luke. We must be quick to point out, however, that John is less at home in this world than Luke and more at a distance from both the implied and real audiences he must accommodate and persuade.

Even more interesting, however, is the fact that John's strategy is a good example of marked speech. John does something unexpected. One would not normally admit that the person being commended in a narrative is a dishonorable lowlife who cannot speak on his own authority. Yet that is the implication when John shifts the locus of authority to God. As the portents and key characters in the story indicate, the Johannine Jesus will eventually be glorified, but that is only after he leaves this world; hence the narrator keeps reminding readers that the hour for this has not yet come (2:4; 7:30; 8:20). Until it does, John leaves the earthly Jesus beneath the threshold of honorific expectation.

It is clear that an ancient audience would notice what John is doing. Luke follows the normative pattern, but John does not. The audience might or might not buy into the notion of delegated authority and eventual glorification, but they surely would have found this a strange way to proceed. However by its very contravention of the expected way of claiming authority, John's narrative choice would have been an attention-getter, a marker. Just as a pause after a handshake draws attention to itself, so also does the radical shift in rhetorical strategy offered by John. Both are clear examples of marked speech.

John's strategy also implies social relations between the author and the outsider audience, social relations quite different from those in Luke. Luke is comfortable with the conventions and assumes his audience is as well; hence, he constructs a narrative along the expected lines. John knows the conventions, knows his audience will expect them, knows he cannot meet them; hence, he creates a narrative, the defensive tone of which belies a genuine strain in the social relations between John and those who hold the normal semiotic expectations. John's strategy is not that of someone comfortable in the world of Luke.

Conclusion

Space does not permit a full examination of the rhetorical strategies of each Gospel author with regard to the honor of Jesus. Luke especially employs a variety of strategies for moving Jesus up the scale of ascribed and acquired honor. But the illustrations we have examined warrant a tentative conclusion that, whereas Luke buys into the logonomic system of the Greco-Roman elite with unhesitating enthusiasm, John is wary and guarded. He is prepared to contravene expectations with the full knowledge that his audience will be wary of the tactic. Thus, in both Luke and John, we can say that social relations and semiotic behavior correspond. Luke's social relations are harmonious. John's are not. It is not just what they say, but how these authors choose to say it that demonstrates their respective stances toward both their audiences and a socially prescribed set of semiotic behaviors.

CHAPTER 5

What Did Jesus Know about Himself and When Did He Know It?

I T IS a commonplace in New Testament scholarship to say that the answers we get are determined by the questions we ask. Yet it does not appear to have dawned on many historical Jesus researchers that ethnocentric results are frequently the result of questions which are themselves rooted in ethnocentric bias. In order to explore this possibility, I would like to examine one of the central questions in historical Jesus research: The question of the so-called messianic self-consciousness of Jesus. Few questions in historical Jesus research have generated more print, or more disagreement, than this one.

To tread upon this ground might at first seem rather dangerous. After all, Western scholars have debated it intensively for a century and a half and yet remain deeply divided. Our purpose here, however, is neither to review nor to analyze the enormous literature on this subject.[1] Rather we intend to examine the question about Jesus's self-understanding in order to determine (1) whether the question itself is inappropriate, and (2) whether the question predetermines a range of answers that are peculiarly Western in character and therefore inevitably ethnocentric. Should this turn out to be the case, it seems likely to call into question a considerable portion of the Western scholarly effort to understand who Jesus was.

The Nature of the Question

First, then, let us explore the nature of the question being asked. It is a question that appears in the titles of books and articles in all the decades of the

---

[1] That has conveniently been done by a number of scholars over the years, though perhaps most clearly and systematically in the recent work of Gerd Theissen and Annette Merz, *The Historical Jesus: A Comprehensive Guide.*

twentieth century.[2] In its most basic form it is an inquiry into the *self*-understanding of Jesus. Exactly who did he think he was? Was he acting out an identity of his own choosing? Did he have a conscious agenda of his own? Did his *self*-understanding define his mission? That is the heart of the matter.

Many researchers of course have asked these questions in rather naïve fashion, as if we could somehow do a psychological inquiry into Jesus's sense of self. Ragnar Leivestad, for example, claims that "if there is no possibility of attaining any psychological understanding and insight," then the person of Jesus will inevitably be an "unapproachable enigma and his proclamation abstract and distant."[3] Others, however, have grasped the fact that this is not really possible. Thus Joachim Gnilka readily acknowledges that the Gospels do not contain any psychological texts with which to work.[4]

What virtually all the many inquiries into this question have in common has been asserted recently and forcefully in an article by Ben F. Meyer: "We take it, for our part, that Jesus was a man with a definite view of himself . . ."[5] That view, that Jesus had a definite view of himself, is taken for granted by virtually all Western scholars addressing the issue. Yet it is precisely this underlying assumption that has remained almost completely unexamined in the historical Jesus literature to date. That is so, I believe, because *self*-understanding is so fundamental to the Western perception of what it is to be human, that it is nearly impossible for us to conceive of a human being without it.

The Self as a Cultural Construct

What is missing in all this is any recognition that the concept of the "self" is a cultural construct that differs markedly from one society to the next. As hard as it is to conceive, social scientists have demonstrated that not everyone on the planet shares our Western understanding of what it is to be a human self. Moreover, as Edward Stewart and Milton Bennett have argued, few cultural realities contain the potential for more misunderstanding than this one.[6]

---

[2] Articles by Western scholars addressing the issue of the "self-consciousness" of Jesus are far too numerous to list in this short chapter. The bibliography at the end of this book offers a representative sample from recent decades.

[3] Leivestad, *Jesus in His Own Perspective*, 12. Theology, it seems, also requires an answer. Wolfhart Pannenberg asserts that, "Christology cannot avoid the question of Jesus' self-consciousness, however difficult it may be exegetically and historically" (326).

[4] Gnilka, *Jesus of Nazareth*, 248.

[5] Meyer, *Jesus' Ministry and Self-Understanding*, 341. Or as Gwilym Beckerlegge puts it, "Any approach to Jesus which accepts both his humanity and his rationality is based on the presupposition that Jesus had a self-consciousness" ("Jesus' Authority," 370).

[6] Stewart and Bennett, *American Cultural Patterns*, 129–47.

According to social scientists, societies may be placed along a continuum in regard to views of the self. On the one hand there are those societies who understand persons individualistically. In such systems, the individual is seen as a bounded and unique center of consciousness, a more or less integrated cognitive and motivational universe. The key to understanding persons in such societies is the psychological makeup of the individual.

On the other hand there are many societies that view the self as fundamentally collective. In this view, persons are so embedded in groups that the group and the individual are in large measure coextensive, both psychologically and in every other way.

Americans, and in varying degrees most other Westerners, stand at the individualist end of this spectrum. Mediterranean persons, however, including those of the biblical period, must be located primarily at the collectivist end. The difference between Westerners and Mediterranean persons is thus rather is substantial. Moreover, the individualist–collectivist difference is one New Testament scholars simply cannot afford to overlook. For as F. Sushila Niles has recently argued, there is now a near consensus among social scientists that such individualist–collectivist differences may be the single most important factor in determining social behavior.[7]

Individualist Cultures

In all the individualistic cultures of the West then, and especially in the United States, individualism rests on the fundamental notion that "each person is not only a biological entity, but also a unique psychological being."[8] The self is fundamentally subjective; hence, individuals are endowed with unique perception, unique personal opinions, their own creativity, and personal preferences.[9] Since it is subjective, this Western self can best be examined via its own subjectivity. As a result, the Western individualistic self is highly introspective and in the last analysis can finally and completely be known only to itself. For Westerners, therefore, *self*-understanding is always the heart of the matter.

Variations among individualist cultures exist of course, and we shall say more about these in a moment. But the differences notwithstanding, most individualists share certain key characteristics. First, they base identity on personal experiences, personal achievements, possessions, abilities, and personal preferences.[10] They tend to attribute actions to internal causes and personal

---

[7] Niles, "Individualism–Collectivism Revisited," 315–16.

[8] Stewart and Bennett, *American Cultural Patterns*, 129.

[9] Ibid., 130.

[10] Triandis, *Individualism and Collectivism*, 71.

choices in ways that collectivists simply do not.[11] They focus on personal rights, needs and abilities. They are relentless in seeking cognitive consistency. Individualists attribute motives to internal needs and aspirations. They give greater priority to attitudes than to norms and treat values as matters of individual choice. They value privacy and private property. Career, life work or mission, purpose, and even religion are all matters to be worked out by individual choice. Above all, individualists assume that ability, effort, and responsibility are the basis for personal success.

The fact is, however, that this sort of individualism has been rather rare in the cultures of the world. It is nearly absent in the Middle East today and almost certainly was absent in antiquity as well. Most important, there is virtually nothing in the New Testament or in the Jesus tradition that suggests anything like what we have been describing.[12] The Western type of individualism simply did not exist in the world of Jesus. To my knowledge, however, recognition of this fact is virtually absent from historical Jesus research to date—even though applying these concepts to the historical Jesus is certainly an ethnocentric mistake. That will be clearer if we take a moment to contrast individualist cultures with the collectivist ones of the biblical period.

Collectivist Cultures

First, it is necessary to clarify what we mean by a collectivist culture. It may be defined as a culture in which persons understand themselves as parts of groups or collectives such as family, tribe or nation.[13] People are defined by the groups to which they belong and do not understand themselves as having separate identities. They are motivated by group norms rather than individual needs or aspirations, and strenuously avoid articulating personal goals or giving them priority over the goals of the group. For most collectivists the primary identity-group is the family, though belonging to additional in-groups is common. Since personal identity and group identity are completely inseparable, however, in these societies separation from a group always involves a loss of self.[14]

It is important to recognize that collectivism is both a historical development and one involving considerable variation. Geography, ecology, language, mode of production, family size, age structures, affluence, urbanism, and the presence or absence of personal choice are all factors shaping human

---

[11] Only individualists could produce countless introspective sermons on the meaning of such biblical terms as *metanoia*.

[12] Malina, "Circum-Mediterranean Person?" 67.

[13] Triandis, *Individualism and Collectivism*, 2.

[14] Malina, "Let a Man Deny Himself," 106–19.

patterns of self-perception. Thus anthropologists see evidence that hunter-gatherers were primarily individualists. By contrast, agrarian societies, and especially agrarian societies in which peasant farming provides a marginal living for the vast majority of the population, have been almost exclusively collectivist. Both agricultural practices and marginal resources require extensive cooperation for simple survival.[15] Triandis argues that 70 percent of the world's population is currently collectivist rather than individualist.[16] Others put the current figure as high as 80 percent.[17] Most important, since nearly all agrarian cultures are and have been collectivist, it likely that ancient Mediterranean society was no exception.

If all this is true, we simply cannot, of course, assume a Western definition of the self when we inquire about the self-understanding of Jesus. Indeed, we have to ask whether the question Westerners have been using since the time of Reimarus (whom New Testament scholars acknowledge as the first to ask about Jesus's historical identity) is in fact appropriate. For as cultural anthropologist Harry Triandis, a foremost researcher on cultural understandings of the human person, has pointed out, the individualism versus collectivism distinction is a fundamental challenge to the universal applicability of Western psychological understandings.[18]

Horizontal and Vertical Cultures

Of course not all individualist or collectivist cultures are individualist or collectivist to the same degree, or for the same reasons, or in the same fashion. Thus we can make an additional set of distinctions that will aid in locating contemporary Western cultures in relation to ancient Palestine. Triandis distinguishes between what he calls "horizontal" and "vertical" cultures, each of which produces individualism and collectivism of a different type.[19]

Cultures that tolerate relatively small differences in status, power, and privilege Triandis calls "horizontal." The range of social stratification in these societies is thus rather small. By contrast, societies in which differences in status, power, and affluence are much greater Triandis calls "vertical." In vertical societies, social stratification is both marked and rigid. Thus if we examine

---

[15] Triandis, *Individualism and Collectivism*, 82–83.

[16] Ibid., 13.

[17] Pilch, "Psychological," 113.

[18] Triandis, *Individualism and Collectivism*. For excellent discussions of collectivist views in relation to New Testament study, see Malina, "Dealing," 127–41; also see Malina, "Circum-Mediterranean Person?" 66–87; and Malina and Neyrey, "First-Century Personality," 67–96.

[19] Triandis, *Individualism and Collectivism*, 44ff.

this particular cultural characteristic in relation to individualism and collectivism we obtain the following:

Types of Individualist and Collectivist Societies

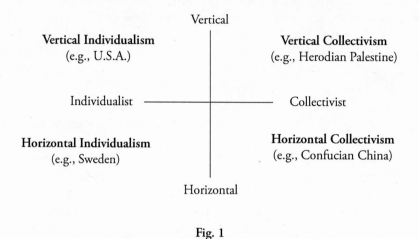

Fig. 1

First, as the diagram indicates, cultures in which persons maintain a high degree of independence and yet which tolerate only small differences in power, status, and affluence produce a "horizontal individualism." Triandis cites Sweden as an example. Second, cultures that likewise tolerate relatively small differences in status and power and yet hold a collectivist view of the self can be termed "horizontal collectivist." Confucian China is perhaps an example. Third, cultures that tolerate significant differences of status are, hence, vertical. But if these vertical cultures are also individualist, then they produce achievement-oriented, hedonistic, acquisitive, and competitive social behavior. A prime example is obviously the "vertical individualism" of the U.S. Finally, cultures that tolerate wide differences of status and power yet are predominantly collectivist in outlook produce the kind of "vertical collectivism" that characterized the Mediterranean societies of antiquity.

Individualism in Vertical Collectivist Societies

Of course it is important to recognize that no society is completely one way or the other, either completely individualist or completely collectivist. For example, it is true that certain kinds of individualists do exist in predominantly vertical collectivist societies. Because of this, we cannot assume that all persons in all collectivist societies are to be characterized in exactly the same way.

Near-individualistic behavior did exist in the vertical collectivist societies of the ancient Mediterranean world, and we must take account of it.

We must point out, however, that these "individualistic" persons in ancient collectivist societies are not somehow the equivalent of the introspective, psychologically minded, self-reliant individualists familiar to modern Americans. Rather, they are of two types: either (1) elite, idiocentric, acquisition-oriented, self-indulgent and competitive persons[20] or (2) rootless, disconnected, marginalized persons.[21] Whether they fit either or both of these two types, all such individualists in vertical collectivist societies display an outlook that derives from the special positions they occupy in the social system. Sharing some but not all the characteristics of individualists familiar to us, perhaps they might best be called quasi-individualists in order to distinguish them from the familiar American individualist model. The following diagram identifies who they are:

Quasi-Individualism in Predominantly Vertical Collectivist Societies

Urban Elite
Competitive, Hedonistic
Quasi-Individualists

Majority
Collectivists

Degraded, Expendables
Isolated, marginalized
Quasi-individualists

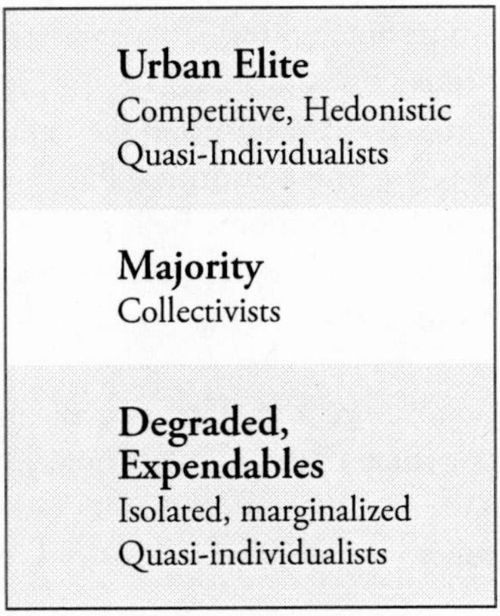

Fig. 2

Especially important for anyone studying the New Testament is that collectivist societies that are strongly vertical, and hence that contain wide variations in status as well as rigid social stratification, tend to produce these pockets of individualistic-like behavior in otherwise collectivist situations. Obviously status and affluence bring independence and choice. Thus the elite members of otherwise collectivist societies can rather quickly become

[20] Malina, "Let a Man Deny Himself," 113.

[21] See Triandis, *Individualism and Collectivism*.

quasi-individualists. They are often motivated by pleasure, personal needs, or achievement aspirations. Harry Triandis cites Latin America as a contemporary example of a place where members of elite groups have become quasi-individualists.[22] There the elite indulge in all kinds of conspicuous consumption, carnivals, trade, luxury goods, and so on. The picture is not at all unlike ancient Rome. In Rome a similar quasi-individualism emerged among the urban elite, who differed markedly from the collectivists that predominated elsewhere in the society.

Equally important for Jesus scholars is another factor that creates pockets of individualistic-like behavior in otherwise collectivist societies. At extreme levels of poverty, what Triandis calls "anomic individualism" appears.[23] This term refers to the most marginalized individuals in a society, who are cut off from the in-groups that guarantee survival and create identity in collectivist cultures. Beggars, prostitutes, disinherited sons, orphans, or children that families cannot support, who are abandoned to the streets to fend for themselves, are all obvious examples of populations in which anomic individualism might arise.

However one caution in adopting Triandis's terminology is relevant to any consideration of Roman Palestine. Beggars, orphans, prostitutes, and the like may not have conformed to the norms of the main stream, but no one in that society (not even beggars and prostitutes) lived outside the social norms prescribed for their respective positions. Behavior fit recognizable patterns. Thus, the term *anomic* is not quite appropriate in our case. The key fact about such marginalized persons is that they are isolated from groups and left to fend for themselves.

It is important to recognize, therefore, that the individualistic behavior of these people does not come from personal choice. It is forced upon them by their circumstances in life. The result is that it does not produce a modern individual with a "definite view of himself." Instead it produces a marginalized sense of isolation.

In sum, then, though the Mediterranean societies of antiquity were predominantly collectivist in outlook, two types of individualistic behavior existed. There was first the narcissistic and hedonistic behavior of the urban elite, and second the solitary, desolate behavior of the marginalized and degraded. The first was an outlook derived from privilege and choice, the second from isolation and despair. It is important to recognize that both types of individualistic behavior are present in the Jesus traditions.

---

[22] Triandis, *Individualism and Collectivism*, 82.

[23] Ibid., 82.

Facets of the Self

There is one additional aspect of the self that will aid our discussion. Anthony G. Greenwald and Anthony R. Pratkanis have identified several facets of the self that play distinct roles in determining who we are.[24] First, there is what they call the *private* self. This is the self that emerges when one's inner audience evaluates its own opinions, attitudes, and actions. It is the foundational self in most of the individualistic cultures in the West and is in fact the classic subjective self so assiduously sought in Western psychoanalysis. Indeed in many respects this private self is what the vast majority of historical Jesus researchers are seeking when they inquire about the *self*-understanding of Jesus.[25]

Second, there is the *public* self that is the result of a general evaluation by others. It consists of both expectations and reports of others that get internalized by an individual. The intense interest of collectivist societies in gossip as a means of evaluating others is ready testimony to the importance that the public self has for them. Moreover, as the study below in chapter 9 indicates, gossip played a critical role in the public evaluation of Jesus.

Third, Green and Pratkanis describe the *collective* self, or what Malina has called the "in-group" self.[26] This self emerges as one internalizes the values, expectations, and opinions of an in-group in which one is embedded. For most ancient Mediterranean persons, of course, this group would have been the biological family. For Jesus, it may have been his biological family early on, but at least according to the Gospels, his in-group eventually became the followers with whom he was most closely associated.

What we wish to recognize now is the fact that the relationship among these three selves—the private, the public, and the in-group—is worked out differently in individualist and collectivist societies. The following diagram indicates the relationship of these selves to each other in individualistic and collectivist societies.

---

[24] Greenwald and Pratkanis, "Self," 158.

[25] It is the psychological self of Jesus sought, for example, by Ragnar Leivestad in his psychologically oriented book, *Jesus in His Own Perspective.*

[26] Malina, "Let a Man Deny Himself," 113.

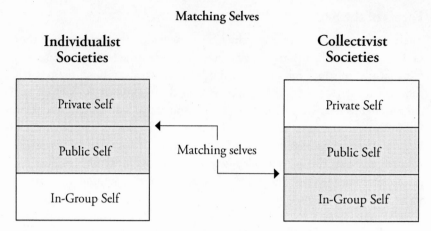

Fig. 3 (Adapted from Malina, 1993a)

As the diagram indicates, in individualist societies the private and public selves are expected to match. Failure in this regard is considered hypocrisy. The result is that individualistic persons are extremely sensitive to the nuances involved in relating private to public self. By contrast, in collectivist societies, persons are socialized to monitor the relation between public self and in-group self. These are the two that must match for collectivists because meeting the expectations of others is the standard by which all collectivist persons are judged.

In addition, of special importance for our inquiry is the fact that in collectivist cultures the private self is never revealed in public. It is hidden behind an intensely maintained mantle of secrecy. In fact, as John Pilch has shown, lying in order to keep the private self concealed is considered honorable behavior in collectivist societies.[27] This is so because in collectivist societies any public declaration of one's uniqueness, that is, of the ways one is different from others, demonstrates lack of loyalty to the in-group—and loyalty to the in-group is, of course, the highest value collectivist societies acknowledge. Thus collectivist people publicly present themselves in terms of what their neighbors want hear; to do anything less is shameless behavior.

Collectivism and Quasi-Individualism in First-Century Palestine

By clarifying these various aspects of the cultural construction of the self, it is possible now to begin locating the historical Jesus in the profile of the ancient Mediterranean society from which he emerged. That society was predomi-

[27] Pilch, "Secrecy," 151–57.

nantly vertical and collectivist. Among the urban elite, however, a narcissistic and hedonistic individualistic behavior resulted from opportunities of status and wealth. At same time, at the lowest margins of the society substantial isolation existed among those the society left to fend for themselves.

A collectivist and quasi-individualist profile of Herodian Palestine can be obtained, at least with a broad brush, if we compare our results with Dennis Duling's macrosociological profile of typical agrarian societies.

Social Stratification in the Herodian Period

Urban Elite 1-2% of the population	Roman emperor (prefect/procurator) Client king, tetrarch or ethnarch Herodians High priests Lay aristocracy
Retainers 5% of the population	Bailiffs Tax farmers Bureaucrats
Urban Nonelite 3-7% of the population	Merchants Artisans Day Laborers
Rural Peasants and Other Villagers 75% of the population	Freeholders (15-50 acres) Small Freeholders (4-15 acres) Tenant Farmers Village Artisans Day Laborers Slaves
Unclean and Degraded 5% of the population	Prostitutes Porters, Dung Carriers Sailors Tanners Etc.
Expendables 5% of the population	Lame Blind Deformed Diseased Etc.

Fig. 4 (Adapted from Duling)

As Duling's diagram suggests, the elite accounted for 1–2 percent of the population. As we noted above, in highly stratified collectivist societies, elite persons were likely self-indulgent, idiocentric, acquisition-oriented quasi-individualists. Survival was not at stake for them, and thus they could afford to act as a law unto themselves, beholden to no one. Their honor was displayed in their achievements and possessions, not in their conformity or loyalty to a group. That of course is exactly what we find among the urban elite of Palestine in the Roman period.

At the other end of the social spectrum were the unclean, degraded, and expendables. Such persons accounted for about 10 percent of the population in the Herodian period, and it is among such persons that the Triandis model would predict the quasi-individualism of the marginal and isolated. A clear example from the Jesus tradition of quasi-individualism on the margins is the beggar in John 5 who had no friend to put him in the pool. Beggars, prostitutes, tanners, sailors, the poorest day laborers, bandits, ass drivers, usurers, dung collectors, shepherds, and the like fell into the category of marginalized quasi-individualists, too. Their individualistic behavior came not from the affluence or status that brought the availability of choice but from their isolation from any group on which to draw for a sense of identity. They had loyalty to no one, and none had loyalty to them.

The Identity of Jesus

We are now in a position to inquire more directly about the identity of Jesus. Was he a typical agrarian collectivist? Or might he have been one of the two kinds of quasi-individualists we have identified as present in a typical agrarian, vertical, collectivist society?

One possibility of course is that Jesus was an individualistic exception of the hedonistic, narcissistic, indulgent, competitive, achievement-oriented sort that emerged among the urban elite. Yet nothing in the texts gives us any reason to locate Jesus here. He was a village artisan from Nazareth, a tiny village in a rural area. Moreover, as the diagram indicates, village artisans were among the lowest-status persons in agrarian societies. Hence, on the basis of his origins, Jesus cannot plausibly be placed in this group. And in fact, the teachings of Jesus do not suggest he shared these elitist values.

The other possibility is that Jesus was among the marginalized whose position resulted from extreme poverty and isolation. Should we place Jesus here? Once again, I would argue, we have no New Testament data that would lead us to do so.

It is true that Jesus appears to have broken with his biological roots. That would mean a loss of group-centered identity. But two things argue against using this as data for quasi-individualism. One is that the break appears to have been voluntary. We learn of nothing in Jesus's life suggesting he was forced onto the streets to fend for himself. Moreover, the teachings of Jesus suggest the very opposite of this type of individualism. They offer a home to the homeless rather than an expression of isolation or despair.

The second argument against seeing Jesus as a marginalized quasi-individualist is that while he broke with one group, his family, he appears to have rather quickly reestablished new in-group relationships, probably at first with the Baptist's movement but then later with followers of his own. My conclusion, therefore, is that we can locate Jesus among neither of the individualistic-like groups present in Herodian Palestine. Rather, we must assume that he shared the collectivist outlook that predominated in the ancient world.

Equally important is to recognize that, as a collectivist person like other collectivists persons, Jesus would have been concerned with his public self and his in-group self and not with his private self. The private self is an issue only for Westerners. That private self is the self that we Westerners see as essential for all human persons. We see it as the seat of motives and the explanation for personal actions. To explain what Jesus did and why he did it, therefore, Westerners require an account of this private self of Jesus. We know nowhere else to locate his motives or sense of mission. Yet it is this very private self that Middle Easterners do not consider central, do not reveal, indeed do not even admit to having in public. So what we should expect to find in the Gospel traditions is material describing the public and the in-group selves of Jesus, not his private self. And as it turns out, this is exactly the case.

Evidence in the Gospels

Space does not permit an examination of all of the relevant New Testament texts, but at least one cannot be overlooked. The *locus classicus* of this entire issue is Mark 8:27–30, a passage that has played a key role in the debate since the time of Reimarus:

> Jesus went on with his disciples to the villages of Caesarea Philippi; and on the way he asked his disciples, "Who do people say that I am?" And they answered him, "John the Baptist; and others, Elijah; and still others, one of the prophets." He asked them, "But who do you say that I am?" Peter answered him, "You are the Messiah." And he sternly ordered them not to tell anyone about him.

The overwhelming majority of scholars consider this anecdote to be a later creation of the church, and indeed in its present form it almost certainly is. As is well known, however, Erich Dinkler was among the first to argue—persuasively, in my view—that much older tradition lies behind this Marcan narrative.[28]

The nearly universal Western interpretation of this passage is that Jesus himself knows who he is, and that he is quizzing his followers to see whether they do.[29] Up to this point of Peter's confession, they have not identified him correctly, so his questions are a kind of test. Peter's half-understood exclamation that Jesus is the Messiah is thus thought to represent a climactic confessional moment in the Gospel narrative.

Yet if it is correct that Jesus was a collectivist person, we can make no assumption that Jesus possesses self-knowledge. Further, we can assume neither that Jesus is trying to determine whether the disciples have understood him correctly, nor that he is trying to provoke their recognition. All this seems to me an entirely Western approach to the matter, based on the assumption of private self-knowledge. Rather, we have to assume that Jesus *does not know who he is*, and that if he wishes to know he will have to ask the significant others in whom he is embedded. His identity can only come from the group in which he is embedded.

Note carefully the questions Jesus puts to the disciples in Mark 8:27–29. He asks first: "Who do the *people* say I am?" This is an inquiry about his *public* self. And the answers to his question appropriately come *from the public*. His followers tell him that people are saying he is "John the Baptist; and others, Elijah; and still others, one of the prophets." Next, look what Jesus asks: "Who do *you* say that I am?" This is an inquiry about his *in-group* self. The in-group is of critical importance in collectivist societies because it is the in-group that *determines* who one is. So in a collectivist culture the answer must come *from the in-group*, not from Jesus. It is his in-group that identifies Jesus as the Messiah. Moreover, note that in each case the answers provided suggest stereotypical roles, *not personal qualities or individual choices*.

In other words, what the anecdote narrates is Jesus asking an in-group *to identify both his public self and his in-group self. Conspicuous by its absence, however, is any talk whatsoever about Jesus's private self,* either from the disciples or from Jesus. It simply is not there, and it can be put there only by importing Western assumptions into the text. This story has in view only the public and in-group selves of Jesus.

Even more precisely, in this story Jesus is inquiring about the *match* between his newly emerging public and in-group identities. Who do people (public) say that I am? Who do you (in-group) say that I am? This is precisely

---

[28] Dinkler, "Peter's Confession," 192.

[29] Scholars (and their writings) espousing the common view include: Schweizer, *Good News*; Williamson, *Mark*; Myers, *Binding*; Hurtado, *Mark*; Hooker, *Gospel*, et al.

the match that is central in collectivist societies. There are thus significant social grounds for assuming, as Dinkler does on form-critical grounds, that a historical tradition may lie somewhere behind the Marcan version of events at Caesarea Philippi.

When one thinks about it, it is not at all surprising that confusion developed over the identity of Jesus, not only in the mind of his followers but in his own mind as well. In addition to the text in Mark 8:27–30 there is widespread speculation about it in the Gospels.[30] In fact the sheer scope of the speculation suggests that behind it lies something genuinely historical. While space unfortunately does not permit an analysis of all the texts here, the point would not be to answer the question about who Jesus thought he was. That question is inappropriate even if it could be answered. Rather the point is that speculation about Jesus identity was going on in public, exactly where it should occur in a collectivist society.

Conclusion

At the beginning of his article on the historical Jesus that we quoted above, Ben F. Meyer makes following claim, here now in its entirety:

> We take it, for our part, that Jesus was a man with a definite view of himself and his time, a man with a mission, equipped with great resources for accomplishing it and confronted with not easily manageable obstacles in the way of its accomplishment.[31]

It would be hard to imagine a more ethnocentric and anachronistic understanding of Jesus. It is a virtual projection of the Western, individualistic, private self onto the Jesus of history. Its plausibility in the collectivist society

---

[30] In Mark 6:1–6 the crowd asks: "Where did this man get all this?" "Is not this the carpenter, the son of Mary and brother of James and Joses and Judas and Simon, and are not his sisters here with us?" In Luke 4: 22 the synagogue goers ask: "Is not this Joseph's son?" In John 7:14 people are puzzled: "How does this man have such learning when he has never been taught?" Later they add, "Can it be that the authorities really know that this is the Messiah?" Yet they are confused because they "know where this man [Jesus] is from" (John 7:27). Finally a division breaks out among the people who can't decide whether Jesus is a prophet, the Messiah, or a fraud. Some cannot believe a Messiah could come from Galilee (John 7:40-43). The similarity between this story and Mark 8:27-30 is truly striking.

Elsewhere in the Synoptics, Jesus's disciples ask: "What sort of man is this?" (Matt 8:27). The authorities ask him: "Tell us by what authority you do these things" (Luke 20:2). They are really asking him who he thinks he is, but he refuses to answer. Elsewhere crowds wonder at him (Mark 1:27; 2:12; 5:20; 5:42; 12:17; Matt 9:33; 12:23; 15:31; 22:22; 27:14; Luke 4:36; 5:26; 9:43; 11:14; 20:26). The disciples also wonder (Mark 4:41; 6:52; 10:32). Even Jesus's parents wonder who he is (Luke 2:33; 2:47). Demons seem to know him (Mark 1:24, 1:34; 3:12; 5:7), but everyone else wonders and speculates about who Jesus is.

[31] Meyer, *Jesus' Ministry and Self-Understanding*, 341.

of antiquity is near zero. Western assumptions about the nature of the self have determined the outcome before the inquiry even starts.

Did Jesus think of himself as the Messiah? I do not know. But I suggest that if he did, and if he was at all typical of collectivist personalities, he would have been extremely careful about asserting it either in public or even in his in-group. To assert a private self would have been shameful behavior. So if Jesus did have a private self, neither his followers, nor his in-group, nor the public, nor you, nor I would ever hear of it during his lifetime.

In the end, however, it seems to me that the question about Jesus's private self is completely inappropriate not just because it is unanswerable but because it is culturally ethnocentric. It is a question only a Westerner would ask. All the legitimate questions about Jesus have to do with groups. In what group was Jesus embedded? What was their opinion of him? In what way did he embody and defend their goals? If he detached himself from biological family, by what means did he reestablish a collectivist identity? All such questions presume the collectivist understanding of human beings that is the only one appropriate for understanding the historical Jesus.

As we said at the outset of this chapter, the questions you ask determine the answers you get. It is important finally to recognize that in seeking the person of Jesus, we have been asking questions of the wrong kind.

CHAPTER 6

Zacchaeus: Defender of the Honor of Jesus

CROSS-CULTURAL READING of the Bible is not a matter of choice. Since the Bible is a Mediterranean document written for Mediterranean readers, it presumes the cultural resources and world view available to readers socialized in the Mediterranean world. This means that for all non-Mediterranean people, including all Americans, reading the Bible is *always* an exercise in cross-cultural communication. It is only a question of doing it poorly or doing it well.

Equally important is the demonstration by sociolinguists that language is by its very nature a form of *social* interaction.[1] Thus, apart from a shared social context that enables both speaker and listener to bring similar expectations to a conversation, words and sentences are meaningless. Indeed without knowledge of a shared social system, meaning is often significantly confused—as any cross-cultural conversation is likely to demonstrate.

Ironically it is often true that the biblical stories with which Americans are the most familiar are the very ones most likely to suffer from inappropriate accommodation to Western sensibilities. And nowhere is that more evident than in the story of Zacchaeus, the diminutive tax collector who climbed a tree in Jericho.

Scholarship on the Zacchaeus Story

It would probably be fair to say that over the last century Western scholars have researched and written this story to death. Saying anything new about it might therefore be difficult. But we begin our attempt to do so by noting

---

[1] See Halliday, *Language as Social Semiotic*; Cicourel, "Text and Discourse," 159–85; and Malina, "Reading Theory," 3–24.

two refrains in "Zacchaeus scholarship" that have been especially common. One has been the attempt to set the story in its literary context, drawing associations between various stories or motifs in the Gospel of Luke and particular elements of the Zacchaeus story.[2] For example, it perhaps addresses the question, how can a rich man be saved (18:18–27) or a tax collector justified (18:9–17)? What must the rich do with their possessions (14:33)? And what about Jesus eating with tax collectors and sinners (5:30)? The Zacchaeus story seems to address these questions and more.

A second scholarly concern, one going back a century and a half, has developed into a protracted argument over whether Zacchaeus's statement in 19:8 should be understood as the new resolve of a repentant sinner or a vigorous defense by this tax collector of his present, perhaps even customary, behavior.[3] The two verbs in the sentence (δίδωμι, ἀποδίδωμι) are both in the present tense, and indeed many translations render them in exactly that fashion (" I give," "I pay back"), including the KJV, RSV, ESV, and others. The statement is thus taken to be one in which a defiant Zacchaeus defends his behavior in the face of the crowd's hostility.[4]

The more traditional view holds, of course, that the statement in v. 8 is that of a repentant sinner resolving to mend his wicked ways and embark upon a new and better path.[5] Viewed this way, the two verbs in question must be taken as "futuristic" presents[6] and rendered accordingly: "I will give," and "I will pay back" (NRSV, NAV, NJB, et al.).[7] Both the NIV and the REV make the statement a vividly present declaration of this new resolve ("Here and now I give") that demonstrates the chosen path of a newly repentant Zacchaeus.

However, we will suggest that, reviewed in light of its culture of origin, this story has little to do with "repentance" (never mentioned in the story yet strangely the focus of traditional interpretation). The story has more to do with Luke's defense of the honor and authority of Jesus. In fact it is not only a story about Zacchaeus, but also and perhaps primarily it is a story

---

[2] See Tannehill, "Story," 201–12; O'Hanlon, "Story," 2–26; Loewe, "Towards an Interpretation," 321–31.

[3] For a review of the debate up to 1988, see Hamm, "Luke 19:8," 431–37.

[4] For expressions of this view, see Salom, "Was Zacchaeus," 87; White, "A Good Word," 89–96; Fitzmyer, *Luke*, vol. 2; Witherington, "Jesus the Savior," 197–211.

[5] For a vigorous defense of the traditional view, see Hamm, "Luke 19:8," 431–37. See also the commentaries by Plummer, Zahn, Grundmann, and I. Howard Marshall.

[6] BDF 168, 323.

[7] Interestingly, while the RSV used the present tense ("I give," "I restore"), the NRSV switched to the future ("I will give," "I will pay back"), thereby eliminating the view that the statement is a defense.

about Jesus. In order to understand this claim about the Zacchaeus story, it is necessary first to review briefly the distinction between ascribed and acquired honor.

Honor: Ascribed and Acquired

The concepts of honor and shame are by now well known to most New Testament scholars; therefore it will be necessary only to summarize a few of the more salient points. First, we have to recognize that honor is indeed the core value in Mediterranean culture. It is one's public reputation, one's standing in the village, one's "face." And it may either be *ascribed* or *acquired*. *Ascribed* honor, perhaps the most important, is the honor derived from birth status, power or public position (*Rhet.* 2.2). It may be understood as the primary cultural indicator of social precedence. *Acquired* honor, by contrast, is the honor gained by achievement or laudable public behavior. As Aristotle put it, honor of this sort "is the prize of virtue" (*Rhet.* 2.2).

Second, honor of either type, either ascribed or acquired, requires public recognition. Without recognition, honor claimed is at least foolish and at most dangerous. Moreover, in a world of limited good, honor gained is always honor taken from another. It is therefore the focal point of intense social competition.

Third, it is essential to recognize that honor is always at stake in any sort of public interaction. Every action, statement, or behavior of whatever kind is relentlessly judged in the court of public opinion. Honor is thereby won or lost as either implicit or explicit claims are validated or rejected by one's social peers.

The Honor of Zacchaeus

Zacchaeus of course is a man with no apparent basis for ascribed honor. We are told nothing about his birth family, so presumably it offered nothing to the stereotype Luke begins to build. Moreover, as commentators invariably point out, Zacchaeus's occupation rules out honor ascribed by virtue of his position. Since this information is cited so often by commentators, we need only sample it here to make the point. Dio Chrysostom, for example, considers tax collection a "base and unseemly" pursuit, comparable to keeping a brothel. The penalty, he says, is to be "hated and abominated by men" (*Disc.* 14.14; also Diogenes Cynicus, *Ep.* 36.2, Lucian, *Pseudolog.* 30). The Mishnah groups tax collectors with robbers and murderers (*m. Tehar.* 7.6; *B. Qam.* 10:2; *Ned.* 3:4); the Talmud includes them in a list of despised trades that observant Jews should not follow (*b. Sanh.* 25b). The Synoptics, of course, nearly always associate them with sinners (Matt 9:10–11; 11:19;

Mark 2:15–16; Luke 5:30; 7:34; 15:1), while Matthew adds an association with πόρναι (Matt 21:31). Even more pointedly for our purposes, Matthew considers them the same as Gentiles (5:46; 18:17).

It may also be relevant that while tax collection in the Galilee was not under the jurisdiction of Roman prefects in Jesus's day, in Jericho it was. This meant that Zacchaeus was probably a contractor (ἀρχιτελώνης) working for Rome. Or to put it another way, he should probably be understood as a Roman retainer. Therefore if any hope for *ascribed* honor exists for Zacchaeus it cannot come from his position as tax collector.

Another possibility is his wealth. This too is usually acknowledged by commentators; we only cite it again because it must be taken into account in assessing the honor status of Zacchaeus. Luke calls him "rich." Calling someone "rich" in antiquity was usually "a moral and social statement as much as an economic one. It meant the power or capacity to take from someone weaker what was rightfully not yours."[8] Thus, being rich was often synonymous with being greedy.

While riches are viewed negatively in the Gospel of Luke (16:13; 18:24), they are not always put in a bad light in the literature of antiquity. Aristotle, for example, can associate wealth and honor in decidedly positive fashion (*Nic. Eth.* 4.1, *Rhet.* 1.5–6). But like many in antiquity, Aristotle is also intensely critical of wealth gotten in inappropriate ways: "Love of base gain," he says, "makes men seek profit from all sources and pay more regard to the profit than to the shame (*Vices and Virtues,* 7.7–8). He is especially clear that one cannot gain honor by feeding at the public trough: "It is not possible to get wealth from the common stock and at the same time honor" (*Nic. Eth.* 8.14). With regards to contracts, he comments that greed is "taking what is . . . contrary to one's desert (*Vices and Virtues,* 7.4). In Luke's Gospel, John the Baptist says pretty much the same of tax collectors (3:12–13).

Yet as negative as Luke's portrait of Zacchaeus is thus far, Luke adds one more descriptor that stereotypes him as a man unlikely to be held in high public esteem. Zacchaeus is short.[9] That information is important because in the mind of the ancients a person's character could be discerned from his/her physical appearance.[10] The science was called "physiognomy," and it is described by Aulus Gellius:

---

[8] Malina and Rohrbaugh, *Synoptic Gospels,* 400.

[9] Some commentators have tried to see the term μικρός as a reference to Zacchaeus being a dwarf. However, there is no real evidence for that view.

[10] Evans "Roman Descriptions," 43–84; "Study of Physiognomy," 96–108; *Physiognomics*; Malina and Neyrey, *Portraits of Paul,* 25–66; Parsons, "'Short in Stature,'" 50–57.

> The word means to inquire into the character and dispositions of
> men by an inference drawn from their facial appearance and expres-
> sion, and from the form and bearing of the whole body. (*Attic Nights*
> 1.92).

Polemo considers this the proper way to form judgments about human character (*Phys.* 31.236).

Moreover, as Mikael Parsons has shown, when it came to being short,
the ancient stereotype was dominantly negative.[11] Pseudo-Aristotle claims
that small people with small limbs are "small-minded" (*Phys.* 808a.30). And
as Aristotle notes:

> It belongs to small-mindedness to be unable to bear either honor or
> dishonor, either good fortune or bad, but to be filled with conceit
> when honored and puffed up by trifling good fortune, and to be un-
> able to bear even the smallest dishonor . . . (*Vices and Virtues* 7.13).

That is why ancient descriptions of great persons who were physically short
usually explain away the shame by noting compensatory features. Often they
say their subjects were physically "well-proportioned."[12] Or, as in the case of
the Apostle Paul, when he is described in the *Acts of Paul and Thecla* as "a man
small of stature," the narrator adds that he is "in a good state of body" and
"has the face of an angel" (*Acts Paul*, 3).

If position, wealth, and stature then are not sources of honorific status
for Zacchaeus, we can turn to the matter of his behavior.[13] This of course
would raise the question of acquired honor or honor as virtue. And it is here
that the debate profiled above plays a role as we seek to clarify the social
dynamics of the Zacchaeus story: Was Zacchaeus a repentant sinner or a defiant self-defender? Our argument will be that there is no need to introduce
the notion of repentance into the story, nor any need to justify doing so by
construing the verbs in the sentence in any way other than as their obvious
present forms. Resort to a "futuristic present" for the sense of the verbs is a
grammatical stretch that is simply not required to make sense of this story.

---

[11] Parsons, "'Short in Stature,'" 54–56.

[12] Parsons, "'Short in Stature,'" 53. E.g., Augustus (Suetonius, *Aug.* 79). See also from
Qumran: [The righteous person is one] whose eyes are neither dark nor light, whose beard
is sparse and medium curly, whose voice resonates, whose teeth are fine and regular, who
is neither tall nor short but is well built, whose finders are thin and long, whose thighs are
hairless, the soles of whose feet and whose toes are as they should be. . . ." (4Q186, Frag. 2 Col
1.1–8; cited in Parsons, "'Short in Stature,'" 52).

[13] While we shall describe Zacchaeus's behavior as highly honorable, some commentators
have seen his climbing of a tree (causing ankles and, perhaps, posterior to be exposed) as a
shameful way to act.

As we will detail below, the "repentance" option can thus be rather quickly left aside.

So let us consider the possibility that the present tense verbs (δίδωμι, ἀποδίδωμι) should be taken as written and in fact refer to the customary practice of Zacchaeus, not to his recent repentance. In order to evaluate this possibility it is best to separate the two halves of the public claim Zacchaeus makes, recognizing, of course, that public claims are *always* made in the service of one's honor status.

In the first part of v. 8 Zacchaeus claims that he gives half his goods to the poorest of the poor.[14] This is laudable behavior indeed. In fact it is behavior that would have had a considerable impact on the lives of whatever poor people he gifted. Perhaps the implication is even that Zacchaeus has acted as a patron for the poor. In speaking of such liberality, Aristotle declares that ". . . the liberal man is praised not in respect of military matters, nor of those in respect of which the temperate man is praised, nor of judicial decisions, but with regard to the giving and taking of wealth, and especially in respect of giving (*Nic. Eth.* 4.1). Or again, "Liberality is accompanied by . . . a compassionate and affectionate and hospitable and honorable nature (*Vices and Virtues* 5.5). Thus Zacchaeus could indeed be defending his acquired honor based on his customary generosity. To quote Aristotle again, "Honor is the token of a man's being famous for doing good. It is chiefly and most properly paid to those who have already done good; but also to the man who can do good in future (*Rhet.* 1.5).

The second half of v. 8 specifies behavior that requires special scrutiny. It is one thing to act generously toward the poor but quite another to defraud people. To do so would mean taking from a contract "beyond one's deserts." Given the fact that Zacchaeus is in Jericho (a gateway city and one possessed of extensive and richly profitable balsam groves, indeed the winter capital of the kingdom) no doubt meant he possessed a lucrative opportunity for farming the transport tolls in the region. Moreover, the fact that Zacchaeus *speculates* about whether he has committed this evil ("*If* I have defrauded . . .") could well represent a real situation: Such greed may have existed among Zacchaeus's employees (after all, he is an ἀρχιτελώνς) rather than in his own dealings. But in any case, the public would have considered him responsible, and if the public knew of any such theft Zacchaeus's public claims to acquired honor on these grounds would have brought immediate howls of protest. [15]

---

[14] The REV translation "charity" is an unfortunate way to render the term for the poorest of the poor, (that is, the beggars)— πτωχοῖς—invisible.

[15] As an ἀρχιτελώνης, Zacchaeus probably had little direct contact with those paying the tolls. That task fell to his employees. Thus no actual knowledge of Zacchaeus was likely to

What is thus in view here is the fact that a public statement such as that made by Zacchaeus in v. 8 is an enormous claim to honor, made in the most public fashion, which thereby puts Zacchaeus at significant risk of public ridicule should the claim turn out to be rejected. We shall return to this statement below when we examine Zacchaeus's role as patron for Jesus, but for now we can simply leave the whole business of "repentance" aside (which, we must emphasize again, is *not* mentioned anywhere in this story) in order to assert that in this story Zacchaeus is making a very public claim to ascribed honor.

The Verbal Exchanges in the Narrative

Enough has now been said so that we can look at the actual interactions in the Lukan story in light of the honor–shame culture of the ancient Mediterranean world. We note that in doing so there is no need to raise the question of the story's historicity.[16] We can simply assert that while it may or may not reflect an actual incident in the life of Jesus, it nonetheless bears the verisimilitude required to treat the story as a Mediterranean cultural artifact. Moreover, our central thesis will be that what Zacchaeus is doing in making his pretentious claim is only indirectly a statement in defense of his own honor. That is involved, of course, but the heart of the matter is rather a defense of the honor of Jesus. That can be seen if we follow the interactions of the story carefully.

The first public statement in the story is that of Jesus telling Zacchaeus that he "must" stay at his house that day (v 5). Two things may be noted here. First, and most important, the honor of Jesus is now on the line. That is critical. Note that it is *Jesus's* public statement that causes a crowd reaction, and it is *his* behavior that is undergoing evaluation by the grumbling crowd: "There was a general murmur of disapproval. 'He has gone to be the guest of a sinner'" (v 7). This honor judgment about Jesus is therefore negative. Recall that honor unrecognized by the public is risky and even dangerous. Western commentators have simply failed to see that it is the honor of *Jesus* around which the story now revolves.

Second, what Jesus's comment in v. 5 raises is the all-important issue of hospitality.[17] Jesus asks Zacchaeus to be his host. Called "receiving strangers" in the Mediterranean world, hospitality was the process of transforming

---

be widespread; his reputation in Jericho would have come from the usual stereotype of his profession rather than from personal knowledge of his behavior.

[16] Perhaps a majority of contemporary scholars take the story to be entirely the creation of Luke for the purpose of summing up motifs in the travel narrative of 9:51—19:10. See especially O'Hanlon, "Story," 2–26.

[17] The Greek in v. 7 (καταλῦσαι) refers to loosing or unharnessing pack animals, hence to preparation to lodge overnight with someone (Fitzmyer, *Luke*, 2:1224).

strangers into guests.[18] Its practice involved a variety of conventions, many of which were common to both the Greco-Roman and Israelite worlds.[19] Among these widespread conventions, three are especially important for our purposes: (1) the need of a stranger for a local patron, (2) the testing of the stranger to evaluate any potential threat to the community, and (3) the obligation of a host to provide protection for a guest.

First, there is a need for any stranger to seek out a local patron. As Bruce Malina has noted, in the ancient world "a stranger possesses no standing in law or custom within the visited group; hence it is necessary for him to have a patron in order to gain the protection of the local laws and gods."[20] This of course is exactly what Jesus seeks in Jericho: "Today I must stay at your house." Jesus is asking Zacchaeus to be his local patron. Moreover, the haste with which Zacchaeus climbs down from the tree adds color to the narrator's claim that Zacchaeus agrees to play that role.[21] He "welcomed him gladly" (v 6). Zacchaeus is willing to be the local patron Jesus needs.[22]

In addition, this agreement of Zacchaeus to play the role of Jesus's local patron puts Zacchaeus's statement in v. 8 in a whole new light. Not only is Zacchaeus defending his own honor when he claims to give half his goods to the poor, he is also indicating that he has both the wherewithal and the inclination to be an effective patron. He has done it in the past; presumably he can do it for Jesus as well. Again, Western commentators have simply missed the point: Zacchaeus's statement is an indication of his willingness and ability to be the patron of Jesus.

Second, testing strangers was equally important because any stranger represented a potential threat to the community.[23] As Malina puts it, without a local protector a stranger could be "destroyed or despoiled with impunity, simply because of his potential hostility."[24] The grumbling of the crowd certainly suggests that such a test is underway in the court of public opinion. The crowd reaction implies a direct and very public challenge to Jesus's acceptability within the village.

---

[18] Malina, "Received View," 181.

[19] See Arterbury, *Entertaining Angels*.

[20] Malina, "Received View," 183.

[21] Note that the opposite occurs in Luke 11:5–13.

[22] It may be worth noting here that according to Andrew Arterbury, "the host's extension of hospitality to a traveling teacher was an indication that the host accepted or agreed with the teaching of the traveling teacher" (*Entertaining Angels*, 123). Luke 9:5 shows, e.g., that refusal to welcome Jesus's disciples correlated with refusal to accept their teaching.

[23] Malina, "Received View," 183; Hobbs, "Hospitality," 11.

[24] Malina, "Received View," 184.

Finally, accepting the role of patron laid heavy obligation on both host and guest. Mediterranean guests are required to honor their hosts, and hosts are required to protect the honor of their guests.[25] Speaking with perhaps more truth than we sometimes acknowledge, the writer of Proverbs observes that making public pledges of this sort to strangers can entangle one in trouble (6:1–3). That obviously is the case here.

Entanglements might arise in part because staying at another's home also involves the sensitive issue of meals. As Jerome Neyrey has pointed out, meals are ceremonies that function to confirm statuses within a group.[26] Above all it is a meal that transforms the stranger into a guest. Of course people in the Mediterranean world normally ate with those whose values they shared and with those who held roughly the same measure of honor in the eyes of the public. Likes ate with likes. Not surprisingly, it was Jesus's habit of eating with tax collectors and sinners that caused so much criticism of him elsewhere in the Gospel of Luke (5:29–32; 15:1–2:). In addition, in the book of Acts Luke reminds us quite specifically of an important taboo: "You yourselves know how unlawful it is for a Jew to associate with or to visit anyone of another nation . . ."(10:28). Thus if tax collectors were seen by the Lukan audience as "Gentiles," as they are in Matthew, (Matt 5:46; 18:17), the public reaction to Jesus's exchange with Zacchaeus would not be in doubt. A public pledge has now entangled both Jesus and Zacchaeus in a pack of trouble.

But given the importance in Mediterranean culture of a host protecting the honor of a guest, we should not be surprised at the immediate reaction of Zacchaeus. He is now under heavy obligation to address the threatened honor of his guest in order to fulfill his obligation as host. This begins to put the very public statement of Zacchaeus ("he stood there and said . . .") in a whole new light. He must respond. But how is he to defend the honor of his guest?

Whatever the statement in v. 8 may have been with respect to his own honor, the fact that Zacchaeus's statement so quickly and publicly follows the crowd's disapproval of Jesus as his guest suggests that Zacchaeus's statement is offered as much to protect the honor of Jesus as it is to assert any honor of his own. To be sure, as we have seen, his statement in v. 8 is indeed a claim to his own honor on the part of Zacchaeus: he claims honor as the prize of virtue. But in asserting his own honorific status, Zacchaeus is actually proclaiming that Jesus is not to be condemned for being received into the house of a "hated and abominated man." Jesus will be welcomed into the house of a man whose honorific status should be beyond question because of his

[25] Arterbury, *Entertaining Angels*, 6.
[26] Neyrey, "Ceremonies," 362.

customary patronage of the poor.[27] In asserting his own honorific status as host, therefore, Zacchaeus defends the honor of his guest in the face of the crowd's initial reaction. In seeking a local patron, his guest has not chosen badly after all.

But of course the public exchange is not finished. Host and guest have mutual obligations. So after hearing Zacchaeus defend him (by defending his own honorific status as host), Jesus reciprocates by publicly defending the honor of Zacchaeus: Jesus declares him part of the essential kin group. Zacchaeus is no Gentile; he is a son of Abraham, the honored mutual ancestor. That is an ascribed honor status of considerable magnitude. Thus if Zacchaeus has protected the honor of Jesus, Jesus hereby does the same for Zacchaeus. The guest fulfills his part in the code of hospitality. The host has protected the honor of the guest, and the guest has protected the honor of host.[28] The public exchanges in the narrative portray both host and guest as mutually supportive in the face of the grumbling crowd.

Before leaving the interactions in the story, however, it is necessary to comment upon the final statement of Jesus that "salvation" had come to the house of Zacchaeus on that very day. Obviously it is this statement that has anchored the traditional view that this is a story of repentance even though, as Joseph Fitzmyer points out, nothing anywhere in the story indicates new-found faith, repentance, or discipleship on the part of Zacchaeus.[29] Nor does Jesus say anything to Zacchaeus that would even suggest a call to repentance, much less its consummation. He simply asks Zacchaeus to be his local patron. Notions of repentance would therefore seem more plausible as a case of presuppositions brought to the story by Western interpreters rather than as anything read from the dialogue in the story itself.

But there is perhaps one more thing to say. Note that after Jesus's declaration of salvation for the house of Zacchaeus, there is no additional reaction from the crowd. Why not? Did they just go away convinced that two scoundrels were now in league? Or were they persuaded by what they had seen and heard? In the end, did they acquiesce to the mutual defense of honor by Jesus and Zacchaeus and thus end their public grumbling?

---

[27] Fitzmyer cites the concern of Alfred Plummer, et al., that taking v. 7 as a statement of Zacchaeus's customary behavior would make him a boaster, which is presumably not a good thing (2:1220). But in the Mediterranean world, public boasting about one's honorific behavior was expected.

[28] Malina, "Hospitality," 105.

[29] See Tannehill, "Story," 203. See also Fitzmyer, *Luke,* . Perhaps it would not be too much to suggest that the Western preoccupation with guilt, which stands in sharp contrast to the Mediterranean preoccupation with honor, has led to the persistent description of Zacchaeus as a "repentant" sinner.

The introduction to the next story in Luke's Gospel may offer a bit of a clue. Luke 19:11 says that the very crowd that had been listening to this exchange between Jesus and Zacchaeus now thought the kingdom of God might dawn at any moment. To be sure, the narrator tells us that this crowd reaction happens because Jesus was nearing Jerusalem. But also implied with this statement may be the assumption that the exchange in 19:1–9 did not convince the crowd to think otherwise. It may be that there was a certain authority granted to Jesus's final judgment of the Zacchaeus matter ("salvation has come to this house"), and therefore no additional note of disapproval is to be heard.[30] If the judgment of Jesus that Zacchaeus was, in spite of his stature and occupation, a man of honor, and if Jesus's judgment of Zacchaeus was finally accepted by the skeptical crowd, then we could say that "salvation" had indeed come to the house of Zacchaeus on that day.

Of course to understand "salvation" as the restoration of honor not only for Zacchaeus but also for his whole house has simply never occurred to American scholars. Surely the term *salvation* has primarily a theological meaning in the New Testament, including in the Lukan writings, but the use of *salvation* as a broad description of rescue from any kind of difficulty is well known in antiquity. Isaiah speaks of the walls of the city as "salvation" (60:18). In Baruch, "salvation" simply refers to the restoration of Jerusalem (4:24). The author of the book of Wisdom thinks there is "salvation" in a multitude of the wise (6:24). Philo, who usually uses the term to refer to the salvation of God, can also use it to describe saving a horse from drowning (*Leg.* 2.104), the cure of a physician (*Deus* 1.66), and the sense of moderation that saves the mind from excess (*Virt.* 1:14). Josephus often uses the term simply to refer to rescue from any kind of danger (*Ant.* 7.314; 11:285). To be sure the term *salvation* has primarily a theological meaning in the New Testament, including the Lukan writings, but the use of the term as a broad description of rescue from any kind of difficulty is well known in antiquity.

Conclusion

In conclusion, then, our argument is that the much-debated issue about whether this is a story about a reformed sinner or about a man defending his customary behavior misses a good deal of what the story involves. The debate overlooks the centrality of honor in the Mediterranean world and the

---

[30] The parable that follows will of course disabuse Jesus's hearers of any naïve optimism in this regard. But the fact that the narrator leaves the final statement of Jesus in the Zacchaeus story unchallenged may well indicate that it won the day and settled the dispute. If that is the case, the honor of Jesus, threatened by his choice of host, has now apparently been affirmed by all.

obligations of a stranger and host in the code of hospitality. Indeed the story's dynamics make clear that in many ways this is not so much a story about Zacchaeus as it is a story about the authority of Jesus. To be sure, the behavior of Zacchaeus is relevant, since his acquired honor plays a key role in the story. But it is not primarily the honor of Zacchaeus that is at stake. It is the honor of Jesus. Zacchaeus the host defends his own honor primarily as a means of defending the honor of Jesus his guest. Zacchaeus is claiming, in effect, that in seeking a local patron, Jesus has made a rather good choice.

The crowd of course is a large one, and it is there because of Jesus's reputation. They have come out to see him. What causes their discontent, however, is the unexpected and seemingly dishonorable behavior of Jesus after he sees Zacchaeus up a tree. Surely no wise or knowing teacher would request this man to be his local sponsor. Yet he is the one of whom Jesus makes his request. Moreover, if we are right about the conclusion to the story, it is not hard to see that this is ultimately a tale about the honor and authority of Jesus being vindicated—as it is everywhere and always in the Gospel of Luke.

CHAPTER 7

A Dysfunctional Family and Its Neighbors: Luke 15:11–32

IN TRADITIONAL exegesis the parable of the prodigal son has been understood as a story about repentance, forgiveness and a churlish older brother.[1] Perhaps it is. However, a number of commentators have pointed out that the term "repentance" is in fact never mentioned, that the younger son's return

---

[1] The list of commentators on this story is truly formidable. Thus there have been literary studies (Sellew, Kozar, Ramsay, Tannehill, Talbert, Crossan), legal studies (Derrett, Pöhlmann), structuralist studies (Patte, Scott, Grelot, Giblin), psychological studies (Tolbert, Via, Hein, King), studies of ancient parallels (Fisher, Foster, Aus, Ernst) and Old Testament motifs (Hofius), studies of patristic use of the parable (Thieme, Frot, Derrett, Barnard), along with a host of theological and homiletical treatments. In fact, articles, commentaries and studies of it abound in such numbers that a comprehensive bibliography is neither possible nor useful. The works included on this parable within the bibliography form therefore a representative rather than an exhaustive list.

It may be helpful to note for the interested reader where good overview treatments can be found. In addition to the standard commentaries, we strongly recommend two important contributions that cover much of the available work on the parable: Scott, *Hear*, 99–125; and Bailey, *Poet and Peasant*, 158–206. Both studies reflect on the literary, legal, and cultural issues, and both take into account earlier discussions of the parable's authenticity. The latter is now not widely questioned, though for an exception see Heiki Räisänen, "The Prodigal Gentile and his Jewish Christian Brother (Luke 15:11–32)," in *The Four Gospels 1992: Festschrift Frans Neirynck*, Vol. 2, ed. Francis Van Segroeck, et al. (Leuven: Leuven University Press, 1992), 1617–36. Räisänen's unconvincing case is heavily dependent on (1) a soteriological reading of the story and (2) heavy speculation about allegorical equivalents (see below) for the story's characters. He is led to the latter because he cannot imagine a "representative equivalent" for the older brother in the *Sitz im Leben Jesu*. The latter would not be necessary, of course, if the former were not a presupposition.

With the best recent studies we also recognize that the story is not an allegory, or as Bailey (*Poet and Peasant*, 159) puts it, "the father is not God *incognito*." Of course this is not to say that the actions of the father cannot be symbolic of the actions of God; that theological possibility remains. So Joachim Jeremias, *Parables*, 103.

seems motivated primarily by his stomach, and that initially he is more inclined to *work* his way back into the family circle rather than to depend on
divine grace or family generosity.[2] Moreover, if an observer steps back from
the traditional title of the parable, it is not difficult to see that the parable is
not really about a prodigal son at all (who does not appear after v. 24). Rather,
it is about the troubles of a generous if somewhat erratic father with his *two*
rather difficult sons. It is really a kinship story. In fact the story could quite
plausibly be titled, "A Dysfunctional Family and its Neighbors."

Instead of coming at this story with the usual preunderstandings of
Western soteriology, therefore, we propose a new approach that attempts
to set the parable as closely as possible in the sociocultural milieu out of
which it came. Above all, this means recognizing what Western exegesis frequently overlook: the parable was originally a Mediterranean story told by a
Mediterranean storyteller for a Mediterranean audience.[3] Our intent is thus
to ask what this type of Mediterranean kinship story might have evoked in
the minds of ancient Palestinian peasants when they first heard it from one
of their own kind.

To some, of course, concentrating on this original audience of Jesus
might seem a risky option since it is unlikely that Luke's setting or audience
corresponds to that of Jesus, and Luke is nearly all we have to go on.[4] It is
plausible, however, to presume a rather general audience that could well have
included Pharisees, scribes, and tax collectors and sinners, as Luke suggests;
but the audience likely included others as well.[5] In fact, since 90 percent of
agrarian populations were typically rural farmers and since the story itself is
about just such a village setting, perhaps we can assume that Galilean peasants were also among the original hearers.[6] The value of this strategy is that

---

[2] Bailey, *Poet and Peasant*, 173–80.

[3] For an introduction to the use of cultural anthropology in the study of the New Testament
see Elliott, *What is Social Scientific Criticism?* and Malina, *New Testament World*. We must also
acknowledge our indebtedness to the groundbreaking work of this type done on the story by
Kenneth E. Bailey. While Bailey does not come at it from the point of view of anthropology
as a discipline, his vast experience living in the Middle East has spawned the most provocative
cultural work on the parable to date.

[4] Scott, *Hear*, 103, has correctly pointed out there are three audiences in view here: the
historical audience of Jesus, the audience in the story-world of Luke, and Luke's own audience
(his implied readers).

[5] Some literary critics would object to looking past the Lukan performance of the parable to
something hypothetically behind it. But our interest is not in the *ipsissima verba Jesu* or some
pre-Lukan form of the parable. We offer no comment on *Traditionsgeschichte* in either the wide
or narrow sense. We are simply trying to ask how this story might have hit someone who came
at it without the preconditioning of the Lukan setting.

[6] As Halvor Moxnes points out, the special parables in Luke tend to focus on full members

it allows us to ask about the impact of the story without treating it as a theologoumenon[7] and without allegorically pigeonholing each of the characters ahead of time.[8] We can simply ask what a story about settling a family quarrel might have suggested to the kind of rural audience Jesus typically addressed.

Family Solidarity

It is difficult for modern North Americans and Europeans reading the New Testament to set aside the individualism with which we view the world. But ancient Mediterranean peasants were not individualistic. Instead they were what anthropologists call "dyadic" or collectivist persons. They "internalize and make their own what others say, think and do about them because they believe it is necessary, for being human, to live out the expectations of others."[9] For them the psychological center is not the isolated ego or the individual; it is the family.

In peasant societies identity is thus family identity, not individual identity. A moniker like "James the son of Alphaeus" speaks volumes: a son's identity is derived from his father. Family members are deeply embedded in each other socially, economically, and psychologically; hence the loyalty they owe each other is simply categorical.[10] They watch each other constantly for hints that kin group loyalty is weak, and any member acting outside the pattern of the family is deeply resented. When describing a family celebration, for example, first-century Roman poet Ovid puts it bluntly: "Let the innocent appear; let a disloyal brother stay far, far away." Interestingly, Ovid counts among the "disloyal" any brother with an excessive interest in inheriting the property, that is, "anyone who thinks his father is still too much alive" (*Fasti*, 2, 61).

(as opposed to either marginales or administrator bureaucrats) of the typical village. Since the parable presumes slave ownership (15:22), the picture is of a substantial village landowner. By contrast he notes that the parables in Mark focus on nature (1988: 55–56.

[7] Scott, *Hear*, 118 *contra* Jeremias, *Parables*.

[8] The typical allegory imagines the father as God incognito, the older son as a Jew (or a Jewish Christian: Räisänen) and the younger son as a Gentile Christian. The subtle anti-Semitism of such interpretations is to be deplored. Whatever claim to sense such a reading makes in patristic exegesis (Ambrose, Augustine, et al.) and elsewhere, it makes no sense whatever at the level of Jesus. As noted above, the recent study of Räisänen in which such allegorical speculation is rife is the result of pre-deciding that this is a traditional soteriological tale.

[9] Moxnes, *Economy*, 67.

[10] du Boulay, "Lies," 393.

Intrafamily Conflict

Just because family solidarity is a peasant ideal, however, does not mean it is always a reality. Family conflict is a fact of peasant life. Conflict between father and sons is often intense and usually centers on inheritance rights, marriage (and the establishment of an independent family), and a son's demand for his own way in matters of work and entertainment (in early youth). When generational conflict of this sort threatens family stability, mothers are often pushed into the role of buffer or family reconciler.[11]

Fraternal rivalries can also cause serious conflict in peasant families.[12] Sons commonly live in a father's house even after marriage, but upon a father's death, a major restraint on fraternal tension disappears. At this point rivalries frequently result in brothers establishing separate nuclear families. If uncontrolled, of course, such rivalries threaten the kind of instability that destroys everyone in the group.[13]

Village Solidarity

If family solidarity was most important, solidarity with the village was second in importance. In a world characterized by social and geographical immobility, the ancient Mediterranean family and village formed what anthropologists call a "closed" social network.[14] Tightly knit circles of family and friends lived in close proximity over long periods of time and developed deeply felt community attachments. Even though peasant families were normally quite self-sufficient, very few of them, even larger three-generation ones, could manage without calling on neighbors for economic and social support.[15] For an isolated individual, it was almost impossible—as the prodigal soon found out.

Equally important to village solidarity was social conformity. Everyone was always subject to the constraints of the village. As May Diaz explains,

---

[11] Perhaps the best-known case is the quarrels in the family of Herod the Great. The troubles were spectacular indeed, including murder, intrigue, multiple divorces, and land and inheritance disputes. Josephus recounts the beginnings of the trouble: "fortune was avenged on Herod in his external great successes, by raising him up domestic troubles; and he began to have wild disorders in his family, on account of his wife, of whom he was so very fond." For a fine kinship study of the Herodian family, see Hanson, "Herodians," parts 1–3.

[12] Péristiany, "Introduction," 8.

[13] The story of sibling rivalry is especially strong in the tradition of Israel. As Scott, Hear, 112, points out, the "younger brother" motif is prevalent in the Old Testament despite Deuteronomy 21:15–17. See in Scott, Hear, 112 for the midrash that he cites on Psalms 9 to indicate that the "younger brother" tradition continued long past New Testament times.

[14] Wolf, Peasants, 84–90.

[15] Diaz and Potter, "Social Life of Peasants," 156.

Characteristically, in the peasant community, where the nonconformity of one frequently is seen as a threat to the cohesion of the whole, the limits are very narrow. The individual wishing to maintain viable face-to-face relations with his fellow villagers, finds that he must play the economic game according to local rules. He dares not risk ostracism by becoming a free agent, for he depends on those around him for extra hands in building a house and for harvest, for spouses for his children, and for assistance at birth, death and famine.[16]

In short, social conformity was a matter of survival. Both social conformity and survival meant that peasant groups had to maintain sharp boundaries between insiders and outsiders, between themselves and all others. "Who belongs and who does not is clearly demarcated; 'we' and 'they' are unmistakable."[17] Obviously, going to a "far country," where one was a stranger, was not really a very good idea.

Such social solidarity has typically been the strongest in what anthropologists call "closed" villages, i.e., those villages where land is not considered by the locals to be alienable.[18] It is stronger still in societies where the population is largely nonliterate. In such settings, land claims are not written public records but are a matter of collective memory. They depend on and are reinforced by open participation in nonkinship-based associations. Thus breaking solidarity with the village can literally result in land claims being "forgotten."

Obviously then, an ancient Mediterranean family's honor was dependent upon constant public reaffirmation of loyalty to the village.[19] A good illustration can be seen in the way those acquiring excess wealth were expected to give back to the community.[20] By spending lavishly on rituals or feasts of various kinds, a family both acquired prestige and demonstrated solidarity with neighbors. Similarly, when dyadic contracts resulted in labor exchanges among neighbors, the contracts were then "validated and celebrated by ritual and ceremony, by drinking, feasting and dancing, so that participants feel they have gained in enjoyment for what they have contributed in work."[21] In this way wealth enhanced rather than weakened community solidarity.

---

[16] Diaz, "Economic Relations," 50–51.

[17] Ibid., 52.

[18] Leviticus 25:23. Elites of course had no such view. For a full discussion of the fact that Israelite peasants in the first century retained the old notion of the unalienability of land, see Fiensy, *Social History of Palestine*.

[19] On the concept of honor and its role in family well-being, see Malina, *New Testament World*, 28–62. For the economic consequences of honor, see ibid., 90–116.

[20] Diaz, "Economic Relations," 54.

[21] Ibid., 53.

Interfamily Conflict

Conflict within a family or village can threaten solidarity, but so can conflict within a family. Interfamily rivalry can be intense. "Eavesdropping, gossiping about neighbors, inventing scurrilous explanations of events, lying to destroy another's reputation" are all common events in village life.[22] If such conflict is the result of friendly rivalry, of course, it might often be construed as "fun."[23] But if over serious matters, corrective measures have to be taken quickly to prevent disaster.

Villagers especially fear the mockery of others:

> On discovery of some offence, the discoverer immediately relates it to his or her friends and relations, and in no time the story is all round the village and everyone is, as they say, 'laughing.' The more serious or ludicrous the offence is, the more people mock the principals of it. The more they laugh, the more the victims of the laughter are humiliated, because the chief ingredient of laughter is lack of respect, and it is this above all that is the enemy of reputation and self-esteem.[24]

As we shall see, conflict of this sort is a serious risk to the family of the prodigal.

Unalienability of Land

A final matter we must address before turning to a reading of the parable itself is the unalienability of land. This simply means that land rights are not exclusively individual; hence land cannot be sold in perpetuity. In many peasant societies this system of collective land rights militated against the use of wills. Land was considered to belong to past and future generations, not merely to present occupants, and thus the current owner was not free to dispose of property according to personal whim.[25] This view began to modify in the late Roman republic, however, as the use of wills became widespread.

Yet as David Fiensy's recent study has shown, the old idea that God owned the land was very much alive among Israelite peasants (though certainly not among elite groups) in the Herodian period.[26] A peasant would even buy the land of a kinsman in economic trouble rather than let it slip

---

[22] du Boulay, "Lies," 392.

[23] Ibid., 395.

[24] Ibid., 394.

[25] Gardner and Wiedmann, *Roman Household*, 117.

[26] Fiensy, *Social History of Palestine*, 1–20.

from family control (Lev 25:25). Endogamous or defensive marriage strategies had the same intent.[27]

One result of these family customs is that a peasant's emotional attachment to the land remained significant. As Robert Redfield put it in his classic study of peasant cultures: "The land and he [the peasant] are parts of one thing, one old-established body of relationships."[28] Thus expulsion from the land was not only an economic disaster, it was a social one. It meant loss of honor, broken survival networks, and disintegration of the family unit. The bitterness of Psalm 137 and the rejoicing of Psalm 126 are witness to this emotional investment in land lost and regained.

Because land is life to a peasant, every effort is made to keep it together and in the family—though not all peasant societies use the same strategies for doing so. Primogeniture is one such strategy and usually means that younger sons are given movable wealth or forced to move elsewhere and find other means of support. Villages practicing primogeniture are usually typified by "alliances based on marriage and fictive kinship between multi-generational groups" with common interests.[29] By contrast, where land is split up among heirs, the resultant community is more likely to be an "intertwined network of nuclear families."[30] Since the land was indeed split in Israel (Deut 21:17), networked nuclear families are to be expected in Israelite society, and a pattern of networked nuclear families is exactly what we see in the parable of the prodigal son.[31]

In sum, we can now say that much more is at stake here than losing and gaining an errant son, traumatic as this event would be. The well-being and future of an entire extended family is at stake within the parable of the prodigal son. The family's honor and place in the village, its social and economic networks, even its ability to call on neighbors in times of need are all at issue. If the family were to lose its "place," no one would marry its sons or daughters, patrons would disappear, and the family would be excluded from the necessary economic and social relations. Families that do not maintain solidarity with neighbors are quickly in trouble.

---

[27] Malina, *New Testament World*, 134–60.

[28] Redfield, *Peasant Society*, 28. See also McVann, "Family-Centeredness," 70–73.

[29] Diaz, "Economic Relations," 51.

[30] Ibid.

[31] This is what Emmanuel Todd calls the "endogamous community family," typical of some portions of the Mediterranean world. It is one of the seven family types he analyzes. See especially Todd, *Explanation of Ideology*, 133–54.

A Cultural Reading of the Story

With this bit of sociocultural background, it is time to turn to the parable itself. If we can presume the attitudes described above for at least some of Jesus's hearers, and at the same time if we can resist traditional soteriological readings, perhaps we can see the story in a new light. It is not that the many traditional readings are necessarily wrong; it is simply that we wish to bracket the received wisdom for the moment in order to concentrate on new possibilities.

Luke 15:11 And he said, "There was a man who had two sons; 15:12 and the younger of them said to his father, 'Father, give me the share of property that falls to me.' And he divided his living between them."

A family with two sons was blessed. Male children were an economic asset and thus considered a gift from God.[32] Keeping sons together, especially in the face of the usual tensions over marriage and inheritance, was difficult but desirable. As J. D. M. Derrett points out, attempts to avoid squabbles after his death might be the one circumstance leading a father to divide an estate ahead of time.[33] Many commentators have noted, however, that it is highly unusual for a son to press a father for his share of the inheritance while the father is still alive. Bailey argues that this means the son wishes his father dead,[34] an attitude reflected in the above quote from Ovid. Scott agrees, though he thinks early inheritance was a possible occurrence, even if it was not the norm.[35]

As Sirach 33:19–23 puts it,

> To a son or wife, to a brother or friend, do not give power over yourself, as long as you live; and do not give your property to another, lest you change your mind and must ask for it. While you are still alive and have breath in you, do not let anyone take your place. For it is better that your children should ask from you than that you should look to the hands of your sons. Excel in all that you do; bring no stain on your honor. At the time when you end the days of your life, in the hour of death, distribute your inheritance.

Or as the Babylonian Talmud comments,

> Our Rabbis taught: three cry out and are not answered: he who has money and lends it without witnesses; he who acquires a master; he

---

[32] Malina, *New Testament World*, 108.

[33] Derrett, "Law in the New Testament," 59.

[34] Bailey, *Poet and Peasant*, 181–89.

[35] Scott, *Hear*, 109–11.

who transfers his property to his children in his lifetime (*b. Baba Metzia*, 75b).[36]

In other words, the father who does not wait is a fool. He has given his place as head of the family to a son and thereby has destroyed his own honor and authority.

The family in Jesus's parable is obviously a family in trouble. The younger son has no (sense of) shame or family loyalty. Moreover, careful reading of Luke's opening line indicates that the older son is no better than his younger brother. Only Bailey, coming as he does from a lifetime of living in Middle Eastern villages, notes that on hearing that the elder was to get his share as well (v 12: "he divided his living between them"), the typical Middle Eastern reader would expect a loud and immediate outcry of refusal from the older brother.[37] That this brother is silent indicates he too is shameless and disloyal. Yet even Bailey has not taken seriously enough the fact that the father too is suspect because he gives in without protest or apparent necessity. Villagers (or readers) hearing this would have been dumbfounded. None of the characters in the story has acted properly to this point; all apparently lack a sense of propriety and shame. What kind of family is this? Villagers would be wondering if the family could even continue to function.

In light of earlier comments about the solidarity of family and village, however, it is necessary to see that more than internal family relations are at stake here. Even if this shameful episode had taken place in private, it would only be a short time before the whole village would know what happened. Since nonconformity is seen as a threat, village gossip networks are very effective in spreading stories about those who break the rules. What the shameful behavior of the father and his two sons would signal to other villagers, therefore, is the need to close ranks against this family quickly, lest the contagion spread. Thus it is not only internally that the family is crumbling, so also are its relations with its village neighbors.

15:13 Not many days later, the younger son gathered all he had and took his journey into a far country, and there he squandered his property in loose living. 15:14 And when he had spent everything, a great famine arose in that country, and he began to be in want.

Given the normal peasant attachment to land and family, this is a shocking notice indeed. The son is expected to stay at home, and it is especially in the interests of his mother that he does so. Obviously he should maintain his father in his old age,[38] but his presence means far more than that to his

---

[36] Quoted in Bailey, *Poet and Peasant*, 110.

[37] Ibid., 168.

[38] As Bailey, *Poet and Peasant*, 166, points out, the father has granted both possession and

mother. He is the surety of her place in the family. J. G. Péristiany describes her position:

> If bearing a son is likened to the growing of roots in one's own home, his departure, especially his premature departure after a quarrel with his father, is responsible for the sentiment of intense insecurity. A mother is thus prepared to make any sacrifice in order not to lose him.[39]

A peasant hearing of the younger son's scandalous departure, then, would recognize that *both* parents had been damaged. We usually forget about the mother, but peasants would not.

The story notes that in taking off, the younger son "gathered all he had"—presumably meaning that he sold off his portion of the land.[40] That of course violates the peasant norm of unalienability. It is not as if the younger son got nothing and *had* to leave; giving him a share of land (presumably the younger son got the expected one-third [Deut 21:17]) was *designed* to keep him tied to family and village! As Derrett points out, "He was not the younger son of an English landed family of the pre-1925 period, to whom the virtue of adventurousness was a necessity."[41] Moreover as the prodigal sells the land, it is lost to the family, and the potential support of the family's extended members is diminished. Indeed the North American concept of a "nuclear family" was not a peasant phenomenon in the Mediterranean world. Land supported larger extended families in antiquity. A lot of people would have had interests at stake in the younger son's actions.

We noted earlier that in peasant societies in which land is split among heirs, the village pattern is normally one of *networked* nuclear families. Thus Jesus's hearers undoubtedly expected the younger son to practice endogamy, that is, to marry locally, at least within the village and preferably within the extended family, thereby forming a new nuclear family close by.[42] The land would remain in or near the family and maintain all the needed networks. But the prodigal left instead, obviating this type of marriage arrangement.

The elder brother's accusation in v. 30 notwithstanding, the Greek text does not indicate *how* the younger son blew the money, only that he did so

---

disposition of the property to the younger son—highly unusual in light of the father's right to the usufruct.

[39] Péristiany, "Introduction," 14.

[40] I. Howard Marshall, *Luke*, 607, argues that the term συνάγω here means to "turn into cash." Also see Fitzmyer, *Luke*, 2:1087, who cites Plutarch's use of it in this sense (*Cato Minor*, 6.7 § 672c).

[41] Derrett, "Law."

[42] As Marshall, *Luke*, 607, notes, the story implies that the young man was unmarried.

(ζῶν ἀσώτως, literally: living wastefully; the RSV "loose" is misleading). The notice is not surprising. Space does not permit a full discussion of peasant behavior when cut off from the restraining social networks of the village, but the prodigal's seemingly irrational behavior is widely attested in social science literature.[43] Dislocated peasants are unfortunately in a situation where "tradition is no longer a sufficient guide to life."[44] Lacking experience with long-term views of managing capital, peasants who go to the cities usually live just as they do in the village: hand to mouth. Frequent stories of third-world peasants who migrate into modern cities and blow all their money illustrate the tragedy all too well. When short-term sources of money dry up, they are in serious trouble.

15:15 So he went and joined himself to one of the citizens of that country, who sent him into his fields to feed swine. 15:16 And he would gladly have fed on the pods that the swine ate; and no one gave him anything.

Traditional studies of the parable focus here on explanations of the "pods" and the degradation involved in a Jewish person feeding swine. These items are significant but have been explained often and need not be repeated here. The line that gets less attention but is equally important is the notice that the young man "joined himself" to a local citizen. Since ancient citizenship was normally in a city, usually the central place in a "region," we can assume the citizen is an urbanite. At a minimum, this citizen is a landowner capable of hiring wage laborers, and thus he is very likely among the elite. It is from this sort of patron that the prodigal seeks aid.

Patronage of course pervades all levels of peasant societies.[45] Meager opportunities beyond basic survival are the usual peasant lot. Anything more, including help in times of trouble, comes from the largesse of patrons who broker resources to the peasant class.[46] The younger son here obviously knows the system and thus seeks aid by becoming the client of a local patron.

There is a certain poignancy to the notice of what the younger son has done here. To get a feel for this poignancy, it is worth quoting George Foster at length:

> The emotional dependence of the peasant on the city presents an especially poignant case. Peasants throughout history have admired the

---

[43] For insightful comment in this regard, see Foster, "Peasant Society," 302–3.

[44] Foster, "Introduction," 8.

[45] A review of patronage in Roman Palestine is available in Moxnes, "Patron-Client Relations," 241–68.

[46] "Patron-client relations, in which peasant villagers seek out more powerful people who may be city dwellers, wealthy hacienda owners, religious leaders, or other individuals with the power to aid, are a significant element of most peasant societies" (Foster, "Introduction," 9).

city and have copied many of the elements they have observed there. The city, with its glitter and opportunity, holds a fascination, like a candle for a moth. But at the same time, and for good cause, peasants hate and fear cities and the city dwellers who exercise control over them. Since time immemorial city people have alternately ridiculed, ignored, or exploited local country people, on whom they depend for food, for taxes, for military conscripts, for labor levies, and for market sales. Peasants know they need the city, as an outlet for their surplus production and as the source of many material and nonmaterial items they cannot themselves produce. Yet they recognize that the city is the source of their helplessness and humiliation, and in spite of patrons half trusted, the peasant knows he can never really count on a city man.[47]

It would be hard to imagine a more telling description of the position of the prodigal son!

15:17 But when he came to himself he said, 'How many of my father's hired servants have bread enough and to spare, but I perish here with hunger! 15:18 'I will arise and go to my father, and I will say to him, "Father, I have sinned against heaven and before you; 15:19 I am no longer worthy to be called your son; treat me as one of your hired servants."'

Through most of Christian history these verses have been seen as the "turning point" in the story—the moment of "repentance" to traditional exegetes who imagine this to be a soteriological tale.[48] However, careful reading suggests that this may not be the case at all.[49] As Scott makes clear, the prodigal is really motivated by his stomach and is therefore not repentant in the truest sense.[50]

The critical issue is the meaning of the phrase, "he came to himself." Various attempts have been made to find Aramaic equivalents or rabbinic parallels for it. Some have claimed Hellenistic equivalents meaning to "have second thoughts."[51] But perhaps closer to the implications in the story is the

---

[47] Foster, "Introduction," 10.

[48] Most notably Schottroff, "Das Gleichnis vom verlorenen Sohn," 27–52 but many others as well.

[49] Bailey, *Poet and Peasant*, 175–77, allows that the prodigal may have repented of blowing the money, but his principal argument is that the prodigal is simply cooking up a self-rescue scheme by which to pay back the father. Obviously the theological axe being ground here is making a case for the prodigal's unwillingness to accept unmerited grace.

[50] Scott, *Hear*, 116. A bit earlier Bornkamm, *Jesus of Nazareth*, 126, took the same view. Marshall, *Luke*, 609, cites *M. Rab. Lam.* 1:7 [53b]; Str-B I, 568; II, 215–16: "When a son (in need in a strange land) goes barefoot, then he remembers the comfort of his father's house."

[51] The evidence or, better, the lack thereof, is carefully reviewed in Bailey, *Poet and Peasant*, 173–76.

suggestion of Dan O. Via that the prodigal is remembering his own past and thereby remembering who he is.[52]

If Via is right, and if this is indeed such a moment of self-recognition, then the recognition that occurs above all is recognition of the family from which the prodigal derives his identity and from which he has separated himself. Granted the envisioned return will only put him on the periphery of the family, nonetheless it will reconnect him with the family's social networks and place him in a social location where he *knows how to operate*. The community's guiding hand, even if not full membership in the family, will be restored. He will no longer be among outsiders who exploit, ridicule, or ignore him. Perhaps that is enough to hope for.

15:20 And he arose and came to his father. But while he was yet at a distance, his father saw him and had compassion, and ran and embraced him and kissed him. 15:21 And the son said to him, 'Father, I have sinned against heaven and before you; I am no longer worthy to be called your son.' 15:22 But the father said to his servants, 'Bring quickly the best robe, and put it on him; and put a ring on his hand, and shoes on his feet;'

Kenneth Bailey was probably the first to set this line fully in its proper social context. Especially important is that he (nearly alone) takes seriously the embedded (and indebted) position of the family in the village:

> The father also knows how the village (which certainly has told him he should not have granted the inheritance in the first place) will treat the boy on his arrival. The prodigal will be mocked by a crowd that will gather spontaneously as word flashes across the village telling of his return. . . . [H]e will be subject to taunt songs and many other types of verbal and perhaps even physical abuse.[53]

The son's return to the edge of the village thus precipitates a crisis.

It also makes the subsequent actions of the father understandable. As Bailey points out, in the Mediterranean world, *old men do not run*.[54] Running is not only shameful (ankles show); it also indicates lack of control. Old men *certainly* do not run to meet or welcome anyone and especially not their children. But if an emergency exists, perhaps it is another matter. This makes sense of the unique Greek term used here: δραμών. The term means "to exert oneself to the limit of one's powers."[55] It implies straining to the utmost. Obviously the father exerts himself here because the boy is in trouble. The

---

[52] Via, *Parables*, 168.

[53] Bailey, *Poet and Peasant*, 180–82.

[54] Ibid., 181. Bailey also cites Aristotle: "Great men never run in public" (undocumented) and Sirach 19:30: "A man's manner of walking tells you what he is."

[55] Arndt and Gingrich, *Greek–English Lexicon*, 833.

villagers would be angry, and the father's "compassion" is well placed. Hence we can argue that the embrace and kiss are not first of all signs of welcome; they are signs of *protection*.

Of course much has been made of the actions of the father as expressions of incredible paternal love. Perhaps that is true, since a Mediterranean audience might have expected instead to see the father beat the son in public in order to signal his disapproval. But we must point out that the villagers here see both a son *and a father* of whom they would disapprove. They would fear that the son's behavior might infect their own sons but would equally deplore the father's foolishness for having given in. Thus we must ask if more is going on here than simply an outpouring of paternal love.

Our contention is that the father's task is not only to reconcile his son to the family but also to reconcile himself and his family to the village. The first step in that process has been taken when the father (1) protects the son and (2) publicly demonstrates his reintegration into the family with the robe, ring, and sandals.[56] Bailey argues that the robe, ring, and sandals would have signaled to the *servants* how the son is to be treated, and that the robe would have signaled the same to the *villagers*. That is probably true, but Bailey is almost certainly not correct in suggesting that the robe would "assure" village reaction.[57] Unfortunately, for the village simply to acquiesce in the prodigal's return would not settle the matter.

The problem is that the *father and older son* have also offended the community and therefore something further is required in order to address *their* offences. In fact something must be done to reestablish confidence in the entire family by demonstrating its respect for and solidarity with the village. Only in this way can the father rescue not only his two sons but also himself and his extended family.

15:23 'and bring the fatted calf and kill it, and let us eat and make merry; 15:24 for this my son was dead, and is alive again; he was lost, and is found.' And they began to make merry.

Here the father takes the necessary action to reconcile himself and his family with the village.[58] As Bailey correctly notes, "the selection of a calf rather than a goat or a sheep means that most, if not all, the village will be

---

[56] If it is the best robe in the house, it is probably the father's. If the ring is a signet ring as is often argued (Derrett, Plummer, Marshall, et al.), it is a sign of authority. Since slaves went barefoot, sandals may well have indicated free status.

[57] Bailey, *Poet and Peasant*, 185.

[58] Scott, *Hear*, 118, argues that this making merry in the family is also designed to "encompass the reader." Perhaps. But Scott's statement is premature. It skips the critical reconciliation with the village that the father's party now provides.

present that evening.[59] To kill a calf is rare and expensive. Not to share it with neighbors would be to add insult to injury. But as we noted earlier, by spending on elaborate feasts, an individual gives back to the community and gains (or in this case regains) honor. A feast is a gesture of solidarity with and respect for those invited.

But there is also a huge risk here. What if the invitees refuse to come? If the father throws a party and the villagers do not come, they will have signaled their unwillingness to reconcile with the family. That is always a risk in such a situation, and if no reconciliation occurs, the family will be worse off than they were before. By making the first move toward the village, therefore, the father risks a disastrous rejection. At this point, listeners to the story would probably have been a bit on edge wondering what might happen next. But when the villagers do indeed show up, the hearer or reader would be much relieved that the desired reconciliation had succeeded.[60] The story would seem to be resolved.

15:25 Now his elder son was in the field; and as he came and drew near to the house, he heard music and dancing. 15:26 And he called one of the servants and asked what this meant. 15:27 And he said to him, 'Your brother has come, and your father has killed the fatted calf, because he has received him safe and sound.' 15:28a But he was angry and refused to go in.

The second half of this parable has been disconcerting to nearly all who have read it. Up to this point, the daring but generous efforts of the (foolish) father have succeeded in rescuing his beleaguered family. The son has been reconciled to the father and the father and his sons to the village. The villagers have acquiesced in what is going on, and all appears to be going well. The older son's refusal to come in, however, is totally unexpected. It is shocking. It is a public humiliation of the family and the father, a humiliation that would have seriously taken aback any Middle Eastern hearer or reader.

The notice that the party has to be reported to the unknowing older son has put off some commentators who see this as an unrealistic situation. However, most commentators argue that the report to the older son is simply a "stage-managed" literary effect designed to set up a contrast between the two sons.[61] The first half of this explanation (that the report is a literary effect) will probably satisfy any who recognize the art in storytelling. But the latter (traditional) notion that the story here contrasts the two sons requires a closer look.

---

[59] Bailey, *Poet and Peasant*, 186.

[60] For an example of an attempt to throw a party when the guests did not show up, see Luke 14:16–24.

[61] Usually following Linnemann, *Jesus of the Parables*, 10.

In fact the contrast here is not between the two sons at all. It is between the villagers and the older son. The contrast between the two sons took place earlier in the story when one asked for the inheritance, both took it, but only one left home. Now we propose to take our clue for this new contrast from what has just been said about the family's need to reconcile with the villagers and about the fear that villagers might signal their disapproval by not showing up at the family party. The villagers do show up. But will the older son? There was never any question of the younger son's showing up at the party. This is a given. The doubt centers on the villagers and the older son. The music and dancing signal that the villagers have indeed arrived and have affirmed the reconciliation. The question then is whether the older son will follow suit.

After all, he is another of the aggrieved parties. The prodigal's loss of the money means the older brother will be the sole support of the father in his old age and likely a support for the prodigal as well. His interests have been damaged. Yet a reconciliation between the brothers is essential to the well-being of *all* members of the family and indeed to its relations with the larger community. If the younger son is to remain at home, a debilitating sibling rivalry would strain family interaction with outsiders—as anyone knows who has tried to stay neutral in a fight between a pair of friends. Whatever tensions remain inside the family belong there and not in public. But once again the public is drawn into the family quarrel.

Obviously the expected public role of the eldest son at a feast would be very conspicuous by its absence. Bailey reports that the current custom in the Middle East is for the oldest son to stand barefoot at the door and to greet guests.[62] I have experienced that same phenomenon on several occasions, notably on arriving for tea at the home of the sheik of Bethany in 1986. The oldest son introduced the father to everyone present and supervised the serving and entertainment. Whether such a role pertained in antiquity is difficult to say, but the older son's deliberate and public refusal to come to the party leaves no doubt that he is trying to humiliate his father.[63]

15:28b His father came out and entreated him, 15:29 but he answered his father, 'Lo, these many years I have served you, and I never disobeyed your command; yet you never gave me a kid, that I might make merry with my friends. 15:30 But when this son of yours came, who has devoured your living with harlots, you killed for him the fatted calf!'

---

[62] Bailey, *Poet and Peasant*, 194.

[63] Note that the elder son disregards the expected respectful address to his father (Luke 15:29). Cf. 1 Tim 5:1.

This is truly a remarkable scene. In the Middle East old men do not entreat their sons. They order them. To beg is demeaning and indicates a lack of shame. This father did not seek out the younger son but ran to protect him when he did return. Now the father's extraordinary behavior in trying to keep his family together gets even more bizarre as he begs the older son to come in. It is safe to say that family reconciliation is indeed a high priority for this father.

Nonetheless the tragedy of these lines in the story is threefold. First there is the fact that the father cannot convince his own son to do what the villagers have so readily done. Instead, the son goes in the opposite direction. As is often noted, the language of the older brother ("this son of yours," v. 30) suggests that he is attempting to dissociate himself from the rest of the family. That is what the younger son had done earlier, and here the parallel between the two sons is clear. Ibrahim Said puts it nicely:

> The difference between him and his younger brother was that the younger brother was estranged and rebellious while absent from the house, but the older son was estranged and rebellious in his heart while he was in the house.[64]

He then adds:

> The estrangement and rebellion of the younger son were evident . . . in his request to leave his father's house. The estrangement and rebellion of the older son were evident in his anger and his refusal to enter the house.[65]

The issue then is plainly drawn. Who is really in and who is out? Who belongs and who does not? The villagers confirmed that the younger son was really in. He is accepted again as a member of both family and village. But at the end of the story, the villagers publicly witness the fact that the older son is really out. He is completely disloyal. Moreover, the consequences of this disloyalty will be no less devastating to the long-range prospects of the family and of its place in the village than the earlier behavior of the prodigal.

A second unfortunate display of the older son is his accusation against his younger brother. He accuses his sibling of spending the inheritance on harlots, even though the story earlier left no such implication. The older brother is mocking. He is cooking up a scurrilous explanation of events in the attempt to destroy his brother. This is what anthropologists call "deviance labeling": the attempt to pin a label on someone in order to undermine them

---

[64] Said, *Sharh Bisharat Luqa*, 402, trans. in Bailey, *Poet and Peasant*, 197.

[65] Said, *Sharh Bisharat Luqa*, 403, trans. in ibid.,197.

in the public eye.[66] As Said puts it, "He [the older son] volunteers this exaggeration in order to label his brother with this polluted accusation" (Said: 404).[67] If he can make the promiscuous label stick, he can destroy the younger brother's place in the family and probably in the village as well. The fear would be that down the road "sons" of the prodigal might show up claiming family and village rights and chaos would ensue. If the older son's label sticks, therefore, the younger son would have to leave the village for good and no progeny of his could ever return.

The final discouraging comment of the older son is that the calf had been killed "for him," that is, for the younger brother (v 30). This is not precisely what is going on here. The calf is for the villagers, not for the prodigal. It is a peace offering aimed at the community. At a secondary level, it is also for the members of the prodigal's extended family, who have been rescued by the actions of the father. They too have much to celebrate. Of course if the older brother joins the party, it will also be for him because his place in the village has been restored as well. After all, he took his share of the inheritance in a manner the village would disapprove and thereby raised questions about his own familial loyalties. By claiming the calf was for his younger brother, then, the older son refuses to recognize the family's need to reconcile with the village and compounds the insult aimed at his father.

15:31 And he said to him, 'Son, you are always with me, and all that is mine is yours. 15:32 It was fitting to make merry and be glad, for this your brother was dead, and is alive; he was lost, and is found.'

Commentators have often noticed the term of endearment used here by the father (τέκνον: *child*; the vocative form indicates affection). Just as the father was compassionate toward his younger son, so he is here toward the elder. He acknowledges the son's place in the family and the fact that everything remaining belongs to him.[68]

The listening audience of course would not miss the father's playback of the older son's line ("this *son* of yours") with the critical substitution ("this *brother* of yours"). The two lines are otherwise identical in the Greek.[69] The comment that the prodigal "was lost and is found" may well be evidence of

---

[66] For a full discussion of "deviance labeling" and of its prevalence in the Gospels, see Malina and Neyrey, *Calling Jesus Names*.

[67] Said, *Sharh Bisharat Luqa*, 404, trans. in Bailey, *Poet and Peasant*,199.

[68] Many commentators have worried over an ambiguity in the Greek text here, and translations differ. It is not clear who is supposed to rejoice. The vast majority opt for "we" as opposed to "you": so the KJV, NAB, JB, TEV, NIV, and the REB. The old RSV retains the ambiguity. The NRSV goes with the majority and reads: "we." But the choice is unnecessary. *Everyone* is supposed to be included in the celebration.

[69] Plummer, *Luke*, 379; Fitzmyer, *Luke*, 2:1091–92; Corlett, "'This Brother of Yours,'" 216.

the editorial hand of Luke since it echoes the two parables earlier in chapter (15:6; 15:9). It nonetheless summarizes beautifully the substance of what has happened here and provides a *family* rationale for why the older son should indeed participate.[70]

Conclusion

The lack of an ending to the parable has frustrated some readers. Yet it has inclined others to see in the parable an artful example of open-endedness that places the reader in the position of the older son: the father pleads, and a decision must be made about whether or not to come to the party.[71] For the moment, however, we are content to leave the story as it is, wondering whether the older brother eventually did or did not come to the party.

Our final question has to do with why Jesus might have told this story about the chaotic life of a village family and the attempts of the father to reconcile things gone wrong. Obviously it is the kind of story any peasant could easily identify with and understand. It clearly commends the valiant struggles of the beleaguered if somewhat foolish father. It is a story that depends on the dynamics of real village life.

Hearers might initially have been scandalized at the behavior of the father and the two sons, but perhaps the audience grudgingly recognized that at least the older son stayed home. As the younger son woke up to his family identity, however, and as the father risked everything to restore the situation, the audience might quickly have recognized that they had judged father and prodigal a bit hastily. Ultimately, both the father and the younger son recognize the gravity of the situation. The actions of the father to protect his son and then to reconcile the family to the village would likely have evoked admiration. The father's respect for the community would have been especially gratifying. Perhaps the erratic members of a community should not be judged too quickly.

Would stories about family reconciliation make any sense in the setting of Jesus? No doubt they would, especially to the quarrelsome fictive kin group (disciples, followers) that Jesus gathered around himself (Luke 9:46–50; 11:23; 22:24–27; *Gos. Thom.* 12; POxy1224). In the face of the all too common family conflict in peasant societies (the ideal notwithstanding), this story affirms responsibility to both family and community. It even affirms

---

[70] While most commentators treat the three parables of chapter 15 as a unit, Michael R. Austin (307–31) argues that the literary connections between 15:11–32 and 16:1–8 are far more significant.

[71] For the parable's conclusion being an open ended invitation see Bailey, Plummer. Fitzmyer thinks the issue inappropriate because it detracts from the Lukan story of a loving father.

generosity of spirit in the face of scurrilous behavior. In the setting of Jesus, such a message seems plausible indeed.

Moreover, if one takes a step back from the details of the story and thinks about what is going on as the plot unfolds, it is obvious that one of the key things being celebrated here is the return of a villager who had gone to the city with tragic consequences. Since the nonelite populations of the cities came primarily from those separated from village families by debt, non-inheritance, or family dispute, the experience of the prodigal would have been all too familiar to peasant hearers of Jesus. The story would celebrate the return of one of their own who had experienced the devastating impact of the city upon displaced peasants. Moreover, if Richard Horsley is correct that the social revolution of Jesus was aimed at the renewal of local community and the resolution of community conflict, then the place of the story in the ministry of Jesus would be even clearer.[72] It would call into question the fatal attraction peasants felt toward the city and offer skepticism about reliance on elite institutions such as patronage. Above all it would celebrate the recon-ciliatory efforts of the father and, through the older son, would force open the question of participation on the part of Jesus's hearers in community reconciliation.

Like many of the stories of Jesus, this one features persons who break all the conventional rules of honor. After all, this is a foolish father who divides his estate while alive, who runs to rescue a shameless son, and who begs to another son bent on humiliating him in public. Like the story of a foolish shepherd who leaves ninety-nine sheep to rescue one, this story also suggests an improbable sort of kingdom in which prudence is not the highest value. In the mouth of Jesus, this sort of comment has a familiar ring. To followers of Jesus who also knew the dynamics of peasant family life and the rancor that could engulf it, a story of family reconciliation might even have sounded like good news.

---

[72] Horsley, *Jesus and the Spiral of Violence*, 246–84,

CHAPTER 8

A Peasant Reading of the Parable of the Talents/Pounds: A Text of Terror?

GIVEN THE avalanche of writing on the parables of Jesus in recent years, wisdom might suggest that one let the dust settle before jumping into the fray. There is after all much to sift and evaluate before new ventures are undertaken. Yet little of this work on the parables has taken into account recent efforts to use the social sciences in New Testament interpretation. That is certainly the case with the parable of the talents/pounds (frequently called "A Man Who Entrusted Money'") about which there are no social science treatments to date. What might be interesting therefore is to look at the parable in light of what anthropologists have learned about peasant economics, and particularly in light of the notion of "limited good" that typified peasants in what has been called the "Mediterranean culture-continent."[1]

In so doing we should make it clear that what follows is not a full exegesis of the parable. It is rather a study of the social relations implied both in the story's narrative world and among the several audiences in which the parable has been heard. As Brandon Scott reminds us, an active imagination is a necessary prerequisite for reading the parables of Jesus.[2] But our thesis will be that having imaginations socialized in the capitalist West, Western interpreters have found it nearly impossible to conjure up images of the agrarian social dynamics to which the story once appealed.

The Basic Elements of the Parable

As with most parables of Jesus, the parable of the talents/pounds has a complex literary history. Much disagreement exists about that literary history,

---

[1] See Braudel, *Mediterranean*; and Gilmore, *Honor and Shame*.
[2] Scott, *Hear*, 67–68.

though we may begin by noting the scholarly consensus that the canonical forms of the parable cannot be original. It has come down to us only in heavily edited form. However, since our interest is in social relations rather than a full exegesis of the text, we may bypass concern for the *ipsissima verba,* the original words, and work instead with what Scott calls the "originating structure" that underlies the canonical versions of the story.[3] Following Scott's lead, we may list what appear to be the basic elements from which the story has been constructed.[4] Note that what follows is not a text, and certainly not a hypothetical original text, but rather a simple list of the actions the narrative includes.

1. A master planning a long journey entrusts money to servants, returns, and asks for an accounting.

2. Some of the servants increase the initial amounts they are given, return the increased capital to the master, and are rewarded.

3. Another servant, who admits being frightened, hides the amount he is given in order to return it intact to the master.

4. The angry master takes the money of the last servant and gives it to the first.

Thus pared of details, the social dynamics on which this story depends stand out in high relief; so it is with this set of core elements that we shall to go work.

As we begin it is important to note, as indeed many commentators have, that stripped of the additions of Matthew and Luke, which turn the story into a warning about diligence among those awaiting the *Parousia,* the story appears to be exactly what one expects of a parable of Jesus. It is indeed a parable and not an allegorical story. It draws upon events familiar from the real world to create an imaginary and open-ended situation—a narrative world we might call it—that hearers are invited to ponder. There is no application or interpretation provided, leaving the hearers to reflect on the possibilities the story holds for their own situations. This being the case, we are led to ask what some of those possibilities might have been for the story's first audience.

The Social Impact of the Basic Ideas

Since the settings provided for the parable in Matthew and Luke cannot be original, we are left to speculate about the parable's original audience. Those

[3] Ibid., 223–25. See also Lambrecht, *Once More Astonished,* 180–81.

[4] Scott, *Hear,* 225–31.

inclined to see the original parable as a warning to Jesus's opponents about their stewardship of divine resources are quick to specify such opponents as among the addressees (Dodd, Jeremias, Lambrecht, et al.). Perhaps such opponents were among Jesus's first audience. But since estimating the audience from the supposed thrust of the parable is both risky and premature, we might prefer at the outset to envision a much more general audience that could have included not only opponents but also disciples of Jesus as well as a wider group of unspecified hearers. Given the fact that upwards of 90 percent of agrarian populations were rural farmers, it may even have included Galilean peasants. Moreover, if it did, the commonly perceived thrust of the parable quickly becomes severely problematic.

It should not take a great deal of thought to recognize a striking similarity between the parable's fundamental ideas we listed above and the basic tenets of modern capitalism—or, at least, so it seems to minds conditioned by the capitalist societies of the modern West. Indeed commentators of the nineteenth and twentieth centuries have genuinely reveled in the parable's seeming exhortation to venturous investment and diligent labor. It appears to be nothing less than praise for a homespun capitalism on the lips of Jesus. Even though such treatments of the parable can be seen as far back as John Chrysostom, and running forward as well into the exegesis of John Calvin, it is a treatment that has been particularly dear to the exegetes of our own time who rarely question this allegedly capitalist motif.

But as soon as we ask how this story might have been viewed by a peasant of first-century Palestine (if indeed such peasants were among the hearers of Jesus), then questions immediately arise. Could such a story possibly have been good news to a peasant? Good news is, of course, always a two-sided affair: good news for thanksgiving diners is obviously bad news for the turkey. If this parable is somehow expected to offer someone good news about the kingdom of God, it is clearly not a peasant. The parable may have been good news to the elite, but to a peasant it would have been nothing less than what Phyllis Trible has termed "a text of terror."

Limited Good

In order to understand the way a peasant might perceive this parable as a text of terror, we need to pause for a moment to lay out the idea anthropologists have labeled "limited good." It has been most clearly spelled out in the cross-cultural studies of peasantry done by George Foster.[5] As Foster explains it,

---

[5] See Foster, "Peasant Society," 293–315; and Foster, "Image of Limited Good," 300–323. See also Gregory, "Image of Limited Good," 73–92; and Malina, "Wealth and Poverty," 354–67.

broad areas of peasant behavior are patterned in such fashion as to suggest that peasants view their social, economic, and natural universes—their total environment—as one in which all of the desired things in life such as land, wealth, health, friendship and love, manliness and honor, respect and status, power and influence, security and safety, exist in finite quantity and are always in short supply as far as the peasant is concerned. Not only do these and all other 'good things' exist in finite and limited quantity, but in addition there is no way directly within peasant power to increase the available quantities. It is as if the obvious fact of land shortage in a densely populated area applied to all other desired things: not enough to go around. 'Good,' like land, is seen as inherent in nature, there to be divided and re-divided, if necessary, but not to be augmented.[6]

What this means is that the pie is limited. A larger share for one automatically means a smaller share for someone else. Good, indeed all goods, are both limited and already all distributed.[7] There simply is not enough of anything to go around or any way to increase the size of the pie.

Use Value and Exchange Value

Of key importance here is the fact that the only markets that existed in the preindustrial world were those among the urban elite. Market economics as we know them in the capitalist world simply do not apply to peasant societies. To the notion of limited good, therefore, we must add a careful description of the mode of production and the pattern of exchange relations among agrarian peasants.

As widely recognized cross-cultural studies have shown, peasant production was primarily for use rather than exchange.[8] Peasant economies are primarily subsistence economies, and thus the purpose of labor was not the creation of value but the maintenance of the family and the well-being of the village.[9] Families and the satisfaction of their needs were the aims of production, not the amassing of wealth. Traders amassed wealth, but peasants did not. They lived at the subsistence level and viewed traders as evil exploiters. As Sirach puts it: "A merchant can hardly keep from wrongdoing, and a tradesman will not be declared innocent of sin" (Sir 26:29).

The necessary distinction here is between a view that evaluates the world of persons or things in terms of *use* and one that evaluates them in terms of

[6] Foster, "Peasant Society," 296.

[7] Malina, *New Testament World*, 81–107; and Malina, "Wealth and Poverty," 354–67.

[8] See Oakman, *Jesus and the Economic Questions*. See also Taussig, *Devil*; Roll, *History of Economic Thought*; Wolf, *Peasants*; et al.

[9] Oakman, *Jesus and the Economic Questions*, 17–91.

exchange. It is a distinction made as far back as Aristotle in his famous comment about producing shoes *(Politics,* I, 9, 2–3). One can make shoes either to use, that is to wear, or to exchange for profit. The former Aristotle sees as legitimate, the latter he does not. He considers it immoral.

The money exchange and banking coming into being in Aristotle's Athens had raised a debate about the validity of exchange, and in *Politics* Aristotle reflects the older peasant view. He makes the case that exchange is an unnatural acquisition of wealth. A natural acquisition is one connected with the household and is intrinsically limited in nature because it has only to serve the needs of the house. As he puts it, natural acquisition is "subject to definite bounds" *(Politics* I, 9, 17). By contrast, unnatural acquisition is a matter of "retail trade," and is concerned "only with getting a fund of money, and that only by the method of conducting the exchange of commodities" *(Politics,* I, 9, 12). Such unnatural acquisition is unlimited by any object that it serves, and in its most hated form, usury, trade in money, or the breeding of money as he calls it, a person "tries to make it increase as though it were an end in itself" *(Politics* 1,10, 5). Exchange as a way of making unlimited wealth is, in Aristotle's mind, inherently evil.

One important result of this shift from production for *use* to production for *exchange* is that money itself takes on new characteristics. Michael Taussig[10] provides a model that draws the distinctions nicely:

Characteristics of Money		
	Use Value	Exchange Value
Aim of circulating money	To satisfy needs	To gain money as an end in itself
Characteristics of money	Means of exchange C-M-C Natural Barren	Means to make more money (Means as ends; capital) M-C-M' Unnatural Fertile

M=Money; M'=Money plus interest, i.e., capital; C= Commodities

From *The Devil and Commodity Fetishism in South America* by Michael Taussig.
Copyright © 1980 by the University of North Carolina Press.
Used by permission of the publisher.

[10] Taussig, *Devil*, 131.

The peasant sells commodities (C) to get money (M) in order to buy other needed commodities (C). The capitalist uses money (M) to buy commodities (C) to sell again at a profit and thereby increase the money (M'). This latter Aristotle considered an unnatural use of money because it implied that money, an inanimate thing, had the power to grow, to multiply. It assumes money is fertile, that it has powers that do not belong to it.

As peasant studies the world over have shown, this perception that money can take on unnatural powers accounts for the frequent association among peasants between money and the supernatural powers of evil.[11] It is also why wage laborers in peasant villages are often thought to have entered a pact with the devil for the purpose of increasing both production and wages. Those trying to gain more are considered to be in league with evil. They often become victims of envy, a fundamental attitude toward others in honor–shame societies, so that by imputing to the successful an allegiance with the devil, "a restraint is imposed on would-be entrepreneurs."[12] Such attitudes of course are the result of a deep-seated belief that profit making is both evil and socially destructive.[13] Moreover, that belief in turn depends upon the distinction we are making between production for use and production for exchange.

Some surplus production for the purpose of exchange did of course exist among peasants, particularly temporary trade-work in the off-season when fieldwork was at a lull. But exchange was never the primary orientation of peasant labor. Moreover, the bulk of that small surplus product that did exist was invariably siphoned off from the peasants in various schemes of centralized redistribution such as taxation and tribute and thereby ended up in the hands of the urban elite.

What is coming into view here is the basis for the widespread notion in agrarian societies, including the one in the ancient Mediterranean culture-continent, that rich people are inherently evil. As Jerome would later put it, "Every rich person is either a thief or the heir of a thief"(*In Hieremiam*, II, V, 2; LCL LXXIV 61). Rich people are associated with thievery because to have gained, to have accumulated more than one started with in a limited-good world, is to have taken the share of someone else.

Comments about the evil of amassing wealth are of course common in the writings of antiquity even outside the New Testament, especially in the writings of Cynics and Stoics. Noteworthy also is the treatise of Plutarch entitled *On the Love of Wealth*, in which he stereotypes the wealthy as invariably greedy. He compares the quest for wealth to madness, a misery. No matter

[11] Ibid., 126–29.

[12] Ibid., 15.

[13] Ibid., 126–29; Weber, *General Economic History*, 355.

how much there is, there is never enough; the rich always want more. He quotes one obsessed fellow with already bulging coffers as saying, "I've put everything under lock and seal or lay it out with moneylenders and agents and yet," he plaintively adds, "I go on amassing and pursuing new wealth, wrangling with my servants, my farmers, my debtors" (*On the Love of Wealth* LCL VII, 525; 17). The greedy rich, says Plutarch, "catch the taint of avarice from their fathers" and later, after the father's death, there is an "interrogation of servants, inspection of ledgers, the casting up of accounts with stewards and debtors" (*On the Love of Wealth* LCL VII, 526; DEF; 27).

Plutarch of course was not a poor man as we count poverty. But it is important to recognize that in Plutarch's world, as well as in the world of the Bible, the terms *rich* and *poor* are political before they are economic. That is, to be rich is to have the power to maintain what one has or even to increase it, while to be poor is to be unable to defend even what one has.[14] The rich are therefore those who prey upon the weak, who take additional shares of the limited pie, and who thereby amass what is not rightfully theirs. To be rich is to be evil. To gain more than one has is to steal from others. As Pseudo-Pelagius put it, "For persons to cease to be greedy, they must cease to be wealthy" (*On Wealth* II, PISupp I, 1381).

Important here is the size of the increases reported in the parable we are studying. Brandon Scott, following J. D. M. Derrett, asserts that the gains reported are "not unusual by the standards of the day."[15] Such, however, is hardly the case. Derrett uses as justification for his remarks a doubtful reading of the Code of Hammurabi in which he mistakes a legal penalty for a presumed measure of profit.[16] Noting that the gains reported by the two servants in Matthew are 100 percent and in Luke 500 percent and 1000 percent respectively, Derrett declares the latter to be a "most satisfactory result."[17] A different view might have been suggested had he consulted Roman sources nearer to the first century. There the legal interest rate is 12 percent.[18] Thus Cicero is reported to have been deeply distressed that so honorable a man as Brutus should have lent the city of Salamis on Cyprus a large sum of money at 48 percent. He tried in vain to have it reduced to the legal amount in order to avoid ill will.[19] In assessing the net return from Italian farms in the imperial period, M. I. Finley argues that the gain of 34 percent claimed by Pliny

---

14 Malina, "Wealth and Poverty," 358–61.

15 Scott, *Hear*, 226.

16 Derrett, *Law in the New Testament*, 24.

17 Ibid., 24.

18 Finley, *Ancient Economy*, 54.

19 Ibid., 54.

is almost certainly an exaggeration.[20] Gains of 1000 percent are thus more likely hyperbole than commonplace and calculated to draw an astonished gasp from the listening audience.

The Parable

What then are we to make of this parable in which we see a master "laying out his money to moneylenders and agents," "pursuing and amassing new wealth," "wrangling and interrogating his servants," "inspecting the ledgers" and "casting up accounts" with the stewards to whom he has entrusted his money? And what are we to make of servants who cooperate with the scheme, proudly announcing their success and, if not anticipating, at least receiving a handsome reward? For whom could such a story possibly be seen as good news?

Such persons as this master can be seen as honorable and such a story seen as good news only if the story is told from the vantage point and value system of the rich—i.e., those who have and use power to extract the shares of others for themselves. Such are the very opposite of those praised by Sirach 31:8–11. Western interpreters, however, overwhelmingly assume that the actions of the master in the story are justified, and that he himself is an honorable person. Some argue that the narrative logic leads inevitably to that conclusion because it nudges the reader to adopt the viewpoint of the master. Is this true? Does narrative logic lead us so? Or is it simply Western acculturation? In a limited-good world, a master getting 1000 percent on his money would be viewed as greedy to the core.

And what of the servants? The "venturesome" and "industrious" pair could be heroes only to those who believed it right to amass wealth by contriving to get a bigger share of the limited pie. The third servant (the one who gained nothing), could be viewed as "wicked" only by persons with this same elitist mentality. He is universally condemned by Western interpreters as a failure.[21] His comments about the master are automatically assumed to be self-justifying and excusatory. Scott sees him as claiming prudence but assumes the claim is invalid and reads it as an attempt to avoid responsibility.

As we shall argue in a moment, the servant's claim may have been quite the opposite. It may have been a claim to have acted more responsibly than either of the other two servants. Scott is among the few to have noticed that in Luke's version of the story, the master never actually condemns the third servant; nonetheless in his own reconstruction of the original, Scott and vir-

---

[20] Ibid., 117.

[21] For example, see Scott, *Hear*, 222.

tually every other Western interpreter to date assumes the judgment of the master toward the third servant to be legitimate.[22]

To a peasant, however, who believes that there is nothing within his or anyone else's power that can increase the size of the pie, who believes that rich people are thieves without mercy and that honorable men seek only what is already theirs, to such a peasant could this text have been anything but frightening? It would have confirmed his worst fears about the kingdom of God, suggesting that it worked exactly as did his daily experience: the strong trample the weak and are rewarded for doing so.

Look again at the actions of the third servant in the story. He tries to protect the existing share of the master. That is exactly what, in the peasant view, an honorable person should do. On Exodus 22:7, Josephus comments that if a depositary loses any portion of a deposit, he must face a tribunal of seven judges, swearing that he has neither used a portion of it nor has lost it through malice or intent (*Ant.* 4.285–87). Thus in Matthew, the servant chooses to bury the amount he is given in the ground, precisely what rabbinic law specified as the proper course. Since burying was safer than other means of protection, the rabbis ruled that the person burying an entrusted amount was not responsible for any loss (*b. Baba Mezi'a* 42b; *m. Baba Batra* 4:8).[23] Though the Lukan servant ties the money in a cloth, thus taking what the Mishnah specifies as the riskier course, he nonetheless preserves the pound as any honorable man would. He does not participate in the scheme to double the master's money but honorably refrains from taking anything that belongs to the share of another. Worth noting in this connection is Leviticus 6:2, which forbids defrauding a neighbor in a matter of deposit. Josephus takes this to mean taking back more than one has deposited with a trustee (*Ag. Ap.* 2.208).

It is important to remember that the third servant acknowledges himself to be "afraid," or, as it is in Luke, afraid of the master. Why? The master is said to be a hard man. The term in Matthew, σκληρός, means harsh or cruel or merciless. In Luke the master is said to be αὐστηρός, meaning strict or exacting. In either case we get a picture of exactly the kind of greedy person described by Plutarch: one who constantly interrogates servants and inspects the ledgers with an eye to profit. Moreover, we are told that he "reaps where he did not sow" and gathers "where he did not scatter seed." What could be a better description of a crook? The man is simply a thief. How this master ever became an analogue for God in Western commentary is hard to imagine.

So no doubt the servant was afraid—especially since he had tried to act in an honorable fashion even though, knowing the greedy master as he did, he had reason to fear reprisal. As Sirach 13:4 puts it, "A rich man will exploit you if you can be of use to him, but if you are in need he will forsake you." And true to form, the master rewarded only those prepared to cooperate with him in his scheme of evil extortion.

A Third Extant Version

But before we ask why Jesus might have told such a story, there is one more piece of evidence we must introduce. There is a third extant version of this story in the so-called Gospel of the Nazoreans, known to us only from quotations and allusions in the Church Fathers and a few later writings. Though the date and character of the Gospel are by no means certain, it is usually assumed to have been a second-century translation of the Gospel of Matthew from Greek into Aramaic.[24] It nonetheless contains a very interesting and important variation on the parable we are considering. The fragment is preserved only by Eusebius, and his comment on it must be quoted in full. We take only the liberty of printing it out in such a way as to make the chiastic structure of the parable clear:

> But since the Gospel [written] in Hebrew characters which has come into our hands enters the threat not against the man who had hid [the talent], but against him who had lived dissolutely—
>
> For he [the master] had three servants:
>
> **A** one who squandered his master's substance with harlots and flute-girls,
>   **B** one who multiplied the gain,
>   **C** and one who hid the talent
> and accordingly . . .
>   **C'** one was accepted (with joy),
>   **B'** another merely rebuked,
> **A** and another cast into prison
>
> I wonder whether in Matthew the threat which is uttered after the word against the man who did nothing may refer not to him, but by epanalepsis to the first who had feasted and drunk with the drunken (Eusebius, *Theophania*, 22).

---

[24] Hennecke, *New Testament Apocrypha*, 139–53; Koester, *Introduction to the New Testament*, 201–202,

From this text several things are clear. First, Eusebius is obviously at a loss to understand how the first servant in Matthew could possibly have been approved. Thus by the contrived notion of epanalepsis he tries to figure out how the rebuke of the third servant in Matthew could really have been meant of the first. Since Eusebius knew canonical Matthew, we must assume he knew that there the first servant was said to have gained five talents in addition to the five he was originally given. He seems to assume, however, that this servant was the dissolute one of the Gospel of the Nazoreans, and it is for his dissolute behavior with the master's money, not simply because he gained new monies, that this servant is thrown into prison.

Of special interest, however, is the second servant in Eusebius's text. Note that if we carefully follow the structure of the Eusebius quotation, the second servant, the one who increased his master's money, is not commended as he is in the canonical stories, but is rebuked. His behavior is seen, if not as criminal, at least as reprehensible. Thus we cannot escape the conclusion that neither Eusebius nor the author of the Gospel of the Nazoreans approved of this servant using the master's money to gain more.

However, the same cannot be said of modem commentators. Typical of many Westerners with capitalist assumptions, Jeremias cannot imagine that the servant in the Gospel of the Nazoreans who increased his master's money is rebuked, or that the one who hid the money is accepted with joy. Hence in his paraphrase of the Nazorean text he takes it upon himself to rearrange the sequence of the servants in order to make the one who hid the money the one who is rebuked.[25] Scott follows suit, claiming that the Gospel of the Nazoreans provides a clumsy rationale for the third servant's guilt.[26] It would be hard to imagine a clearer example of forcing a story to conform to one's (Western) cultural assumptions.

But if we again follow carefully the structure of the Eusebius quotation and do not undertake to rearrange it as Jeremias and Scott have done, it can be seen that the servant who was accepted with joy was the one who acted honorably in a limited-good world and who, in the canonical versions, held fast his convictions in spite of his fear of the greedy master. He faithfully guarded the master's money and returned it to him intact. As the chiastic structure clearly demonstrates, it is the approval of the behavior of the third servant that is the centerpiece of this Nazorean version of the story.

In sum, we have in the Nazorean text a hitch in the flow of tradition. It appears to be occasioned by the fact that neither the Nazorean author nor Eusebius its commentator could imagine commending servants who used a

---

[25] Jeremias, *Parables of Jesus*, 58.

[26] Scott, *Hear*, 232.

master's money for additional gain. While they lay out no reason for their disapproval such as the one we have been developing, the simple fact that they disapprove suggests that we take another look at our traditional inter-pretations of the story.

The Parable in the Setting of Jesus

Given all we have said to this point, it remains an open question whether this parable, even in its basic elements, goes back to Jesus.[27] However if anything like the canonical version does trace back to Jesus, we are left to wonder how Jesus told a story so obviously given from the vantage point of the elite and so sharply out of touch with the peasant perception of the world. In answering this question, several choices lie open to us.

First, we might simply acknowledge that Jesus did not share the peasant viewpoint and that attempts to turn him into a peasant are a vestige of late nineteenth-century romanticism about a peasant Jesus. But the convenience of such a view for those of us with self-interest in finding modem capitalist ideology in the New Testament ought to give us pause for thought.

Alternatively, we might simply suggest that the parable, at least in its canonical forms, is not from Jesus, and that it represents a later attempt by affluent Christians to justify their worldview in the name of Jesus. After all, the allegorizing motifs in the canonical versions, especially in Luke, seem to do exactly that. Jeremias long ago pointed out that Luke's additions about a nobleman who goes away to seek a throne, who gets it, and who then returns to ruthlessly slaughter those who had opposed him not only confuse both the parable of the pounds and the so-called parable of the throne-claimant but in the process project an unimaginable Jesus.[28]

Perhaps, then, the parable is not from Jesus at all, and we should write it off as the product of the later church. This might even go together with a hypothesis that the version in the Gospel of the Nazoreans that condemns increasing capital is the more original, and that the canonical trajectories adulterated the story early on. While taking on the question of authenticity lies beyond the scope of our inquiry, it is not difficult to see that the so-called

---

[27] Funk, et al., *Parables of Jesus*, 54–55.

[28] Jeremias, *Parables of Jesus*, 59–60; Weinart, "Parable of the Throne-Claimant," 505–15; Resenhofft "Jesu Gleichniz," 318–31; Zerwick, "Die Parabel vom Thronwärter," 654–74. It is telling indeed that someone, perhaps Luke, thought to combine the story of the ruthless and evil throne claimant with this story about a greedy master. For whoever combined them, the two stories obviously appear to be about similar people. We can thus ask once again, how in the world did this thieving, murdering, greedy crook ever become an analogue for God in Western exegesis? Perhaps the only answer is that our acculturation in the capitalist West has trumped what the story actually says.

environmental criterion for authenticity comes into play here. The Nazorean rendition fits the environment of Jesus much more easily than either of the canonical versions of the story. Moreover, if the environmental criterion is taken seriously, it becomes much easier to explain how the canonical versions derive from the Nazorean text than to treat the matter the other way around. While such considerations may not be sufficient reason to reverse the present scholarly judgment about the secondary character of the Nazorean text, they surely provide warrant for a new and closer look at the Nazorean version.

Finally, then, we should consider the possibility that the story is indeed from Jesus and that whatever form the original may have taken, its basic elements that we identified above are his. Could Jesus have told such a story?

Much depends on how we view both the master and the third servant's comments about him. The third servant acknowledges that he is afraid, as well one might expect a servant to be who had been drawn into such a situation. After all, he did not ask for the money; he was simply summoned and given it. He was asked to take on a responsibility that was potentially disastrous.

He tells us that the master is a "hard" man. If we follow the Lukan reading, αὐστηρός, he is indeed a man who keeps strict ledgers, accounting for every penny that is his. Thus when the third servant characterizes the master as a hard man, is he merely justifying his fear, hence explaining away his inaction with the money—as we usually assume? Or is the servant explaining that his fearful but correct perception of the master is what led him to the honorable course of preserving the money? Is he in effect saying: "I knew I had better be careful, and I have been"? We need to see a self-serving justification in his comment only if we take the viewpoint of the master. By contrast, peasants hearing the story would probably have heaved a sigh of relief that the poor fellow understood what to do and did it well.

Westerners of course universally assume the third servant has failed. John Dominic Crossan, for example, categorizes this parable as one of "action."[29] He then sees the third servant as having failed the "call to act." The same is true of Scott, who thinks the third servant, frozen by fear into inaction, has failed a classic test and thereby suffered the "loss of a future."[30] However, the view that a peasant should have had a prudent concern for the future is seriously anachronistic.[31] This is a modern view derived from capitalist ideology. Even more important, neither Crossan nor Scott notices that the third servant does indeed act; he just does not act as the master wishes. (Moreover,

[29] Crossan, *In Parables*, 100–104.

[30] Scott, *Hear*, 217–35.

[31] Malina, "Christ and Time," 1–31.

if John Pilch is right that "being" rather than "doing" is the dominant value of Mediterranean societies, the business about acting or not acting is ethnocentric and anachronistic as well.[32])

So much depends on the way we view the master. He is angry with the third servant. Is he rightfully angry? Yes, would say the elite in the audience. No, would say the peasants. Yes, says Jeremias, because Jesus is telling a "crisis-parable" to warn his audience against a false sense of security.[33] No, the peasants might say, because Jesus is warning rich people about their unholy reactions to peasant behavior. We know that the master condemned the third servant. But did Jesus? How do we know that? And did Jesus commend the master? Modern readers of the parable assume that he did. But pruned of its later Lukan and Matthean additions, where does the text say that?

It is just as possible that Jesus did not commend the master, that he is in fact condemning the master's viewpoint, in the same way his peasant hearers would quickly have done. After all, we have from Thomas 95 the statement of Jesus judged to be authentic by recent scholarship: "If you have money, do not lend it at interest, but give it to one from whom you will not get it back." Jesus makes a similar statement in the Luke 6:35. Perhaps, then, we should assume a Jesus who would never have commended putting out money for gain. Perhaps we too are expected to infer Jesus's condemnation of the master's attitude—unless of course we cannot do so because we also have adopted an elitist point of view. Apparently Eusebius and the Gospel of the Nazoreans did figure out Jesus's condemnation of the master. Matthew and Luke did not, but perhaps they thereby tell us more about themselves than about the Jesus they purport to quote. It all depends on the assumptions you bring to the text.

Assumptions about the audience are important here as well. Scott et al. assume that the audience was made up of peasants. We would agree, but we assume there were others there as well. Scott is among the few who have seen that, from the audience, peasant sympathy or pride would have been with the third servant, and that peasants in the audience would have found the master's condemnation of the third servant "arbitrary." Yet in the end, even Scott assumes that thereby the peasants in the audience are misled, and that on this potential for misunderstanding hangs the tension in the parable. He makes no comment about the way elite persons in the audience might have viewed the story, or about what tensions it might have held for them. Scott is silent on this point because the underlying assumption throughout his work is that the master (read: Jesus) offers the point of view being legitimated. It is

---

[32] Pilch, "Healing in Mark," 142–50; and Pilch, "Understanding Biblical Healing," 60–66.

[33] Jeremias, *Parables of Jesus*, 59.

precisely this assumption, so dear to Western hearts, that the agrarian social dynamics of the parable call into question.

In other words, the parable of the talents contains a good deal of ambiguity. Like thanksgiving dinner and like a good many of the parables of Jesus, it is capable of more than one reading. The elitist reading is bad news for peasants. The peasant reading is bad news for masters. The fact that we Western capitalists find the peasant reading so difficult to imagine may be little more than a function of our socialization in a world where amassing wealth is the accepted norm. In a world where the overwhelming portion of the population had no such view, this story of Jesus, if indeed Jesus told it, would have been heard and read with assumptions you and I would never make. It is therefore extremely unlikely that the majority of Jesus's hearers would have jumped to the conclusion either that the behavior of the master is praised or that the master is somehow a paradigm for the divine. Jesus's audience more likely would have nodded their heads in knowing agreement as Jesus pegged the unholy greed of the elite for what it was.

In sum, then, we may say that the parable is a warning. But to whom? We in the twentieth century have always assumed that it is a warning to those not sufficiently venturesome or industrious with what they have been given. We theologize about responsible stewardship of the gifts of grace, by which we mean, of course, a profitable (capitalistic) investment before the return of the Master. Yet Jesus's peasant hearers would almost certainly have assumed that the story was a warning to the rich about their exploitation of the weak. Is it possible that they were right?

CHAPTER 9

Gossip in the New Testament

IN HIS poem "Gossip," Ogden Nash claims there are two kinds of people who sail effortlessly through life: gossipers and gossipees. The writer of James had a somewhat less whimsical view. "But no human being can tame the tongue—an unruly evil, full of death-dealing poison. With it we honor the Lord and Father, and with it we curse human beings, the ones in the likeness of God. Out of the same mouth come blessing and cursing. My brothers, it ought not to be" (Jas 3:8–10). A few verses later, the writer warns readers: "Do not slander [καταλαλέω] each other, brothers. He who slanders a brother or judges his brother, slanders the law and judges the law" (Jas 4:11). Or as the proverbialist puts it: "A scoundrel rakes up evil (רעע) and his speech is like a scorching fire upon his lips. A perverse man stirs up dissension and a gossip (נרגן) separates close friends." (Prov 16:27–28).

While gossip has been enjoyed by virtually all who have participated in it (and roundly condemned by all who imagine themselves the keepers of the civil discourse), it has not always been the subject of thoughtful inquiry. Yet Max Gluckman kicked off a flurry of debate among cultural anthropologists in an insightful article. In it he argued that gossip is among the most important social phenomena we can study.[1] He made the case that it is a much more complex and far-reaching phenomenon than is usually suspected, and is indeed a significant means of informal social formation and control. Moreover, given the unique role gossip plays in oral cultures such as the culture of first-century Palestine, we suggest it should be of special interest to those studying the cultural world of the New Testament.

Before looking at specific studies of gossip in Mediterranean village life, however, a cautionary note is in order. We must recognize that gossip is a nearly universal phenomenon, and thus it cannot be claimed that there is

---

[1] Gluckmann, "Gossip and Scandal," 307.

something uniquely Mediterranean about its existence. At least nothing like this claim has been identified to date. Nonetheless two things may be said in this regard. First, the claim does appear to be justified that gossip plays a different role in nonliterate societies than in literate ones, not only in scope and impact, but also in shape and social function.[2] There is justification therefore in looking at studies of gossip in all nonliterate settings in order to gain an understanding of its complexity.[3] Second, as we shall see below, it may also be true that there are things about Mediterranean societies that make the study of gossip there a special case. Of course gossip has not been the same in all Mediterranean societies at all times in history, and therefore we cannot assume that gossip in Greek villages today is the exact equivalent of gossip in the Greek villages of antiquity. But ethnographers argue that several lasting features of Mediterranean culture have had a marked impact on gossip there; hence these must be taken into account. And obviously if that is true, the topic becomes one of special interest to scholars of the New Testament.[4]

Definition of Gossip

Before thinking more systematically about the social function of gossip, it is important to define gossip carefully. David Gilmore offers a succinct definition that will serve our purposes. Gossip, he argues, is simply "critical talk about absent third parties."[5] This definition will suffice. However, two things

[2] In an early study of preliterate societies, Paul Radin made an observation that has been noticed by nearly every ethnographer since his time:
Primitive people are indeed among the most persistent and inveterate of gossips. Contestants for the same honours, possessors of the sacred rites of the tribe, the authorized narrators of legends, all leave you in little doubt as to the character and proficiency of their colleagues. "Ignoramus," "braggart," and not infrequently "liar" are liberally bandied about" (*Man*, 177–78).
That this should be true in oral cultures is not surprising (we note the prevalence of complaint about gossip in the literature of antiquity), but it is important. Among those trained in the study of literate antiquity, including New Testament scholars, informal oral culture has not always been taken as seriously as it should have been.

[3] While ethnographic studies of gossip are not abundant, enough work has been done to warrant initial attempts to develop models that are cross-culturally applicable. See Goldsmith, "Gossip from the Native's Point of View," 163–93.

[4] Our proposal in what follows is simply that Mediterranean ethnography offers *heuristic* aid in looking for evidence of the scope and function of gossip in the New Testament. Perhaps then we can lay to rest the frequently expressed fear that models drawn from modern ethnography are being "forced" onto the New Testament data. No claim is being made here that Mediterranean villages now are the exact equivalents of those in antiquity. Nor is there anything "necessitarian" about our use of these models. They are heuristic, nothing more. They simply offer insight about what to look for and what questions to ask.

[5] Gilmore, *Aggression and Community*, 92. Interestingly, a Talmudic sage offers an identical

in it are especially important. One is that gossip is "signed" (i.e., face-to-face) talk about people who are not present. This distinction leads some theorists to distinguish gossip from *rumor*, which is "unsigned" (i.e., anonymous) talk about events.[6] So at least three parties are always part of a gossip event: the gossiper, the party listening, and the gossipee. The second important factor to note is that gossip is evaluative talk. It may be either positive or negative, but it usually implies assessment of one kind or another.[7] Given the pervasive competition for honor in Mediterranean culture we spoke of earlier, both social ranking and moral evaluation are usually involved in gossip.[8]

Information may be involved in gossip as well. We shall have more to say in a moment about gossip as "information management," but gossip is often the principle means of information exchange in nonliterate villages.[9] It thus overlaps with simple word-of-mouth news about what is going on, though simple information sharing frequently lacks the peculiar characteristics of gossip. We might also note that for gossip to occur (that is, critical talk about third parties), participants must (1) know each other (at least minimally), (2) understand the import of the situation, and (3) share evaluative categories.[10]

Nearly all definitions of gossip recognize the importance of "self-interest" in the matter. The theoretical debate alluded to earlier has to do with whether gossip is a purely individual phenomenon (Paine) or a group activity (Gluckman). While that debate polarized for a while, recent theorists are inclined to see gossip as involving both individuals and groups (e.g., Gilmore, du Boulay, Bailey, Rosnow and Fine, Wilson). This seems especially clear since gossip often serves the interests of both individuals and groups. The point, then, is that in the degree to which evaluation or moral judgment is involved, gossip becomes a way of manipulating moral status (acquired honor) or other prospects in the "interests" of some person or group.

While most definitions of gossip assume it to be an oral medium, written comment about others might also qualify. When verbal reports come to Paul in 1 Corinthians (1:11) it is easy to see that evaluative comments about absent others are being made and that a gossip event is occurring. When *writ-*

---

view: "'What constitutes evil speech?' —Rabbah said: 'Whatsoever is said in the presence of the person concerned is not considered evil speech.' (*Arak.* 15b)

[6] Paine, "Informal Communication and Information," 186.

[7] "Criticism and evaluation of others, which involves ranking, is the subject of gossip, said to be the chief pastime of the village" (Bailey, *Gifts and Poisons*, 45).

[8] Bailey, *Gifts and Poisons*, 45; Yerkovich, "Gossipping as a Way of Speaking," 192–97.

[9] Arno, "Fijian Gossip," 343; Paine, "What is Gossip?" 282.

[10] Yerkovitch, "Gossipping as a Way of Speaking," 192–97.

ten reports of a similar character come to Paul (1 Cor 7:1; 8:1; 12:1), perhaps they too should be construed as gossip.

Finally, when thinking about what constitutes gossip, we note its common association with women (1 Tim 3:11; 5:13). A Talmudic comment offers the typical stereotype: "Ten kabs of gossip descended to the world; nine were taken by women" (*Kiddushin* 49b). Juliet du Boulay observes that in her Greek mountain village, gossip is an activity "indulged in pre-eminently by women."[11] She argues that while men do indeed gossip, their typical location in public spaces tends to inhibit gossip, whereas the private space occupied by women is conducive to gossip.[12] Alexander Rysman's studies suggest that the English term *gossip* developed particularly pejorative connotations only after it came to be associated with women in the nineteenth century.[13]

Interestingly, Rysman's studies of Chicano groups suggest that condemnations of gossip there were really condemnations of female solidarity which men feared (180).[14] Having noted the prevalent stereotype, then, we also note a certain irony in the fact that the vast majority of ancient texts which either condemn gossip as such or criticize particular instances of it refer either to male participants or make no gender reference at all.

Mediterranean Gossip Studies

A variety of studies in recent years have shown that gossip is indeed prevalent in the villages of the Mediterranean region.[15] Moreover, Juliet du Boulay's study of a Greek mountain village (Ambeli) convinced her that the prevalence of gossip there is not a matter of accident. In fact the peculiar character of Mediterranean village life makes gossip almost inevitable. Du Boulay observes that the nature of gossip in Greek villages is

> determined by the various features of the society - the nature of the value system, the importance of a limited number of roles which express these values and which provide ideal standards of behaviour, the privacy of the home, the publicity of communal life, the intense

[11] Du Boulay, *Portrait*, 204.

[12] Ibid., 204.

[13] Rysman, "How the 'Gossip,'" 177.

[14] Ibid., 180. Guss, "Enculturation," 259–69, studying the Makiritare tribe in Venezuela, suggests that gossip among women there is considered a social necessity to mediate conflicts between men. Jones, "Gossip: Notes on Women's Oral Culture," 193–98, makes the point that little is known about language use in all-female groups, a nearly irremediable problem in the study of antiquity because of the lack of sources and so the lack of data.

[15] See Campbell, *Honor, Family and Patronage*; du Boulay, *Portrait*; Gilmore, "Varieties of Gossip," 89–99; Goitein, *Mediterranean Society*.

relevance of every member of the community to every other member, and the unceasing competition for reputation.[16]

Competition for reputation, of course, is a matter of honor, and as we have noted frequently, honor is the core value in the Mediterranean world. J. K. Campbell's study of Greek shepherds in the area north of Corinth (the *Sarakatsani*) affirms this same connection. Gossip, he argues, is "closely related to the two concepts of self-regard and shame."[17] The result is that failure of any kind, but especially failure to defend honor, is the subject of taunts and even songs of ridicule. Songs are especially feared because they keep the memory of failure alive for long periods. They are never sung to the victim's face (recall our definition of gossip), but the songs are always learned of and deeply shameful.[18]

A variety of studies has also recognized that gossip "trades on" the sharp separation of the private and public domains, a separation characteristic of Mediterranean societies.[19] In theory at least, inside and outside worlds are kept apart. Family secrets are closely guarded. The result is a "continual battle between secrecy and curiosity waged between various families" in a village.[20] Basically, then, gossip consists of "leakage from one domain into the other."[21] Moreover, as du Boulay found out, "once a secret is let out of the family [private domain] there is little chance that it will not, sooner or later, be circulated to the entire community [public domain]."[22] It is always just a matter of time.[23]

Because gossip by its very nature is the telling of secrets, it is much feared for the damage it can do. In peasant communities where everyone knows everyone else so well, "people know exactly where to go to extract certain bits of information, and they know equally well the danger points of the community where a leak could be fatal."[24] In fact gossip is often a form

---

[16] du Boulay, *Portrait*, 204. She argues that these features of village life also make gossip an activity "indulged in pre-eminently by women" (204). She suggests that while men often gossip, frequently their associations are sufficiently public that care must be taken how gossip is passed along. On why and how gossip "became a woman" in the English speaking world, see Rysman, "How the 'Gossip,'" 176–80.

[17] Campbell, *Honor, Family and Patronage*, 312.

[18] Ibid., 314.

[19] Haviland, "Gossip and Competition," 186–91; du Boulay, *Portrait*; Gilmore, "Varieties of Gossip," 89–99.

[20] du Boulay, *Portrait*, 202.

[21] Haviland, "Gossip and Competition," 188.

[22] du Boulay, *Portrait*, 208. See also Zinovieff, "Inside Out," 121.

[23] *Honor, Family and Patronage* 313.

[24] du Boulay, 207.

of envy-aggression. Some have even seen it as the verbal equivalent of the evil eye.[25] Not only can words hurt, they can create actual situations that limit or destroy.

Ancient Comment

This of course accounts for the nearly universal condemnation of gossip by ancient authors. Plutarch, for example, devoted a classic essay to the topic entitled "On Being a Busybody":

> Just as cooks pray for a good crop of young animals and fishermen for a good haul of fish, in the same way busybodies pray for a good crop of calamities, a good haul of difficulties, or novelties and changes, that they, like cooks and fisherman, may always have something to fish out or butcher. (*Moralia* VI:518E [7])

He complains that gossips pass up nearly anything beautiful or worthwhile so they can

> spend their time digging into other men's trifling correspondence, gluing their ears to their neighbor's walls, whispering with slaves and women of the streets, and often incurring danger, and always infamy. (*Moralia* VI:519F [9])[26]

In one of Plutarch's insights, he offers as poignant a comment as one might ever read—from antiquity or any other time:

> Since, then, it is the searching out of troubles that the busybody desires, he is possessed by the affliction called "malignancy," a brother to envy and spite. For envy is pain at another's good, while malignancy is joy at another's sorrow." (*Moralia* VI:518C [6])

The cogency of this observation in an honor–shame society is considerable.

Another ancient writer who devoted an essay to the subject of gossip was Lucian. As in the essay of Plutarch, so in this one there is a bitterness that is unmistakable:

> What I have in mind more than anything else is slanderous lying about acquaintances and friends, through which families have been rooted out, cities have utterly perished, fathers have been driven mad against their children, brothers against their own brothers, children against their parents and lovers against those they love. Many a friend-

---

[25] Zinovieff, "Inside Out,"126.

[26] For other pithy comment see *Moralia* VI:516A (2); VI:516B (2); VI:516D (3); VI:517E (5); VI:517F (6); VI:518E (7); VI:519C (9).

ship, too, has been parted and many an oath broken through belief in slander. (*Slander* 1)

Were we to sample other Greco-Roman comment (which is abundant), we would find it is almost universally condemnatory of gossip.

But it is no different in the Jewish world. There is extensive comment in both Mishnah and Talmud that we can only sample:

> "One who bears evil tales almost denies the foundation [of faith]." (*b. Arachin* 15b)

> "Any one who bears evil tales will be visited by the plague of leprosy." (*b. Arachin* 15b)

> "Of him who slanders, the Holy One, blessed be He, says: He and I cannot live together in the world. As it is said: Whoso slandereth his neighbor in secret, him will I destroy." (*b. Arachin* 15b)

> "Whoever relates slander, and whoever accepts slander, and whoever gives false testimony against his neighbour, deserves to be cast to dogs." (*b. Pesachim* 118a)

Once again the bitterness in the comments comes through clearly.[27]

Causes of Gossip

Ancient writers of course focus on the negative. But the fact is that gossip has many social functions, including some positive ones. It also has many causes. We have already noted several of these, including the separation of private and public domains, the intense relevance of people to each other in the constant close contact of village life, and the intense competition for public reputation. In addition to these, a primary cause of gossip is the simple practical need to focus on the character of individuals with whom one might do any kind of business. In the nonliterate communities of antiquity, business deals, contracts, sales arrangements, and the like were not written down. If oral arrangements could not be trusted, serious trouble was likely. Keeping close tabs on anything and everything that might indicate the character of others with whom one might do business was thus a basic matter of survival. As Sofka Zinovieff puts it:

> Gossip can be a precious resource: people in business learn about their competitors; politicians require details about their rivals and support-

---

[27] For additional comment see: *b. Kiddushin* 49b; *Arachin* 3; 15b, 16a.

ers; citizens discover who are their friends and who their enemies, and so on.[28]

To put it succinctly, close scrutiny of the character of others was not "mere pastime," it was a vital necessity.[29]

Yet another cause of gossip has to do with the anthropomorphic world-view that sees personal causality behind nearly everything that happens. The ancient question was not the one we hear in the modern world, *what* caused something to happen? Rather the question for the ancients was, *who* caused something to happen?[30] As du Boulay points out, "The vivid memory and graphic mind of the villager, coupled with a natural philosophy which sees the working of superhuman forces or a supernatural law revealed continually in the doings of others, give to talk even about neutral subjects the remorseless tendency to turn into talk about personalities."[31] In other words, it was simply critical to find out not only *what* was happening but also *who* was doing it.

Zinovieff offers yet another powerful motivation for gossip: the simple need to learn from the experiences of others.[32] It is part of the socialization process that provides everyone the opportunity to discuss and analyze human behavior in an informal but potent way. Because it provides a "close, oral, daily history" of a village, gossip also provides a "map" of the social environment that is constantly being updated with new experiences and new expectations. People learn from everything new or different they hear about other people. Gossip thus allows people to participate in "interpreting and constructing" their own social milieu.[33] To be in that game one has to talk and listen constantly.

Finally, a motivation for gossip that is not often recognized by Westerners is the simple desire for entertainment. There are few organized entertainments in peasant villages, hence people enjoy simply gathering for talk.[34] As du Boulay suggests, "it is natural that people should derive their entertainment from the human comedy around them."[35] Obviously the victims of this entertainment are not always amused.

---

[28] Zinovieff, "Inside Out," 124.

[29] Goitein, *Mediterranean Society*, 190.

[30] Malina, " 'Let Him Deny Himself'," 109.

[31] Du Boulay, *Portrait*, 205.

[32] Zinovieff, "Inside Out," 121.

[33] Ibid., 126.

[34] Gilmore, "Varieties of Gossip," 90; Zinovieff, "Inside Out," 125.

[35] Du Boulay, *Portrait*, 205–6.

Semantic Field

One obvious way to get a sense of feel for a particular culture's attitude toward gossip is to survey the semantic field.[36] David Gilmore's studies of an Andalusian village provide a good example. Gossip there was a much favored pastime, and Gilmore discovered eleven distinct terms being used to describe the phenomenon:

1. *Criticar:* "to criticize." A rough equivalent of the English term *gossip.*

2. *Rajar:* "to cut." (with a clear intention to harm)

3. *Darle la lengua:* "to tonguelash." (a sustained campaign of vilification)

4. *Cuchichear:* "to whisper." (uninformed talk)

5. *Murmurar:* "to murmur." (informed talk)

6. *Chismorear:* "to speak of trifles." (harmless exchange of information)

7. *Paliquear:* "to chatter or talk idly of nothing." (often with sexual undertones)

8. *Cortar el traje:* "to cut the cloth." (idle talk without malice—entertainment)

9. *Charlar:* "to chat." (a euphemism for *criticar*)

10. *Hablar oculto:* "to speak secretly." (secret talk about those in power)

11. *Contar:* "to tell." (to betray a confidence; hence the worst form of gossip.)[37]

This semantic field is of interest to biblical scholars, not only because it comes from a Mediterranean society, and not only because of its scope and depth, but also because nearly all of these Andalusian terms have biblical equivalents.

Before looking at the semantic field in the Bible, however, it is worth noting that the semantic field above can be sorted into a model of gossip forms. It assumes that *criticar* and *charlar* are the more general terms and then distinguishes the other nine in light of four factors: social status of the subject, legitimacy, purposefulness, and number of participants.[38] By differentiating gossip forms and events in this way, we avoid simply lumping all gossip activity together for indiscriminate condemnation.

---

[36] The English word *gossip* lacks the specificity and nuance often seen in terms drawn from other languages. It developed from an earlier term *God sib*, a reference to a godparent. For an account of the development of the term and its association with women, see Rysman, "How the 'Gossip,'" 176–80.

[37] Gilmore, "Varieties of Gossip," 94–97.

[38] Goldsmith, "Gossip from the Native's Point of View," 180.

Biblical Examples

Space does not permit listing all the instances of the following terms in the Bible. The list provided, however, will suffice to indicate that the semantic field in the biblical literature is no less rich than in Gilmore's Andalusian dialect.

Old Testament Terms

Hebrew	English
רכיל (Lev 19:16; Ezek 22:9; Prov 20:19)	*slander, gossip*
דבה (Num 14:36; Ps 31:13; Prov 10:8)	*slander, slanderer*
רכיל (Jer 6:28; 9:4)	*slandering, talebearing, gossip*
רגל (2 Sam 19:27; Ps 15:3)	*slander*
לשן (Ps 101:5)	*slander*
אכל (Ps 27:2)	*slander*, lit. *devour*
קרץ (Ps 35:15)	*slander* lit. *cut, tear apart*
דפה (Ps 50:20)	*slander*, lit. *ruin*
רגל (2 Sam 19:27)	*go around slandering, backbiting*
לשון (Job 5:21; Ps 10:7; 15:3; 31:20; 64:3; 109:2; Prov 25:23)	*tongue*
איש לשון (Ps 140:11; Prov 30:10; Ezek 36:3)	*slanderer,* lit. *a man of tongue*
שמעה (1 Sam 2:24; 1 Kgs 10:7; Prov 15:30; Isa 28:19; 53:1)	*what is heard, report*
שמע (Exod 23:1; Deut 2:25; Josh 9:9; Isa 23:5; Jer 50:43)	*report*
דבר (Num 14:37; Josh 22:33; 1 Sam 11:4; 1 Kgs 10:6; 2 Chr 9:5)	*word, report*
דבר (1 Kgs 13:25; Ps 41:6)	*to speak*, sometimes in sense of *to spread news* (1 Kgs 13:25), or *to spread gossip* (Ps 41:6)

Hebrew	English
אמר (Neh 6:19; Num 14:14; 1 Sam 23:22)	*to say*, sometimes *to report* (Neh 6:19); *to spread news* (Num 14:14; 1 Sam 23:22)
דבה (Gen 37:2; Num 13:32; 14:36; Jer 20:10)	*to spread slander, to bring an evil report* (Gen 37:2; Num 13:32; 14:36), sometimes *to whisper* (Jer 20:10)
לחשׁ (2 Sam 12:19; Ps 41:7)	*to whisper together*
נרגן (Prov 16:28; 18:8; 26:20; 26: 22)	*whisperer, busybody*
שׁמץ (Job 4:12; 26:14)	*whisper*
נגד (Job 17:5; Jer 20:10)	*to bring to light* (hiphil), sometimes *to betray* or *to inform against*
חרפה (Ps 15:3; 42:10; 79:12)	*reproach, scorn*, as a result of being gossiped about
לוץ (Prov 22:10)	*to deride, to scorn*
חרף (Ps 69:19–20; 89:51)	*scorn, reproach*
לון (Num 14:36; 16:11; 17:5)	*murmur*
רגן (Deut 1:27; Ps 106:25)	*murmur*

The similarity between this list of Hebrew terms and the Spanish list is indeed striking.

New Testament Terms

Greek	English
φλυαρέω, φλύαρος (1 Tim 5:13; 3 John 10)	*slander, gossip, talk nonsense*
κενοφωνία (1 Tim 6:20; 2 Tim 2:16)	*empty talk, foolish chatter*
ματαιολογία, ματαιολογός (1 Tim 1:6; 1:10)	*idle, meaningless talk*
μωρολογία (Eph 5:4)	*stupid talk*
λῆρος (Luke 24:11)	*utter nonsense*
σπερμολόγος (Acts 17:18)	*information scavenger*, lit. *one who picks up seed*, also implies passing it along
αἰσχρολογία (Col 3:8)	*shameful speech, slander*
εὐτραπελία (Eph 5:4)	*coarse jesting, indecent speech*

Greek	English
πρὸς τὸ οὖς λαλέω (Matt 10:27; Luke 12:3)	to whisper, to speak secretly
βατταλογέω (Matt 6:7)	to babble, to speak senselessly
λαλία (John 4:42)	talk
καταλαλέω, καταλαλία (Wis 1:11; 2 Cor 12:20; Jas 4:11; 1 Pet 2:1)	slander, talk against
κατάλαλος (Rom 1:30)	slanderer, gossiper
κατηκέω (Acts 21:21; 21:24)	to report, to tell
μηνύω (John 11:57)	to inform, to reveal secretly
φάσις (Acts 21:31)	news, information, report
ἀκοή (Matt 4:24; 14:1; Mark 1:28; 7:36; 13:7; 2 Pet 2:8)	news, rumor, report, information
γλῶσσα (Wis 1:11; Sir 5:14; 51:2; Jas 3:6–8; 1 Pet 3:10)	tongue
γλῶσσα τρίτη (Sir 28:14–15)	slander, gossip, lit. third tongue
φήμη (Matt 9:26; Luke 4:14; 4:37)	news, report, information
διαγημίζω (Matt 9:31)	to spread news around
εὐαγγελίζω (Luke 1:19; Acts 8:35)	to spread news about
δηλόω (1 Cor 1:11)	to report
ψεύστης, ψεῦδος, ψεύομαι (Rom 9:1; Rev 2:2)	lie
ψευδολόγος (1 Tim 4:2)	liar
μαρτυρία, μαρτυρέω (Acts 10:22; 22:12; 1 Tim 3:7; Heb 11:2; 11:39; 3 John 12)	report, usually to speak well of someone
καταμαρτυρέω (Matt 27:13)	to witness against
ψσευδομαρτυρία, ψευδομαρτυρέω (Matt 26:59; Mark 14:56–57)	false witness
εὐλογία (Rom 16:18)	praise, flattery
κατακαυχάομαι (Rom 11:18)	to boast against , to put another down
γογγύζω, διαγογγύζω (Wis 1:10–11; Luke 15:2; John 6:41; 6:61; Acts 6:1)	to grumble, to complain
γογγυστής (Jas 1:16)	habitual grumbler

Greek	English
στενάζω (Jas 5:9)	*to compain strongly about someone*
ὀνειδίζω, ὀνειδισμός (Heb 10:13)	*to shame, insult, disgrace, disparage*
ὑβριστής (1 Tim 1:13)	*insulter, slanderer*
λοιδορέω, λοιδορία, λοώδορος (1 Cor 4:12; 6:10; 1 Pet 2:23; 3:9)	*insult, slander*
ἐκβάλλω (Luke 6:22)	*to slander, to insult*, lit. *to throw out* (a name)
διάβολος (Sir 19:15; 26:5; 51:2; 51:6; 1 Tim 3:11; Titus 2:3)	*slanderer*
δυσφημέω (1 Cor 4:13; 2 Cor 6:8)	*to defame*
κακολογέω (Matt 15:4)	*to slander in a vile manner*
βλασφημέω, βλασφημία, Βλάσφημος (Matt 15:19; Mark 7:22; Rom 3:8; Eph 4:31; 1 Tim 1:13; Titus 3:2)	*to insult, to defame, to revile*
ψιθυρισμός, ψιθυριστής, ψιθυρίζω, διαψιθυρίζω (Sir 12:18; 21:28; 28:31; Rom 1:29; 2 Cor 12:20)	*habitual gossiper, whisperer*
διακρίνομαι, ἀνακρίνομαι (Acts 11:2; 1 Cor 9:3)	*criticize*
μωμάομαι (2 Cor 6:3)	*to find fault*
ἀκατάγνωστος (Titus 2:8)	*above reproach*
ἀναπίλημπτος (1 Tim 6:14)	*above reproach*
ἀπελεγμός (Acts 19:27)	*serious criticism*
θρυλέω (3 Macc 3:7)	*to babble*
διαβάλλω (Luke 16:1)	*to accuse, to slander*
κατηγορία (1 Tim 5:19)	*accusation, charge*
μεμθίμοιρος (Jdt 1:16)	*habitual fault-finder*
συκοφαντέω (Luke 3:14)	*to falsely accuse someone*
ἀπαγγελλώ (Matt 8:33; 14:12; Luke 7:18; 8:36; 13:1; Acts 5:25; Rom 1:8; 2 Cor 7:7)	*to tell, to report, to spread news*
εὐφημία (2 Cor 6:8; Phil 4:8)	*good report*
περίεργος (1 Tim 5:13)	*busybody*
περιεργάζομαι (1 Thess 3:11)	*to be a busybody*

Greek	English
ὀνειδισμός, ὀνειδίζω, ὄνειδος (Matt 11:20; Luke 1:25; Rom 15:3; 1 Tim 3:7; 1 Pet 4:14)	reproach, insult, disgrace

We note once again the striking similarity to the Spanish list. But especially astonishing is the sheer magnitude of the field and obvious frequency of comment about gossip in the Bible (even though the above is only a partial list of instances). Gossip, backbiting, criticism, spreading lies, and the like were obviously a major concern in the world of the Old and New Testament writers.

Social Function of Gossip

We turn now to the social functions of gossip. These are more complex than is usually imagined, though any one of them is likely to be more or less prominent in a given society (or even a given village). The list that follows has been gleaned from the work of a wide variety of social theorists.

1. Clarification (consensus building), maintenance (reaffirmation) and enforcement (sanction) of group values

It should be obvious that successful gossip heavily depends on shared history and common values among at least some part of every community.[39] Talk about values, in the form of talk about the behavior of other people, is the means by which public opinion on moral behavior first emerges and then begins to solidify. It also provides an avenue for constant updating and renewal of group norms and expectations. Each time gossip is repeated group values get reasserted and reinforced. Moreover, whatever community consensus is built up over time becomes the norm into which all newcomers must fit and into which children are socialized. In fact without backbiting and gossip, small-group values of all kinds would simply disappear. Roger Abrahams has summed it up nicely:

> The subjects discussed or gossiped about commonly deal with the proper maintenance of the household and the appropriate practice of interpersonal relationships within the family and among friends. Talk about such matters constantly serves to remind those involved of the importance of the norms of the community, but also rehearses the

---

[39] du Boulay, *Portrait*, 211.

necessity of working within the decorum system by which household and friendship networks are maintained.[40]

Clarifying values and setting moral standards via informal conversation is especially important at the level of what has been called the "Little Tradition," that is, the tradition prevalent among the nonliterate, nonelite. It is a principal means by which a village takes on a cohesive identity and develops its own level of expected participation in a wider tradition. Where community consensus on moral standards is lacking, however, and where people begin to take sides on a matter of individual conduct, gossip about the "others" frequently becomes a campaign in which one side seeks social control.[41]

A good example of gossip working to clarify values at the level of the Little Tradition can be seen in Matt 15:10–20. Matthew's setting is pointedly away from Jerusalem, where representatives of the Great Tradition (Pharisees and scribes) have come to challenge Jesus over purity practices. After a counterchallenge in which Jesus charges his questioners with hypocrisy, he calls the crowd aside and begins clarifying his own values: "It is not what goes into the mouth that defiles a person, but it is what comes out of the mouth that defiles" (15:10). The disciples then report some gossip to him, asking if he knows he has offended the Pharisees. (Their report is itself gossip, since the disciples are talking to Jesus about a third party.) In response, Jesus tells a parable about the blind leading the blind, which is clearly evaluative talk about his opponents, and Peter then asks for an insider explanation. The explanation Jesus provides is a direct insult to his rivals that charges them with slander, among other things. In the process of talking about his opponents, therefore, that is, about others who are not like him, Jesus has clarified and defended his little-tradition behavior.

Above all, in social settings where small group interaction is pervasive, as would be true in peasant villages, gossip is an informal method of social control. As people comment on or condemn the failings of others, they reinforce behavioral norms. Conformity to the norms develops social reputation and thus competition for honor places sharp controls on individual behavior. Especially in societies with a dyadic view of personality, "conscience" is external to the individual: it is the group, the community, that monitors behavior. It is the community that "accuses," not an internal voice. And it is the community which comments. Thus nonconformity is quickly highlighted and condemned by gossipers, not only damaging reputation but also providing negative examples.

[40] Abrahams, "Performance-Centered Approach," 296–97.

[41] Suls, "Gossip as Social Comparison," 165.

Fear of being talked about is especially effective as an informal means of control over people attempting to be part of a religious group.[42] Gluckman, for example, notes that religious control of morals operates very effectively through a gossip network—or the fear of it.[43] His argument is not that gossip creates morality, but that it creates the *appearance* of morality. It motivates people to put up defenses, to hide sins, and to keep up appearances. Of course this pressure to conform in appearance creates some conformity in fact, but it also means that appearance is not quite to be trusted as reality. People work very hard at manipulating impressions. Ironically, however, this very unreliability of gossip allows people margin for breaking the rules. Accusations can be dismissed as the shameless lies of a gossip because "everyone knows that only a fool believes gossip unconditionally."[44]

2. Group formation and boundary maintenance

An important function of gossip is to clarify group membership. We recall that a gossip event involves at least three parties. One person is usually talking to a second person about an absent third. Usually the first is implicitly seeking solidarity with the second against the third, thus reaffirming who is "in" and who is "out." When the third party is embodied as public opinion, the gossip event serves to differentiate the two talkers and their soul mates from nearly everyone else. In this way adherents can be recruited, affirmed, and reinforced.[45] In fact Gluckman argues that a critical step in gaining membership in any group is learning its gossip.[46]

The important point here is that gossip serves to differentiate insiders from outsiders. Obviously anyone expecting to be an insider must be trusted with the tales others in the group tell. "To be a true insider, one must know and be able to gossip about the present membership [of a group] as well as their forebears."[47] To tell tales you have to know the characters personally or at least know their histories.[48] This is one reason anonymous outsiders do not make good subjects for gossip.

The gossip circle thus marks a group off from all other groups which are not privy to its secrets.[49] It does the same with individuals who are marked

---

[42] Ibid., 164; Paine, "What is Gossip?" 278; Gluckmann, "Gossip as Scandal," 312.

[43] Gluckmann, "Gossip as Scandal," 308.

[44] Zinovieff, "Inside Out," 122.

[45] Abrahams, "A Performance-Centered Approach," 290–301.

[46] Gluckmann, "Gossip as Scandal," 314.

[47] Rosnow and Fine, *Rumor and Gossip*, 90.

[48] Zinovieff, "Inside Out,"123.

[49] Gluckmann, "Gossip as Scandal," 311.

as outsiders because they are not given access to the group's gossip circle.[50] Pamela Dorn quotes a Turkish (Jewish) proverb: "No one knows what is happening in the pot except for the spoon that turns." The point is that while everyone can talk about what goes on inside the house, only an insider really knows.[51] In Luke 24:18 Cleopas assumes Jesus is a πάροικος, a resident alien, an outsider, because he seems "unaware of recent local events."[52] He appears to be an outsider; insiders always know.

One interesting twist on this is the observation by Gluckman that the more exclusive the membership of a group, the more prevalent gossip is likely to be among the members. This is so because they have to work harder to differentiate themselves from all other people. Minority groups that cannot overcome the exclusive status thrust upon them by a society provide one good example.[53] A second is the tendency of higher status groups to talk constantly about how they are differentiated from those beneath them. Of course gossip of this sort was endemic in the socially stratified societies of antiquity.

Group unity is also maintained by these same processes. Gossip becomes a form of boundary maintenance.[54] Those who push the boundaries too far are quickly sanctioned by the gossip network. Even those who gossip excessively and do not follow group protocols for gossip are subject to group sanction. Group unity is also served by a gossip network because gossip can function as an informal method of adjudicating conflict in small groups where face-to-face confrontation would do irreparable damage.[55]

3. Moral assessment of individuals

The need to evaluate nearly everyone with whom a villager comes in contact has already been described as a matter of survival. This evaluation allows villagers to differentiate friends from enemies, those who are kin of heart and those who are not. All of those processes we have noted above by which moral control is maintained serve in this evaluative capacity as well. Because moral assessment is the very nature of gossip, gossipers rank people in relation to others on an ongoing basis.[56] In fact not only do people use gossip to measure others on the scale of community values, they use it to measure themselves

---

[50] Ibid., 312.

[51] Dorn, "Gender and Personhood," 299.

[52] Elliott, *Home for the Homeless*, 34.

[53] Gluckman, "Gossip and Scandal," 309.

[54] Zinovieff, "Inside Out," 122.

[55] Arno, "Fijian Gossip," 343.

[56] du Boulay, *Portrait* 211.

(Mark 8:27–30). Self-comparison with group norms often lies in the background as two people talk about others not present.[57]

This kind of moral assessment is especially important in honor–shame societies where the give and take of challenge and riposte is the means by which gains and losses of (acquired) honor are accumulated. Since honor is always a *public* matter, the gossip network is the means by which these gains and losses are validated, and since that process is ongoing, as people gossip the relative honor status of group members is constantly being updated.[58] Such notices that public assessment of Jesus is going on are frequent in the Gospels (Mark 1:27–28; 1:45; 2:12; 9:15; 10:24; 10:32; 12:17; Matt 4:24; 9:31; 12:23; 14:1, 21:15–17; Luke 2:47; 4:22; 4:36; 7:17; 8:56; 18:43; 19:37; 23:47).

4. Leadership identification and competition

As the moral assessment proceeds, individuals begin to differentiate themselves within a group. Leaders are identified as those who embody (and can articulate) group norms.[59] Thus competition between leaders can often take the form of gossip. The comment of Paul Radin cited earlier spoke about the name-calling one leader can aim at another. As leaders talk about their rivals, and as followers pass along the gossip, factions owing allegiance to particular individuals begin to emerge.

An obvious example of gossip being used in leadership competition is the long diatribe against the scribes and Pharisees in Matthew 23. There Jesus directs intensely critical and insulting comment about his rivals to the crowds and his disciples. Still another example is reported in Matthew16:5–12. As a follower of Jesus, Matthew passes along the evaluative talk about the Pharisees and Sadducees talk that Jesus himself had offered to his immediate disciples. Matthew's readers are thereby warned about straying allegiance.

This competition between leaders also engenders one of the key features of gossip, what anthropologists call "impression management."[60] Gossip is manipulative talk. It is highly selective in terms of both audience and content. By what one says or does not say and to whom one does or does not say it, impressions can be managed for best effect. Leaders (read: politicians) often make a living doing this. They develop self-protective instincts that are finely tuned to the boundaries between insiders and outsiders, friends and enemies.

---

[57] Suls, "Gossip as Social Comparison," 164–68.

[58] Rosnow and Fine, *Rumor and Gossip*, 90.

[59] Gluckman, "Gossip and Scandal," 307; Paine, "What is Gossip?" 278.

[60] Cox, "What is Hopi Gossip About?" 88–98.

One of the key ways that impression management is carried out is through the management of information. "The gift of the gossiper is information and the thirst for all sorts (who knows what might be useful?) is unending."[61] By controlling who knows what, a gossiper can pit factions against each other, separate friends, support or undermine a cause. Given that in peasant societies the spread of information depends on word of mouth, information management becomes critically important to those in power or to those seeking power. An example of information management is to be seen in Luke 7:18–23, where we are told that information about Jesus comes to John the Baptist. In response, the Baptist seeks confirmation of Jesus's messianic status by sending two of his disciples to Jesus, who then offers a succinct summary of his ministry of healing and good news. Jesus concludes his comments with directions about the impression one is to get from all this: "Blessed is anyone who takes no offense at me."

Both spreading news and keeping it secret at appropriate times can play a role in information management. It is perhaps in this light that we should understand the so-called messianic secret in Mark. By asking his followers to withhold information, Jesus manages information and thereby manages impressions. Of course the one form of information management which causes very special anguish is the betrayal of confidence (in Spanish, *contar*; see above). No doubt betrayal is common to all societies and viewed in all societies with equal bitterness (Job 17:5; Jer 20:10).

Before leaving the notion of information management, it is important to point out that gossip is a "network" phenomenon.[62] People who gossip usually know each other or know of each other. Usually gossipers also have both mutual and exclusive friends. In turn, the same can be said of each of these friends of the gossipers, and so on. In fact most of the social functions of gossip depend on networks that can spread information in a relatively short time (stale news rarely excites the gossip instinct). Close-knit networks (kin, near kin, close associates) circulate some kinds of gossip that would not be allowed into wider circles. Loosely knit networks, however, can encompass an entire community. and indeed what consensus exists in a community on behavior and morality exists because the gossip network is functioning properly. Of course, given that the spread of information cannot be completely controlled, the feeling of betrayal is often the result of poorly (or maliciously) managed information that escapes the networks for which it is intended.

While this list hits the key points, it exhausts neither the social functions of gossip nor the functions of gossip networks. We have already noted

---

[61] Zinovieff, "Inside Out," 124.

[62] Hannerz, "Gossip Networks," 39–40.

that gossip can be a matter of simple entertainment. It can also be a form of catharsis for individuals, or gossip can relate a community to its living past. Negative gossip campaigns can be a form of status degradation ritual. They can break up marriages, friendships, political alliances, or business partnerships. Positive gossip can affirm values in the same way that negative gossip proscribes others. It can create intimacy between friends who develop a closeness over against the person or people being talked about. Of course when a community begins to cease functioning properly, gossip can even accelerate its disintegration (see 2 John and 3 John).

New Testament Examples

In this short chapter it is impossible to survey all of the biblical evidence for the phenomenon of gossip. In order to provide a summary of sorts, however, we may look at three types of New Testament texts having to do with gossip. First, there are the many texts *about* the topos, that is, about gossip as a phenomenon. Like the texts cited earlier, most of these are extremely negative.

The astonishingly frequent comment about gossip in the pastoral epistles is noteworthy in itself. The pastoral epistles also provide typical examples. There women (wives?) are enjoined not to be "slanderers" (1 Tim 3:11; Titus 2:3, διάβολος). Widows are to be "beyond reproach" (I Tim 5:7, ἀνατίλημπτος). It is feared that younger widows will "learn to be idle, gadding about from house to house." The writer fears "they are not merely idle , but also gossips (φλύαρος) and busybodies (περίεργος), saying what they should not say" (1 Tim: 5:13). Those who are bishops are enjoined to have a "good report" (μαρτυρίαν καλὴν) among outsiders lest they fall into "disgrace" (ὀνειδισμός). Many of the examples in the semantic field, noted above, are this sort of comment about the topos.

Second, there are a large number of texts which are reports about gossip occurring. These are more numerous than one might suspect. As representative examples we may take those texts from the Synoptic Gospels that report people talking evaluatively about Jesus when he is not present. There are at least twenty such instances in Mark, interestingly concentrated entirely in the Judean section of the narrative (1:28; 1:45; 2:1; 2:16; 3:8; 3:21; 5:14; 5:20; 6:2–5; 6:14 [three references]; 6:15; 6:16; 6:55; 7:24, 7:25; 7:36; 7:37; 9:14). One gets the impression that in the story-world of Mark we are very much in a word-of-mouth environment in which the gossip network functions very well.

The gossip network in Mark is widespread indeed. It includes both peasant villagers (1:28) and the royal aristocracy (6:14). Both town and country (5:14) are included. Whole regions are covered (1:28). In one of the turning points of the narrative Jesus inquires of his followers what the nature of the gossip about him is among ordinary people (8:27) and even in his own group (8:28). Here, as indeed in the other Synoptics, gossip notices inform the reader that the reputation of Jesus is constantly being updated even as it spreads.

It is interesting to note that of the twenty Markan references cited above, Matthew eliminates fifteen of them. In one case he omits a Markan reference to the wider gossip network (14:1) and in another he restricts the network to the city (8:33). He adds two references to gossip that come from M (9:26; 17:24), and another from the Q source, in which Jesus muses about the gossip circulating about himself (11:19). In 22:34 Matthew adds a report that the Pharisees heard Jesus had silenced the Sadducees. In general, however, one does not get the sense from Matthew that we are in the same kind of oral (gossip) environment as we are in Mark.

Luke eliminates eleven of the Markan references to gossip and also changes some of the notices that he does include. In 4:37 he removes a reference to the Galilee from a rather sweeping Markan gossip notice. What Mark has as a complaint of the scribes and Pharisees to the disciples about Jesus's eating habits (2:16), Luke turns into a complaint to Jesus about the eating habits of the disciples (5:30). Luke changes Mark's reference to gossip spreading in the Decapolis (5:20) to one about it spreading in "the whole city" (8:39).

Luke also adds a few references. In Luke 2:17 the shepherds return and report what they had seen at the manger. In 4:14 Luke adds a classic reference to the gossip network functioning to update the reputation of Jesus in the area around Nazareth.[63] Three other new references come from special L (7:17; 23:8; 24:19). Of course exactly how many of these added references to gossip about Jesus that can be attributed to Matthew and Luke is difficult to say. The tendency of both writers to eliminate such references in texts that they share with Mark suggests that most of their added references may have come from their sources rather than from themselves. A noteworthy exception, however, may be the notice in 4:14. It seems to fit the Lukan rhetorical strategy in a very special way.[64]

Finally there is a third text type that should be illustrated. In addition to (1) texts about the topos of gossip itself and (2) texts which report gossip occurring, there are (3) some texts that are themselves gossip, that is, they are actual critical talk about third parties who are not present. In Mark 2:18

---

[63] This report is usually (but erroneously) labeled a "summary." For more extensive comment see chapter 3, "Luke's Jesus."

[64] Ibid.

a group of unidentified persons comes to Jesus with critical questions about his (absent) disciples. Presumably the parties present know each other in at least a minimal way and thus can undertake an evaluative discussion of the disciples' behavior. A similar incident is reported in Mark 7:1–15; it occasions a long discussion about standards of behavior. In Mark 6:14 there is a report of the exact content of some gossip that was occurring about Jesus, gossip that had come to Herod's attention. Unidentified persons ("some") had been saying that Jesus was either John the Baptist raised from the dead, or Elijah, or one of the prophets. This of course is exactly what the disciples report to Jesus in 8:28 when he inquires about the way the gossip network is treating him. A third example of actual gossip (rather than a report *about* gossip) is one Paul puts in writing. In Galatians 2:11–14 Paul gossips about Cephas, evaluating his inconsistent behavior in the controversy over compelling Gentile Christians to live like Jews. His complaint serves a number of the social functions noted above, but is an especially clear example of leadership identification and competition.

Conclusion

We began with the comment that gossip is especially widespread in nonliterate societies. Comment about gossip by ancient authors is extremely common and represents an interesting case of written observations about an oral phenomenon. At a very minimum, it would be accurate to say that the New Testament is in touch with this oral world; the frequency with which gossip is evaluated, reported, or actually recorded is truly astonishing. The claim is also justified that the Synoptic writers take the oral environment around Jesus seriously. They record his gossip about other leaders and groups as well as gossip from other groups and leaders about him. They constantly acknowledge that word is spreading orally. For the nonliterate persons who heard the Gospels read aloud, and who like most nonliterate people shared a deep distrust of written words, these reports and records of the oral environment might well have been critical. They are a way of suggesting that the reputation of Jesus was secured first of all in that world a peasant implicitly trusts. As Papias would later put it, "I did not consider that I got so much profit from the contents of books as from the utterances of a living and abiding voice" (*Expositions of the Oracles of the Lord*, Eusebius *H. E.* III. 39).

■ CHAPTER 10

The Preindustrial City in Luke–Acts: Urban Social Relations

A Study of Luke 14:15–24

FULLY ONE half of the references to the city in the New Testament are in the Lukan writings, equally divided between the Gospel and the book of Acts. Whether any significance should be attached to this fact has not been altogether clear to New Testament scholars,[1] nor has the possibility been explored that Luke uses the special characteristics of the urban setting in order to articulate his understanding of the Good News. What initial inquiries into the matter have lacked, and what might advance our understanding in new ways, is a sociological model of the urban system and preindustrial city that can provide conceptual tools for analyzing a Lukan text in which the city plays a key role.

Using the Term City

Before we jump into a discussion of our model it might be helpful to think about the way the term city has been used in the Bible. In the New Testament, ninety different places are named that may have been cities, though not all of them can be identified today. The chart below lists those named in Luke-Acts that are in direct or implied association with the word "city" (πόλις):

---

[1] See, for example, Conn, "Lukan Perspectives," 409–28.

Luke	Acts	
Arimathea	Azotus (Ashdod)	Joppa
Bethlehem	Antioch (Pisidia)	Lasea
Bethsaida	Athens	Lystra
Capernaum	Caesarea	Philippi
Chorozin	Corinth	Tarsus
Jerusalem	Damascus	Thessalonica
Nain	Derbe	Thyatira
Nazareth	Ephesus	Tyre
Sidon	Iconium	
Tyre	Jerusalem	

Obviously other cities, such as Rome or the Antioch in Syria, are mentioned by Luke, but our list above shows all of the sites that he specifically designates "city."

Several items on the list are worthy of comment. Note that Luke 2:4 calls Bethlehem a "city" (πόλις), while John 7:42 calls it a "village" (κώμη). Similarly, Bethsaida is called a city by Luke (9:10) and a village by Mark (8:23). This kind of inconsistency is also reflected in the writings of Josephus, who calls Jotapata both "city" and "village," and who labels Hebron and Gischala both "city" and "small hamlet" (πολίχνη). Capernaum, a location that Luke does consistently call a city, is a name that actually means "village of Nahum." In Jesus's day, Nazareth, another location Luke exclusively designates a city, was off the main roads of lower Galilee and was no more than a hamlet of a few hundred people. It is usually assumed that by calling Nazareth a city, Luke betrays his lack of familiarity with Palestine, but it may also be that like many ancient authors, he simply uses the term *city* in a nontechnical sense. For readers of the English New Testament, the problem of terminology is compounded because translators frequently translate the same Greek word (πόλις) both "city" and "town" (Luke 8:1 and 8:4 in the RSV), words that can have different connotations for the modern reader.

In antiquity a city was nearly always linked to a group of surrounding villages that the Old Testament sometimes called "daughters" of that city (Judg 1:17 [See also 1 Macc 5:65: "He struck Hebron and its villages"; Mark 8:27: "the villages of Caesarea Philippi"]). The exception was the cities of the Levites that were given pastureland rather than villages (Num 35:1–8). Josephus indicates that Julia was the capital of a toparchy that had fourteen villages associated with it (*Ant.* 20.8.4). These villages often provided the city with a major portion of its income, and Nazareth may have been such a village belonging to the nearby city of Sepphoris.

In the Old Testament (Lev 25:31) the city is distinguished from the village by having surrounding walls; moreover, legal distinctions in the disposition of property were drawn on the basis of this definition. Whereas a village house could never be sold in perpetuity and could always be redeemed, after the sale of a house in the city, a buyer had only one year to change his mind (Lev 25:13–17; 25:25–31). In the New Testament this distinction between cities and villages is maintained (Matt 9:35; 10:11; Mark 6:56; Luke 8:1; 13:22), though no criteria for the distinction are provided. In the period after the New Testament, Jewish rabbis came to designate a village as a place lacking a synagogue.

Writing late in the second century of our era, Pausanias reveals something of the Greco-Roman understanding of a city. In a kind of travel guide to the Greek cities of Phocis, a region opposite the Peloponnesus near Delphi, Pausanias first calls Panopeus a "city" but then raises doubts by wondering ". . . if indeed one can give the name of city to those who possess no public buildings, no gymnasium, no theatre, no market-place, no water descending to a fountain, but live in bare shelters just like mountain huts on the edges of ravines" (X.iv.1). Obviously he expects cities to be more than containers for large numbers of people. Exactly how the term *city* should be used, however, is something even contemporary social theorists have been unable to decide.

Anachronistic Understandings of the Concept

In the same way that our understanding of what a city is can cause confusion, so also can projection of the patterns and dynamics of modern cities back onto those of antiquity. For example, Wayne Meeks, in his book *The First Urban Christians*, tries to imagine what led the city dwellers of the Greco-Roman world to join Christian communities like those described in the book of Acts. He imagines a harried city life not unlike that in the fast-paced cities of today:

> Urban life in the early Roman Empire was scarcely less complicated than our own, in proportion to the scale of knowledge available to an individual and the demands made upon him. Its complexity—its untidiness to the mind—may well have been felt with special acuteness by people who were marginal or transient, either physically or socially or both, as so many of the identifiable members of Pauline churches seem to have been.[2]

[2] Meeks, *First Urban Christians*, 104.

It doesn't take too much thought, however, to realize that the city being described here is one from the twentieth century rather than the first.
Incredible complexity, physical and social mobility, and information overload
are things we today deal with all the time. They produce in us strong feelings
of loneliness, anxiety, and alienation. "Finding" such feelings in the ancient
city, Meeks uses them to explain why these ancient city dwellers joined the
Christian movement.[3] But what he is really doing is resorting to modern
popular psychology to provide an explanation for the growth of Pauline
churches.

In part Meeks is led into this line of thought by uncritically applying a
theoretical concept, the notion of "status inconsistency" (poor but honored,
rich but despised) designed to study the social tensions of modern societies
as compared to the societies of the ancient Mediterranean, thereby imagining
in ancient cities the rising social aspirations and accompanying emotional
stresses of socially mobile groups in America. Jerome Murphy-O'Connor
takes a similar tack in his otherwise excellent descriptions of the ancient city
of Corinth. Citing status inconsistencies in Corinth, he writes: "A feeling
of frustration was inevitable: what was the point of a life in which the full
exploitation of one's talents was blocked by circumstances outside one's control?"[4] Modern notions of self-actualization are not hard to spot here.

But equally problematic are the assumptions made about the ancient
city itself. Information overload was not much of a problem in ancient cities,
and social mobility was nearly nonexistent. Social mobility was not a conceiv-
able expectation for most people; in fact social mobility was no more conceiv-
able in the ancient world than the idea of "full exploitation of one's talents." It
is highly unlikely that information overload and the desire for social mobility
were prime causes of alienation and social isolation for inhabitants of ancient
cities. Since what social mobility did occur was usually downward, and since
ancient people imagined the struggle to be hanging on to what they had, not
gaining more, fear of loss or depression over having lost out already was more
likely a motivator than rising aspirations.

Typical would have been the artisans who inhabited preindustrial cities.
As Gerhard Lenski has shown: "In most agrarian societies, the artisan class
was originally recruited from the ranks of the dispossessed peasantry and their
non-inheriting sons and was continually replenished from these sources."[5] He
adds that they were lower on the status scale than peasants and had lower in-
comes. Having lost their connection to the land and to their extended fami-

[3] Ibid., 191.

[4] Murphy-O'Connor, "Corinth," 153.

[5] Lenski, *Power and Privilege*, 278.

lies when they had migrated to the cities, they had consequently lost the status and the protection of their previous connections. Getting reconnected to a group would therefore have had little to do with the psychology of harried and overly complicated city life or with rising social expectations. It would have had much to do with fear for the next meal.

What is needed, then, is an understanding of cities and the broader urban system of which they were a part that is appropriate to the preindustrial world rather than to our own. Our primary purpose in what follows will be to sort out the confusion introduced into comment on Luke's use of urban settings by inappropriate projection of the patterns of industrial cities onto those of antiquity. As a case in point, our model of the urban system will be used as a heuristic device in looking at the parable of the Great Supper in Luke 14:15–24, a story that not only takes place in the city, but does so in a uniquely knowing way. Finally, in the process of looking at the text in Luke 14, it may also be possible to make a few comments about recent discussion of the audience, setting, and purpose of Luke-Acts.

A Model of the Urban System

Our approach to the city in Luke's writings will begin with a discussion of current theory of urban "systems," focusing particularly on what Anthony Leeds has called "social urbanization," that is, on the integration and interaction of component parts of urbanized societies.[6] For reasons that will become obvious as we proceed, we have chosen deliberately to avoid treating the city as an isolated construct that can be understood apart from a regional system. Instead we shall follow the basic thesis set out by Leeds: "that in human settlement patterns in general all aggregations or nucleations ('localities'), from 'tribal villages' to 'megalopolises,' can only be fully understood if looked at as nodal points within societal systems or between hierarchic levels of such systems. Explicit in the model is the argument that nucleations (villages, towns, or cities) can never be looked at in isolation, as closed systems, as tightly bounded entities."[7] It is thus the urban society, not simply the city within that society, which must first be understood.

This also means that we shall not try to define the term *city* as an isolated phenomenon. Modern attempts to do so have produced little agreement in the anthropological literature to date. Among the widely followed (if now abandoned) attempts at doing so was that of Louis Wirth, who believed that on the basis of three variables (number, density, and heterogeneity of population), it would be possible to "explain the characteristics of urban life and to

---

[6] Leeds, "Forms of Urban Integration," 227–47.

[7] Leeds, "Towns and Villages in Society," 6, 11.

account for the differences between cities of various sizes and types."[8] Gideon Sjoberg expanded Wirth's list of criteria slightly by adding that essential to the city is ". . . a wide range of non-agricultural specialists, most significant of whom are the literati."[9] It was on the basis of such a definition that Sjoberg formulated his now classic cross-cultural typology of the preindustrial city.

More recent theorists, however, have not seen Wirth's definition (or the numerous variations thereof) as adequate, not only because the variables chosen demonstrably lack the explanatory power claimed for them, but also because this approach isolates the city from the system of which it is a part. That is particularly true of those definitions assuming the now widely discredited notion of a rural-urban contrast (Sorokin) or continuum (Redfield) that treats the urban and rural as closed or even opposed social systems.

Model One: The Urban System as a Whole

The approach we shall use thus begins not with an allegedly universal definition of the city as such, but with a regional model of the urban system as a whole. It begins with the idea that within a regional system, at least at a very general level, all human "nucleations," including villages, towns, and cities, in all types of societies, have the same function: to facilitate various forms of exchange, transfer, and communication, while linking any one locality with other localities and with the society at large. Such localizations may vary in size and complexity (family, village, town, megalopolis), but at the most general level their function is the same.

HORIZONTAL DIFFERENTIATION

Among these nucleations, however, specializations begin to occur which create what we might call "horizontal" differentiation within a total system. This means that at a less general level, the same things are not done at all nodes in the system, and that some localities take on specialized roles. Moreover, since one specialization necessarily requires another (specialties usually come in sets), "a structure of interrelated differentiations" is created in which the city and village take on different (though frequently overlapping) roles.[10] What distinguishes them is not that some particular functions are typical of the city and others are typical of the village. Instead it is simply that some localities become collecting points for more of these specialties and end up with a greater diversity of function. What distinguishes cities therefore is an ac-

---

[8] Wirth, "Urban Society and Civilization," 744.

[9] Sjoberg, *Preindustrial City*, 11.

[10] Leeds, "Forms of Urban Integration," 231.

cumulation of specializations, not the presence of any particular one. As Eric Lampard puts it: "The city is, in this sense, a multifaceted central place, a focus of generalized nodality."[11]

A major implication of all this is that the terms *urban* and *rural* do not describe polar opposites or closed systems. Cities and hinterland are inherently linked and the specialties present in them are intrinsically parts of a single system. As Leeds sums up the model:

> . . . all people, all action, all culture, all social organization, all technology become specialized. Hence, insofar as such systems display those properties conventionally designated as "urban," we are obliged to regard the entire society as urban and cities merely as concentrations of more or less large ranges and arrays of certain types of specialties.[12]

Or to put the matter another way, a peasant is an urban man. The peasant has a native understanding of the complexity of urban systems. He knows how the system works, in whose interests it is organized (that is, in the interests of the urban elite), and that his special struggle is to hang on to what place he has in it. Likewise, peasantry cannot be seen as a "stage" of evolution somewhere between the tribal and the urban. It is rather one specialization within the whole system of specializations that includes the city.

Vertical differentiation

A system functionally differentiated into rural and urban components nonetheless remains an integrated whole. The pattern that links the parts of the system, however, can vary substantially from one society to the next. Leeds argues that what determines the organizational pattern in a particular society, including the pattern within the cities themselves, is above all else the character of social class relations.[13]

In order to illustrate what this means, several organizational aspects of the preindustrial urban system deserve comment. They will suggest that not only is there a horizontal differentiation (certain nodes becoming collecting points for specialized functions), but that a vertical differentiation—a hierarchy—between city and hinterland typifies the system as well.

This can be seen in the fact that the urbanization of antiquity was the result, at least in part, of the organization and appropriation by cities of an agricultural surplus produced in the hinterlands.[14] Villages had the capacity

[11] Lampard, "Historical Aspects of Urbanization," 540.

[12] Leeds, "Towns and Villages in Society," 7.

[13] Leeds, "Forms of Urban Integration," 234.

[14] Lenski, *Power and Privilege*, 190–297.

neither to store nor to protect a social product of substantial variety or size. Thus cities accumulated what was produced beyond the subsistence needs of the peasants. By bureaucratic, military, commercial, or fiduciary means, they became centers of control—primarily over land use and raw materials—and thereby determined the conditions under which all other parts of the system operated. The diagram below illustrates the way the system worked.

The City and Its Daughters

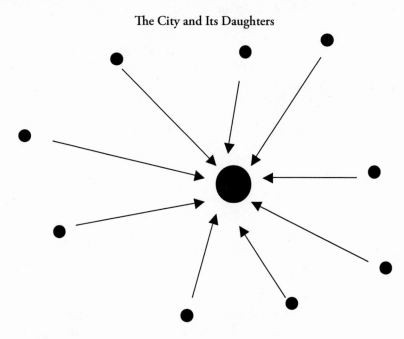

We may further illustrate how all this worked by comparing the labor needs of the industrial and preindustrial city. In contrast to agrarian societies in which the primary economic unit was the family, in the industrial city of to-day the labor unit is necessarily the individual worker. Capital concentration, cost efficiency, and exploding specialization of the labor process (as opposed to specialization of the product in antiquity) all require concentration of a large, mobile labor force composed of persons who can be detached from their geographical and social place of origin. These people thus constitute a flexible workforce for employers seeking to adapt to changing market conditions at minimum cost.

Such a pattern within our cities is directly related to the pattern linking city and hinterland. That relationship is a tightly knit one insuring the flow of capital and labor toward the cities. Marketplace and channels of communication/transportation come to include the hinterlands along with the city.

What is created is a system—an urbanized system—in which the necessary roles and exchanges are structured and enhanced.

By contrast, preindustrial cities existed in a system that required a socially and geographically fixed labor force. Specialists in the city primarily produced the goods and services needed by the urban elite—the only existing consumer market. Since that market was small, the labor force needed to supply it was also small, and as Leeds notes, it thus became a "major interest to keep others than these out of the towns, fixed in their own agrarian, mining or extractive areas."[15] In fact most agrarian societies established legal restrictions on city residence that kept the peasants out.

Preindustrial city and agricultural hinterlands were thus linked neither through the flow of labor and capital nor through mutual participation in a common marketplace but through centralized land control and the religious and political systems of taxation. The need for a socially or geographically detached labor force was small and sporadic. Contact between persons in the two areas was minimized and usually mediated by a politically or religiously defined group of persons. The hinterlands were not a general source of labor, nor were efficient means of transportation/communication necessary to link the system. As Lampard concludes:

> Justified by the liturgical authority of priestcraft, enlarged and defended by the combative force of captains and kings, the mobilization of a net social product at the center constituted an unprecedented concentration of energy potential on a minute territorial base. This implosion of energies, to adopt Lewis Mumford's term, was henceforth subject only to the limits of control techniques at the disposal of decision-making groups lodged at the node. Their demands gradually shaped the composition of the social product and their purposes governed the allocation and utilization of the crucial net.[16]

In sum, the pattern in antiquity was far different than what we see today. The system depended on " . . . the geographical as well as the social distancing of classes and separation physically of their functions in the productive and sociopolitical processes."[17]

Model Two: The Preindustrial City

Horizontal differentiation of a center from its surrounding territory is thus only part of the urbanizing process. It is matched by a concurrent vertical differentiation, what Lampard calls "social-structural stratification," that perme-

---

[15] Leeds, "Forms of Urban Integration," 238.

[16] Lampard, "Historical Aspects of Urbanization," 542.

[17] Leeds, "Forms of Urban Integration," 240.

ates the system. It begins in the hierarchical relation of city and country and extends to the well-known two-class stratification cited by Sjoberg and others as an internal characteristic of preindustrial cities themselves.[18] In order to see how this worked, it is necessary to flesh out a model of the preindustrial city itself.

Demography and Ecology

The cities of antiquity were small and in most areas no more than 5–7 percent of the population lived in cities. Earlier estimates that Rome and other major cities had populations in excess of one million are almost certainly wrong. Recent studies suggest 200,000 for Rome, though very few ancient cities exceeded 100,000. Douglas Oakman has suggested that in Roman Palestine no city exceeded 35,000, and that perhaps no more than two or three cities there exceeded 10,000. Because density was extremely high by modern standards, the area occupied by urban sites was small. The Jericho and Megiddo of the Old Testament period covered about twelve acres. Debir was about eight. The Jerusalem of Jesus' day was about forty-six.

In general, preindustrial cities housed two different populations: the elite, who occupied the center of the city, and the nonelite, who occupied the outlying areas. The elite, though usually no more than 5–10 percent of the total population, dominated both city and country. As the only group with disposable income, the elite formed the only real market population in antiquity. Their control of the political and economic systems was usually legitimated by a religious and educational bureaucracy that became the keeper of the so-called Great Tradition. Usually written down, this is the "official" version of a culture's religion, values, and worldview. It articulates the values and mores that the elite manifest.

Physically and socially isolated from the elite was the bulk of the city population, the nonelite, whose presence in the city was required to serve the needs of those in control. Though birthrates were high in all segments of the city population, survival rates meant that large extended families were characteristic only of the elite. Nonelite city populations were continually replenished by the dispossessed of the countryside, whose lack of skills often relegated them to menial tasks as day laborers.

Function

In our model of the urban system we learned that cities became collecting points for a wide variety of functions. Chief among these were political and

---

[18] Sjoberg, *Pre-Industrial City*, 108–44.

economic functions. Yet if kept apart from centralized political power, the economic control of the elite (a control enabling the elite to expropriate the economic surplus of the hinterlands) would have been impossible. Few cities became prominent by virtue of religious importance alone, yet the religious, educational, and cultural systems of a city acted powerfully to integrate and legitimate the network of other functions the city performed. Since control by the elite was essential to their dominance, temple and palace became the twin foci of most preindustrial cities.

Only nonelite and outcaste groups engaged in manual labor and all but the largest-scale trade. Production was on a small scale, limited mostly to homes and small shops. Very few businesses had employees who were not members of the family. The collection of taxes and tribute from the villages and hinterland controlled by the city were the major source of income for the elite.

Spatial Organization

As Sjoberg and others have pointed out, both the internal social stratification of the city and its peculiar functions in the system were mirrored in the physical configuration of nearly all preindustrial cities. The central area contained the palace, the temple, and the residences of both the political and religious elite. Such centers often were surrounded by internal walls of their own and were tightly bunched to facilitate both communication and protection. The temple centers of Mesopotamian cities are a well-known example. So also would be the acropolis areas of many cities in the Greco-Roman world. Jeremias's description of Jerusalem in the time of Jesus is another, though in Jerusalem's case Herod's palace and the Temple dominated the upper and lower areas of the city respectively.[19] Market areas were usually alongside the religious center; those in Jerusalem clustered in the Tyropoeon Valley near the Temple.

Elsewhere in the city, internal walls divided populations who served the elite in different ways. Ethnic or occupational groups often lived together in separate sections of the city; moreover, walls were usually arranged so that watchmen could control traffic and communication between sections, or so that guards could be advantageously positioned in times of military emergency. Most streets were unpaved, narrow, badly crowded, and impassable for vehicles with wheels. Many streets would have been choked with refuse and frequented by dogs, pigs, birds, and other animal scavengers. Shallow depressions in the streets allowed some drainage but also acted as open sewers. Large open spaces were few in most cities, and those that did exist were often at

[19] Sjoberg, *Pre-Industrial City*, 18–21.

intersections of the few paved thoroughfares. Such open squares often served as gathering places for ceremonies or public announcements.

Particular families or occupational groups, frequently organized into guilds, might control an entire street or city sector. Many guilds had their own internal hierarchical social structure. As Sjoberg has suggested, the non-elite usually fanned out toward the periphery of the city with outcaste groups, often including ethnic groups, small-time merchants and those practicing despised occupations (e.g., tanners), living at the very edge of the city or outside the city walls.[20] Gates in the internal city walls controlled interaction between these various groups and were closed at night, thereby cutting off intergroup communication.

The following diagram will help to visualize the spatial organization we have been describing:

The Preindustrial City

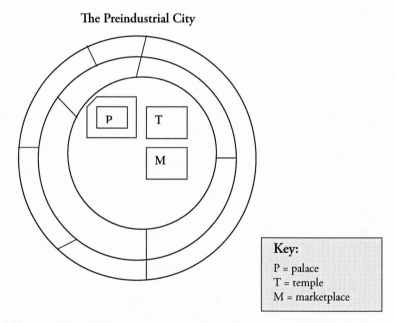

Key:
P = palace
T = temple
M = marketplace

Preindustrial cities were thus clear examples of what R. David Sack has called "human territoriality." By that he means "the attempt by an individual or group to affect, influence or control people, phenomena, and relationships, by delimiting and asserting control over a geographical area."[21] Because territoriality is a social construct, it is by its very nature a means of social control. (In addition, however, by regulating access, it is can also be a way of controlling both land and the flow of resources, especially when land and resources

---

[20] Ibid., 97–100.

[21] Sack, *Human Territoriality*, 19.

are in short supply.) And as Sack points out, geographic territoriality is an effective means of communicating as well as creating both the classification of people and the reification of power. It can make relationships across boundaries impersonal at the same time that relationships within boundaries are personalized and solidified.[22]

PATTERNS OF INTERACTION

Coming from the perspective of urban studies, Lenski and Lampard have also shown that such systems of hierarchical control tend to produce strong feelings of solidarity among people or groups that are differentiated by the system in similar ways. Thus people of the same occupation, age, sex, ethnic group, or social class often see in their category identification a set of interests at odds with the larger system. Thus marriage, as well as most other types of social intercourse across these lines, was nearly nonexistent. A member of the urban elite took significant steps to avoid contact with other groups except insofar as necessary to obtain needed goods and services. Such a person would experience a serious loss of status if found to be socializing with groups other than his own. Thus social and geographical distancing, enforced and communicated by interior walls, characterized both internal city relations and those between city and country.

COMMUNICATION

The means of communication were not well developed nor did they need to be. Proximity facilitated communication among the elite as did their near monopoly on writing. Town criers, street singers, storytellers, actors, priests, astrologers and magicians all served to keep up a flow of information among the majority, though word-of-mouth served as the primary means of communication. Record-keeping, another important tool of control, was inconsistent but largely in the hands of the elite.

In sum, the patterns of preindustrial cities were very much the consequence of the role played by the city in the larger urban system. As the center of control, the city gathered to itself only those nonelite necessary to serve its needs as it carried out the specialized functions it had collected. It was a system characterized by the dominance of a small center, by sharp social stratification, and by a physical and social distancing of component populations that were linked by carefully controlled hierarchical relations. The city was a ready example of human territoriality in which the elite occupied a fortified

[22] Ibid., 32–34.

center, ethnic, socioeconomic and occupational groups the periphery, and outcastes the area immediately outside the city walls.

Testing the Model: The Great Supper in Luke 14:15–24

Analysis of Luke 14:15–24 provides a ready test case for the heuristic value of our model of the urban system. In applying the model, our thesis will be that Luke's version of this parable makes knowing use of features of the urban system in order to make its point, and that these features would have been readily apparent to Luke's intended audience. Along the way we may also have occasion to make observations about anachronistic assumptions introduced into comment about the text by modern scholars who have drawn their perceptions from the modern city rather than the preindustrial one.

The Text Unit

Luke 14:15–24 is a text that has occasioned extensive comment and is therefore one on which we can begin by summarizing certain aspects of the work of others. To begin, it has frequently been noted that 14:1–24 appears to be a unified whole, though disagreement exists about whether the unity is to be attributed to Luke or to a hypothetical source. The chiastic pattern seen in this section of Luke by C. H. Talbert may or may not be there, though there can be little doubt that the arrangement of the traditions within the unit is intentional.[23] The entire unit is set at a Sabbath dinner in the home of a leading Pharisee. It begins in 14:1–6 with the healing of a man with dropsy and a comment by Jesus about healing on a Sabbath day. In 14:7–11 there is a parable criticizing those who choose places of honor at a marriage feast. Luke 14:12–14 is a saying about inviting the "poor, the maimed, the lame and the blind" to dinners or banquets, to which has been added (by Luke?) a comment interpreting the saying eschatalogically. The comment in 14:15, "Blessed is he who shall eat bread in the kingdom of God" then serves to introduce the parable of the Great Supper, a saying that has led many, following Jeremias, to assert the eschatological character of what follows.

It may be, however, that 14:1–24 is not the unit at which we should be looking. James Resseguie suggests that the whole of 14:1–33 should be viewed together as a narrative in which conflicting ideological points of view are juxtaposed and contrasted. One view is "exaltation-oriented," seeking to gain recognition before others, the other "humiliation-oriented," avoiding the self-promotion of the first outlook.[24] In the first half of the unit (14:1–24) the

---

[23] Talbert, *Reading Luke*, 196.

[24] Resseguie, 46.

audience (Pharisees and lawyers) is hostile to Jesus, whereas in the latter half (14:25–33), the audience addressed includes potential disciples (44).[25] Karris agrees that Luke 14:1–33 belong together, noting that 14:25–33 presses the issues raised in 14:1–24, making them a matter of discipleship for those following Jesus. That is especially true for those with possessions.[26] Pointedly, the section concludes: "So therefore, whoever of you does not renounce all that he has cannot be my disciple" (Luke 14:33).

We might also add that the parables in Luke 15 follow up this train of thought, suggesting that the kingdom will include unexpected or overlooked people who epitomize the humiliation-oriented point of view. Moreover, chapter 15 is introduced with the comment that "tax collectors and sinners were all drawing near" and then describes the murmuring of the Pharisees that Jesus not only receives such people, he "eats with them." The point is that the parable of the Great Supper is placed in the context of a larger discussion of eating and associating with the unexpected people the kingdom includes. The question to which we must return then is one about the reason that meals, rich hosts, and unexpected guests are of such obvious concern to Luke.

The Origin and Form of the Parable

The much-discussed origin and form of the parable are not altogether clear. Three versions exist: the one in Luke, a near parallel in *Thomas* (64:1–2), and a heavily edited version in Matthew (22:1–13). Some scholars have argued that Luke's is the most primitive version (Plummer), others that the earliest is the one in *Thomas* (Jeremias, Perrin, Crossan, Fitzmyer). Still others have seen a common source behind all three texts (Funk). A few have argued for the independent origin of the synoptic and *Thomas* versions (Perrin), with some suggesting "Q" as the source behind the parable in Luke and Matthew (Schulz, Fitzmyer). Many would agree with F. W. Beare that the parable is now sufficiently "mangled," so that if the parable does go back to Jesus, "it is no longer possible to tell in what form it was first uttered, or in what context."[27]

Luke's Version of the Story

For our purposes, however, it is less the original version of the story than that which appears in Luke that is of interest. That is so because only Luke appears

---

[25] Ibid., 44.

[26] Karris, "Poor and Rich," 121.

[27] Beare, *Matthew*, 432.

to make knowing use of the features of the urban system described above. In order to make his usage of this system clear, however, it is necessary to draw attention to certain features of the Lukan story that are unique among the three extant accounts. Of interest are the following:

The Host

In Matthew the host of the meal is a "king." In Luke, as in *Thomas*, the host is designated simply a "certain man." In spite of the indefinite pronoun, however, the Lukan setting of the text in the home of a leader of the Pharisees suggests that we should assume Luke has in mind someone like this person hosting Jesus.

The Occasion

In Matthew the occasion is a "wedding feast." In *Thomas* it is simply a "dinner," while in Luke it is a "great supper." The impression one gets is that Luke is talking about a host with the means to hold festive dinners of considerable size. Some see in the adjective *great* a reference to the messianic banquet, thus allegorizing the setting in line with allegorical features usually held to exist elsewhere in the story.[28] Yet no textual warrant for this exists whatsoever and, as we shall argue below, the heavy-handed allegorization of the story in Matthew need not be imported to Luke.

The Original Invitation

In Luke, as in Matthew, but contrary to *Thomas*, the original guests are invited twice. Crossan thinks the *Thomas* version more likely original because Crossan cannot explain the refusal of the second invitation by the original guests.[29] (He also argues that the double invitation fits the allegorizing needs of both Matthew and Luke, a point with which we shall again take issue in the case of Luke.) We may note, however, that evidence of just such double invitations exists in papyrus texts, and, as we shall see, the double invitation serves a clear purpose in the urban system of preindustrial cities.[30]

---

[28] Jeremias, *Jerusalem in the Time of Jesus*, 69.

[29] Crossan, *In Parables*, 72.

[30] Kim, "Papyrus Invitation," 397.

The Excuses.

Both synoptic versions of the story contain three excuses by those initially invited to the feast. *Thomas* contains four. The excuses in *Thomas* appear to have been adapted to the appended logion (64:2) excluding businessmen and merchants from the places of the Father. Two of those in Matthew are similar to the first two in Luke, while the third is adapted to fit the fact that feast being held in Matthew is itself a wedding.

The Reaction of the Host

Only Matthew and Luke recount the anger of the rejected host. Although this rejection and anger are also taken by some as evidence of allegorization (i.e., of the occasion for rejection of the Jews and for evangelization of the Gentiles), we shall again propose that it is so only in Matthew. Our model will suggest that we follow Karris and a number of others in treating the refusal of the supper invitation as a problem within Luke's community rather than a dispute between Luke and recalcitrant Judeans. The anger of the host must then be seen in that context as well.

The Final Invitations

Since all extant versions of the story describe the servant(s) as going out onto the city streets to obtain the needed guests, Scott suggests that this is part of the "originating structure" of the parable.[31] In Matthew the newly invited guests are "the good and the bad." In *Thomas* they are whomever the servant should "happen to meet." Only in Luke are there two groups: (1) the "poor and maimed and blind and lame" from the city streets, and (2) those from the "highways and hedges" outside the city walls. This double invitation to the new guests is thus Luke's alone and, as we shall see, it is significant.

The Banquet Hall

In Matthew and Luke, though not in *Thomas*, the banquet hall is filled. The fact is simply noted in Matthew, but has been heightened considerably in Luke by the addition of the second invitation. The significance we should attach to this will remain unclear, however, until we arrive at a better understanding of the second invitation itself.

---

[31] Scott, *Hear*, 26.

THE CONCLUSION

Finally, we note that the conclusion of each version of the story is different. Matthew's king spots a wedding guest with no wedding garment, leading to a conclusion required by his allegorical reworking of the tradition to fit salvation history. The concluding logion in *Thomas* is a clear addition, perhaps to be seen as a "warning not to let material cares distract one from the invitation to true gnosis"[32] or, as some have seen it, as an "otherworldly ethic." Luke's conclusion is quite different. He adds a saying that Crossan somewhat disdainfully characterizes as "moralizing" about a "rather doubtful ethical greatness."[33]

It can be more appropriately treated as a simple warning to those the parable addresses, though it will of course be important to understand exactly who that is.

In thus summarizing these special features of the Lukan version, we note again that we call attention to them not in order to ask what the original parable may have been like, but in order to highlight its form in Luke. We are also choosing to leave aside the question of the form of the tradition Luke may have received, interesting as that question may be. Our concern is the particular form Luke used and the special features thereof.

Luke's Use of the Patterns of the Urban System

It is time now to turn to our primary task: using the model of the preindustrial urban system as an aid to understanding Luke's version of the parable and the use he makes of it in his own community. In doing so we shall focus on the special Lukan features of the story which, as listed above, can serve as a convenient outline for our study.

THE HOST

We began by noting that the host of the great supper is simply "a certain man." The fact that he can hold a banquet of such proportions clearly places him among the urban elite; moreover, unless the response to the second set of invitations was extremely spotty, we are talking about a very large banquet indeed. The adjective *great* simply underscores this and need not be seen as cryptically eschatological. Hearers of the story would immediately catch the idea that we are talking about a host with considerable means, making the contrast between him and the final guests as stark as possible. The person being talked about is therefore a leading member of that urban group, the group

[32] Crossan, *In Parables*, 73.

[33] Crossan, *In Parables*, 72.

that both sets the terms for and controls access to social interaction between itself and others in the society. This host's social obligations to his peers would thus have been considerable, and maintaining his position among them depended on how well he carried out these obligations. As in all honor–shame societies, social approval of the way these obligations were met was critical for the host and his family.

THE OCCASION

The fact that the story is told while Jesus sits at a dinner in the home of a leading Pharisee would, as we noted above, lead the hearer to assume that the host being talked about in the story was not unlike the host listening across the table. Later readers in the time of Luke, however, would obviously be thinking less about the hosts of Jesus's time than of their own.

THE ORIGINAL INVITATION

As we noted above, in Luke (and in Matthew) the servant of the host is sent out to summon those who had been previously invited. As the papyrus evidence indicates, this kind of double invitation was not uncommon among the upper classes of the city (Cf. also Est 5:8; 6:14; Philo, *Opif.* 78). In fact the double invitation fits well with the dynamics of the preindustrial urban system and is a common pattern in Middle Eastern village life today.

It is not, as many have anachronistically suggested, simply a matter of giving the guests ample notice. Crossan takes this approach, assuming that "[a] man decides on a sudden dinner that very day and sends out his servant to his friends as the dinner is being prepared. Because of a lack of warning each one finds a perfectly reasonable excuse."[34] Crossan goes on to suggest that it is the "untimeliness" of this first invitation in the story that has led Luke to construct a second one. This view, we suggest, is a simple but obvious anachronism on the part of a modern interpreter with a busy schedule.

In the preindustrial city such a double invitation would serve several purposes. Initially the potential guest would have to decide if, as the system required, this was a social obligation he could afford to return in kind. If it was not, he would not attend. But more important, the time between invitations would allow opportunity for potential guests to find out what the festive occasion might be, who would be coming, and whether all had been done appropriately in arranging the dinner. Only then would the discerning guest be comfortable showing up. The nearly complete social stratification of preindustrial cities required keeping social contacts across class lines to a

---

[34] Crossan, *In Parables*, 73.

minimum, and elaborate networks of informal communication monitored such contacts to rigidly enforce the social code.

The point is nicely illustrated by a rabbinic commentary on the Old Testament book of Lamentations. When arguing that the sons of Zion are "precious," the midrash asserts: "None of them would attend a banquet unless he was invited twice" (*M.Rab.Lam.* 4:2). The meaning is clarified by the following text where we read a story about a Jerusalemite who mistakenly invited the wrong person to his banquet, with tragic results.

Thus in the Lukan parable, the host has properly offered this courtesy of a double invitation to his intended guests. Peer approval is not forthcoming, however, as the excuses offered by those invited clearly show. Such excuses, seemingly irrelevant (to the western, industrialized mind), are standard fare in the dynamics of honor–shame societies. The point is not the excuse at hand, but social disapproval of the arrangement being made, a point to which their seeming irrelevance of excuses contributes. Something is wrong with the supper being offered, or the guests would not only appear, social opinion would demand that they do so.

The question then is what is wrong with the supper. In suggesting what might have been wrong, Jeremias cites the well-known rabbinic story (*j.Sanh.* 6.23c) of Bar Maʿyon, in which a tax collector who had become wealthy attempts to provide a splendid banquet for the city fathers. But they uniformly decline his invitation on the flimsiest of excuses. In light of this story, Jeremias argues that we can understand the odd behavior of the guests in Luke 14:18–20. "The host is to be understood as a tax-collector who has become wealthy and has sent out invitations in the hope that this will enable him to be fully accepted in the highest circles."[35] But like the guests in the story of Bar Maʿyon, these guests also refuse to show.

The parallel nicely illustrates the dynamics of dinner invitations in pre-industrial societies. Either all the guests come or none does because none would risk coming to a banquet shunned by important others. What does not follow is that the host in Luke 14:15–24 is a wealthy tax collector. If he were, the story would lose its point (Cf. Luke 19:1–10). In a story told in the home of a leading Pharisee, identifying the host as an aspiring tax collector would elicit a nod of understanding approval toward the guests who refused to come and a condemnation of the host who invited such a person—clearly not the intention of the story. The story depends for its point on readers being forced to face the possibility that it approves the host and contains serious criticism of the guests who do not show. The double invitation to the original guests thus plays on the pattern of social interaction common in preindus-

[35] Jeremias, *Parables of Jesus*, 141.

trial cities by setting up a situation in which the invited guests must decide whether the meal is one they should attend. Likewise, the story leads readers to anticipate acceptance or refusal on the part of the invitees as an important clue to the possibilities the story holds.

THE EXCUSES

As the story unfolds then, the double invitation leads to a considered judgment on the part of the invited persons that something is wrong. They signal this with excuses that are clearly beside the point, though nowhere are readers given a clue as to what really causes the trouble. Why do the original guests stay away? The question is critical because the question is itself the means by which the parable functions as parable. If, as we shall argue, Luke is using the parable to confront the rich of his own community who are avoiding association with poor Christians, the question about why guests stay away is exactly the question that the parable intends to force upon the reader. The typical diversionary answers of Middle Eastern honor–shame social interaction thus function perfectly to assert a challenge that readers must answer for themselves.

Given their diversionary nature, the excuses nonetheless give us additional information about the guests and the proposed supper. In the exploitive urban system of the preindustrial world, much of the land outside the city was owned by the urban elite. The first person to offer an excuse has bought a field outside the city and is thus in this group of absentee landlords. As Kenneth Bailey has pointed out, no one in the Middle East would buy a field without having walked every square inch of it and without having investigated both its past ownership and profit record.[36] The second excuse is from a fellow who has bought five yoke of oxen. Luise Schottroff and Wolfgang Stegemann estimate that ten oxen could plow about forty-five hectares, or something over one hundred acres.[37] Douglas Oakman cites evidence of some families owning as much as three to six acres per adult, though a subsistence plot in Palestine in the first century was about one and a half acres per adult.[38] Since half the land would have been left fallow each year, the owner in need of ten oxen is obviously the owner of a very large piece of property. The third person making excuses has recently married. Some have seen warrant for this excuse the Old Testament provision that a newly married man was excused from both business and military obligation for one year (Deut 24:5). While this is possible, it may also be that what the newlywed is claiming is that he

---

[36] Bailey, *Through Peasant Eyes*, 96.

[37] Schottroff and Stegemann, *Jesus and the Hope of the Poor*, 101.

[38] Oakman, *Jesus and the Economic Questions*, 61.

has burdensome social obligations of his own and cannot take on the reciprocal obligations that accepting this dinner invitation would entail.

These three guests are thus very much a part of the urban elite, perhaps even among its leading members who could be expected to signal for the remaining guests (since clearly the banquet was intended for more than a host and three guests) whether attendance was socially appropriate. It is also clear that these elite guests play according to the rules: their excuses conceal the real reason for the social disapproval as the system demands. They do not break ranks. If one does not show, none do. None will risk cutting himself off from his peers.

THE REACTION OF THE HOST

Both Matthew and Luke indicate the anger of the refused host. In Matthew this anger becomes the occasion for an allegorical account of the burning of the city belonging to those who refused the invitation. Our thesis is that in Luke the problem is different. In Luke's community the problem is not one of the Jews refusing Jesus, but one of elite Christians within the community refusing table fellowship with the poor. Since we shall be in a position to spell this out more fully a bit later, it is enough for now to say that we see little warrant for treating the host or his anger allegorically in Luke's version of the story.

THE FINAL INVITATIONS

So far the story has raised a series of unanswered questions to challenge the perceptive reader. Now it takes its most surprising turn. The angered host sends a servant to the streets and lanes of the city to invite "the poor and maimed and blind and lame." Unlike his peers who are unwilling to break ranks, by inviting this sort of people to his home, the host breaks ranks both physically and socially.

From our description of preindustrial cities, readers will recall that the central areas where the elite lived were walled off from the outlying precincts where the nonelite were located. Furthermore, outlying areas of the cities often had walls separating ethnic, occupational, and income groups from each other. Yet without regard for the distinctions these walls imply, the servant in our parable goes out to all, and all are invited. Moreover, those invited are asked to come into a part of the city where they do not belong. For nonelite to be there serving the commercial or domestic needs of the elite is one thing, but for members of the elite to invite nonelite to a social occasion is a physical breech of socially loaded space. It would have been bad enough had the elite host gone to a dinner in a nonelite area of the city. Deliberately to bring the nonelite into the sanctuary of the elite after dark would have struck the readers of Luke's parable as behavior beyond comprehension.

But Luke presses the issue even further. In describing how the servants went out into the city streets, Matthew had used the somewhat general term "thoroughfare" (τὰς διεχόδους—lit.: the passing of the road), probably referring to the place where the main street exited the city gate. Luke, however, deeply conscious of the pattern of the city, is far more specific. He tells that the servant went to both the wider streets or squares (normal locations for communication with the nonelite [τὰς πλατείας]) and also to the narrow streets and alleys (along which the poorest of the nonelite people lived [ῥύμας]). Often these lanes were little more than open sewers, and so narrow that donkeys could not pass along them. In other words, the host has gone far beyond the normal method of communication in seeking out guests totally unlike those first invited. These are not the aspiring poor of the city, as anachronistic capitalist readings would have it; nor are they those who might have been expected to jump at the chance for social advancement. Rather, these new guests are persons whom the walls and gates of the central precincts of preindustrial cities were designed to shield from view. They are the very ones that walls were meant to keep in their proper place.

The Banquet Hall

Luke is then the only one who tells us that the banquet hall was not yet filled. As we suggested earlier, this allows Luke to describe an invitation to yet another group of people: those outside the city walls along the roads and hedges (ὁδός, φραγμός). ὁδός is of course the usual term for roads, while φραγμός describes the fences or hedges built to enclose fields or other property. Once again, therefore, Luke is specific in pointing to a location in the urban system that housed a particular population: the area immediately outside the city was inhabited by both outcast groups and those requiring access to the city but not permitted to live within it.

These final guests are not, as is frequently assumed, country people. The peasant population lived in villages, not along the roads just outside the city; moreover, an already-prepared banquet would not allow travel to neighboring villages to seek participants. Instead, those just outside the walls usually included ethnic groups, tanners and traders (along with the more commonly noted beggars and prostitutes), many of whom would have had business in the city (serving the needs of the elite that required proximity to it), but who were not allowed to live inside its walls.

What thus becomes clear is Luke's curious statement that these final guests should be "compelled" (ἀναγκάζω) to come in. Sanctions were strong that prevented those living immediately outside the walls from coming into the city for reasons other than business. Those living outside the city walls would thus have immediately understood the invitation as an inexplicable breech of the system and no doubt required considerable compulsion to be induced to attend the supper. They are hardly people who "need a free meal."[39] They are wary outsiders who are rightly suspicious of those who break the system. These were a group of people who were neither of the city nor of the country. They were afforded neither the protection of city walls nor attachment to a village. Socially they were isolated from city elite, city nonelite, and villagers alike. Thus Luke's second invitation, like the first, pointedly specifies a particular group in the urban system.

THE CONCLUSION

If our understanding of the parable has been correct to this point, Luke's conclusion for the parable may also have to be seen in a new light. It is usually construed as an eschatological statement, and it may well be, in some measure. But at a more basic level, the parable's conclusion may also be a rather blunt statement about participation in the Christian community. Those who reject the community by shunning association with its less reputable members will no longer be invited to participate.

In sum, our analysis of the urban system shows that Luke understands those finally invited to be (1) the urban nonelite and (2) those dependent on the city who live just outside it. Moreover, these new invitations are broadcast by word-of-mouth to any and all comers. The original invitations would have gone only to known persons whose social rank could be carefully scrutinized. The elite did not socialize with people they did not know. Those among them who did would be immediately and permanently ostracized because they could not be trusted to protect the system. We come then to what this story is really all about: a member of the elite—a host—making a break with the "system" in the most public and radical sort of way.

How far will the host go in making the break? The second invitation removes all doubt. The sight of the master's servant inviting and even compelling outsiders to breech the bounds of the system by entering the precincts of the elite would have been enough to sever whatever shaky ties the host may have had with his own kind of people. (The tenuousness of those ties is shown by the refusal of the original invitation.) This is a host who is prepared to go all the way.

[39] Tannehill, *Narrative Unity of Luke-Acts*, 129.

Luke's Use of the Parable

This analysis brings us squarely to the question of Luke's use of the parable in his own situation. Half a century ago H. J. Cadbury saw that the Jesus of Luke spoke to "possessors, not to the dispossessed" and that his rebuke of wealth "betokens a concern for the oppressor rather than simply pity for the oppressed."[40] More recently, attempting to explore the *Sitz im Leben* of Luke, Robert J. Karris has collected evidence that "Luke is primarily taken up with the rich members, their concerns, and the problems which they pose for the community."[41] As he puts it: "Their concerns . . . revolve around the question: do our possessions prevent us from being genuine Christians?"[42] In the same vein, Schottroff and Stegemann offer a cogent and perceptive portrayal of Luke as the evangelist to the rich, who uses the tradition about Jesus and the poor (of whose lives he knows little other than what he has learned from the tradition) to confront the rich of his own congregation with the meaning of the Gospel.[43]

Do possessions prevent the rich from being genuine Christians? In light of our study of Luke 14:15–24, we can construe that question a bit more broadly: Does remaining part of the social network with one's fellow elite prevent one from being part of the Christian community, which includes the nonelite? Using the parable of the Great Supper, Luke has given an unequivocal and uncompromising answer.

Table fellowship within the Christian community is thus the issue Luke uses the parable to address. Elite Christians who participated in the socially inclusive Christian community risked being cut off from the prior social networks on which their positions depended. It is not simply "worldly cares" or "excessive materialism" that holds them back. It is nothing less than the network in which they have been embedded since birth. At stake in their decision to join an inclusive Christian community are their friendships, their place of residence, their economic survival (and probably their health as well), the well-being of their extended families, and even the elite "system" itself.

If becoming part of the Christian community provided a social haven for the poor, it occasioned a social disaster for the rich. For many rich Christians, social position in elite circles was no doubt shaky enough, so that preparing a banquet for their peers might seem like a good way to solidify it. They would invite only the right people (exactly what Jesus criticizes in Luke 14:12–14) as a way of reassuring their friends that they had not broken faith

---

[40] Cadbury, *Making of Luke-Acts*, 262–63.

[41] Karris, "Poor and Rich," 124.

[42] Ibid., 124.

[43] Schottroff and Stegemann, *Jesus and the Hope of the Poor*,

with the system. They would choose the best seats at whatever dinners they did attend, to signal the same thing. But in Luke 14:15–24, the writer shows them that in so doing they face rejection not only from peers but also from God. Their bind is an excruciating one that Luke sees with startling clarity: a decision must be made that might cost them everything in their former world. Just this cost is made clear in vv. 26–33, the section immediately following the parable of the Great Supper. Luke inserts the words of Jesus: "If anyone comes to me and does not hate his own father and mother and wife and children and brothers and sisters, and even his own life, he cannot be my disciple." The point is then driven home: "He who does not renounce all that he has cannot be my disciple" (v. 33).

In sum, by using the patterns of the urban system with knowing effect, Luke shows just how far it is necessary to go to maintain one's place in the inclusive urban congregations that are his world. As a man of the city, Luke knows the costs peculiar to the elite. He also knows that table fellowship is the litmus test the elite will watch. The story of the Great Supper thus stands alongside the heavy emphasis Luke places on Jesus's table fellowship with tax collectors and sinners. Both that tradition and the parable provide the positive examples that the rich Christians must confront, examples that warn them of the consequences of trying to hang on to an old way of life.

Beyond Luke 14

In applying the models of the urban system and preindustrial city to other texts in Luke-Acts, we must think again about the term *city*. As we have seen, Luke himself is not very precise in using it. Jerusalem, for example, was undoubtedly a city by any technical definition available. Nazareth and Bethlehem certainly were not. It is also interesting to note the places where Luke adds the term *city* where other Gospel writers do not have it (4:31; 4:43; 5:12; 7:37; 8:4; 8:27; 8:39; 9:10; 10:1; 14:21; 19:17; 19:19; 23:19). Comparing these Lukan texts with the parallels in Matthew and Mark will yield a sense of the environment Luke imagines for Jesus.

In spite of the frequency of the term *city* in Luke, much of Jesus's Lukan ministry takes place outside cities. In fact most of the largest cities in the region (Sepphoris, Scythopolis, Samaria, Caesarea) are never mentioned in the Gospel. Why? Compare this with Acts. How many incidents in Acts take place in the countryside?

Careful readers will also recall that we refrained from defining the term *city* by specific characteristics such as population. We decided instead that the name *city* could be given to "central places" that serve a variety of functions. What might be interesting therefore is to see the way certain locations in Luke-Acts function as central places. Interested readers might go through the texts, for example, and make a list of the reasons that people or groups enter "cities," or other places that Luke names. Are people entering central places for political reasons? Economic reasons? Religious reasons? Remember that not all central places have the same function. Equally important is where these people entering cities come from. Do the starting points for these journeys tell us anything about who the travelers are, and where in the city they might stay?

Readers interested in intercultural exploration of the New Testament might take special note of the reasons Luke gives for people coming to Jerusalem (2:22; 2:41–42; 4:9; 9:51–5; 13:33; 24:33; Acts 8:27; 9:2; 9:26; 11:2; 12:25; 13:31; 15:2; 18:21; 19:21; 20:16; 20:22; 21:12–13; 22:5; 22:17; 24:11; 25:1; 25:20). Many scholars have noted the special role Jerusalem plays in Luke. Luke refers to Jerusalem twice as often as any other Gospel writer, and Jesus's final pilgrimage to Jerusalem (Cf. 9:51; 9:53; 13:22; 17:11; 19:11) plays a central role in Luke's story (Cf. also 13:33). What kind of central place is it? Note that only Luke portrays Jesus weeping over Jerusalem as he enters the city (19:41).

Of course Jerusalem is also the city from which the mission in Acts begins. Yet Luke ends his story of the early mission in Rome. Is this a shift of "central place"? How and why does this shift occur?

It is also instructive to use the model of the urban system to reflect on the reactions of city people to events around them. What is implied about the urban system in passages such as Luke 8:34–37; 9:5; 10:10–15; or Acts 13:50–51; 16:19–39; and 19:23–41? What would be the effect of the "great crowd" approaching the city in Luke 7:11? Why does Luke note the crowd in 7:12? Why does Jesus withdraw from the city so frequently (Cf. Luke 21:37; 22:39)? What is the city afraid of in Luke 8:26–39?

Think about the model of the city itself. In light of the size of ancient cities, what are we to make of the numbers in Luke 9:14; 12:1; Acts 2:41; 4:4 (cf. 1:15)? Note also the frequent references to the presence of ethnically mixed populations (Acts 2:5; 6:6–8; 9:22; 11:19; 13:1; 13:5; 13:44; 14:1; 17:1,10,17, 21; 18:4; 18:3,19; 21:17. Where would these mixed populations have lived? What status would they have had? Why is Arimathea pointedly called a "Jewish" city (Luke 23:50)? What is implied by the designation of a city as one's "own" (Luke 2:3; 2:39)? Why are people designated by the name of their city (e.g., Luke 4:34)?

At the beginning of the chapter we provided a list of the places that Luke specifically designates as cities, though obviously cities are in view at many other points in the text as well. Careful readers of the Third Gospel or of the book of Acts might list every time an event takes place in an urban environment and of all the people mentioned. What kind of people are they? What roles do they play in the story? With whom do they interact? In what space? What is implied about internal city dynamics in Luke 20:45–47; Acts 13:50; 15:5; 16:19–20; 19:23–40?

Pay special attention to indications of status. What dynamics are involved? Are they typical of the preindustrial city? What occupations are mentioned? Though there are not a large number of them designated in the text (note that only Mark and Matthew designate Jesus' occupation), those that are should be seen in light of our comments about both guilds and occupational areas and about those who do and do not belong in the city (e.g., Acts 10:5; 10:34; 18:3; 19:23). Why is Simon's house by the sea?

Conclusion

By using the model of either the urban system or the preindustrial city, we are trying to imagine the situation that would have been evoked in the minds of early readers of Luke-Acts. It would have been a situation quite different than what we might imagine for a city environment today. Cities were not commercial centers, the locus of public agencies providing services to residents, or the marketplace for the surrounding countryside. There were no suburbs for the upwardly mobile. Nor can we imagine harried commuters, or the home as a private retreat at the end of the day (for any but the small number of elite), or weekend flight to the beach.

The cities of antiquity simply did not look, smell, or sound like cities of today. People were not in them for the same reasons we are. Nor did life in them match what urban life has become today. We are likely to make ethnocentric and socially anachronistic readings of the New Testament in whatever degree we fail to recognize that this is so. Models drawn from cross-cultural study of preindustrial cities can therefore be a tool to help us imagine the environment that Luke anticipated among his ancient readers. Cross-cultural models can also help us modern readers to let the Bible speak to our world on its terms rather than on our own terms.

CHAPTER 11

What's the Matter with Nicodemus?
A Social Science Perspective
on John 3:1–21

THE STORY of Nicodemus in John 3:1–21 has attracted voluminous attention from scholars, clerics, and laity alike, including people of nearly
every imaginable theological persuasion. In fundamentalist circles the story
serves as the touchstone of a "born again" theology and has thereby motivated
innumerable sermons extolling the new birth experience. Among scholars,
however, John 3:1–21 has become the classic example of so-called double
entendre, misunderstanding, and subsequent explanation that appears so frequently in the Gospel of John.[1] It has even been understood as a Johannine
literary gem overflowing with ironies[2] (both subtle and heavy-handed) that
become nothing less than the occasion for Jesus's self-revelation.[3]

Not only the story but also the particular character of Nicodemus has
been the subject of endless debate. Was he finally, in the end, a believer
(John 19:39)? Was he an inadequate believer, perhaps one who came to Jesus
only because he saw "signs" (John 2:23; 3:2; 4:48; 6:2; 6:26; 7:31; 9:16;
11:47; 12:37; 20:30)? Was he a "timid half-disciple" as some have called him?
Or is Nicodemus perhaps to be understood as an ambiguous figure, a repre-

---

[1] A good review of John's (supposed) use of misunderstanding, double meanings, and
subsequent explanation can be found in Culpepper, *Anatomy of the Fourth Gospel*, 152–65 See
also Richard, "Expresssions," 96–112.

[2] Treatments of ambiguity and double meanings as "irony" are especially common in the
literature (Duke, O'Day, Culpepper, Gibbons, Snyder, et al). Schneiders, "Born Anew," 189–
96, argues that John 3 is "profoundly and pervasively ironical." Munro, "Pharisee," 710–28,
assumes the use of irony in John's Gospel is a "well-established" scholarly consensus. Our
contention is that treating Johannine language as irony represents a serious misunderstanding
of Johannine anti-language.

[3] The view of O'Day, "Narrative Mode," 657–68.

sentative of the uncertain response of many to the historical Jesus? Of course it has also been argued that there is no indication whatsoever in the Gospel that Nicodemus is anything other than an outsider, a symbol of those who finally did not become real followers of Jesus?[4]

Interesting as this question may be, we will leave it to others to determine the final state of Nicodemus's faith. Instead our interest is in Nicodemus's initial approach to Jesus: the moment of the first encounter. What kind of experience is described here? Does it replicate real experience? Is this strange sort of conversation the kind of thing that actually happened?

This is not of course an inquiry about whether the episode in John 3:1–21 is a report of an actual event in the life of the historical Jesus.[5] The story may simply be a literary construct on the part of the author. If that is the case, however, it is still germane to ask about its verisimilitude: does a story like this in some measure reflect the kind of actual social experience that would make it plausible or believable to a Johannine reader? Is it thus a scene an author could use as a device to reflect on the experience of his own community in its encounter with outsiders?

This raises another set of questions that bear on the literary nature of the story. Is this really an example of double entendre, misunderstanding, and explanation—as is almost universally assumed? And above all, is it really an example of Johannine irony, a literary technique designed to tease readers into exploring its meaning on more than one level? That, after all, has been the dominant understanding of this text in recent literary criticism.[6]

Our contention will be that it is neither. While misunderstanding is in fact involved, this is not a simple case of double entendre as that is usually understood. And while ironical elements may be present at many points in the Gospel of John, to treat Johannine language as fundamentally ironic is to misunderstand the nature of the Gospel's peculiar rhetoric. Moreover, it will be our contention that a by-product of this misunderstanding is to obscure what is actually happening in the Nicodemus episode. But in order to understand our contention it will be necessary to review the basic nature of what anthropologists call "anti-language" and its use in the Gospel of John (existing work on that topic makes necessary only a brief summary here).[7]

---

[4] For a review of the various options and arguments see Bassler, "Mixed Signals," 635–46. Also O'Day, "New Birth," 53–61; Gibbons, "Nicodemus," 116–28; Schneiders, "Born Anew," 189–96.

[5] See Brown, *John*, 1:135–36 for a discussion of the historicity issue.

[6] See especially Schneiders, "Born Anew," 191. There she argues the conversation is "supremely ironical." Also, Duke, *Irony*.

[7] The initial work on anti-language was done by sociolinguist M. A. K. Halliday. For a full treatment of the Gospel of John as anti-language, see Malina, *Gospel of John*; and Malina,

Anti-Language and Anti-Societies

A genuine anti-language, as opposed to simple slang or idiom, is the product of an alienated group of people. That is, it derives from an anti-society: a group "set up within another society as a conscious alternative to it."[8] Anti-language is not mere affectation or literary flair. It is not a "technique," and certainly not a *literary* technique. Anti-language lives only among the genuinely marginalized who protest the values of the society in which they live. Anti-language is an insider way of speaking that functions as a primary boundary marker between those inside an alienated group and all outsiders. An anti-language, along with its anti-society, is therefore a profound form of social protest from the margins of a dominant social order.

Three important characteristics of anti-language are critical for understanding what is happening in the Nicodemus story. The first is what M. A. K. Halliday calls "re-lexicalization."[9] By this he means that old words are given new, insider meanings by a socially alienated group of people. As Halliday puts it, "same grammar, different vocabulary."[10] Moreover, as Halliday's studies make clear, this new vocabulary is concentrated in precisely those areas that are central to the protest of the subculture and which distinguish it most sharply from the surrounding society.

It is important to stress here that anti-language does not consist of new words. It uses old words, common to the vocabulary of the dominant culture, but gives them distinctive meanings. The result is that insider and outsider use the same vocabulary, but not in precisely the same way.

It is this kind of re-lexicalization that abounds in the Gospel of John. Words like *world, grace, truth, light, glory, door, vine, way, life, abide, shepherd, believe, see, above,* and *below* are all common vocabulary in the dominant culture of the first century. But not the way John uses them. His meanings are fundamentally distinctive, and sometimes, at least to us, incomprehensible. So that while John's special words frequently obfuscate matters for the ordinary reader—secrecy and mystery are *necessary* properties of anti-language—they function as closed communication that fosters solidarity in an antisocietal group. Moreover, in the Gospel of John this social function of the distinctive vocabulary is *at least as important as its "meaning."* In fact to press for the meaning of the Johannine vocabulary before recognizing its social function, as we exegetes are wont to do, is emphatically to miss the point.

John's; Malina and Rohrbaugh, *Gospel of John.* See also the excellent work by Norman R. Petersen, *Gospel of John.*

[8] Halliday, "Anti-languages," 570.

[9] Ibid., 571.

[10] Ibid., 571.

A second characteristic of anti-language is what Halliday calls "over-lexicalization." Think about the way John multiplies synonyms, at least terms that are synonymous for him if not for the dominant society: *spirit, above, life, light, not of this world, freedom, truth, love.* All are basically synonymous. So also are their opposites: *flesh, below, death, darkness, this world, lie, hate.* All these terms describe contrasting spheres of existence, opposing modes of living and being. But there are more of them than strictly necessary. John multiplies words, not concepts. Thus with very little appreciable difference in meaning, John speaks of *believing* in Jesus, *following* him, *abiding* in him, *loving* him, *keeping his word, receiving* him, *having* him, and *seeing* him.

Like re-lexicalization, over-lexicalization has an important social function. Part of this function is to continue searching for originality vis-à-vis the dominant society. To be an anti-language, a way of speaking must be original and distinctive. It cannot coalesce with ordinary language, or it loses its social function. It fails to draw boundaries. Hence John provides the reduplication that draws out, lingers over, extends, and fine-tunes the linguistic differences between his anti-group and all others.

Over-lexicalization also has to do with competition, opposition, and display. Synonymy, the piling up of signposts displaying one's difference from the dominant order, betrays a group with attitude. The Johannine community has attitude in abundance.

There are several key points here. One has to do with the role of re-lexicalization and over-lexicalization in group boundary maintenance. If an anti-language becomes comprehensible to outsiders, it can no longer function as anti-language. It becomes ordinary language. This can easily be understood with a rough analogy.

Even though it is often more slang than anti-language, "teenager talk" makes heavy use of both re-lexicalization and over-lexicalization.[11] Take the ordinary English word *cool.* In teen talk it means "hot." Both are ordinary words used differently. The original effect was to draw a line between those who talk this way (teens) and those who do not (adults). But eventually adults learned how these words are used in teen talk and began to use them themselves. So teens began to over-lexicalize, to pile up synonyms. Along came "rad." Later it was "the bomb." All are ordinary words given new meanings. All are synonyms. Each creative addition to the vocabulary reestablished (for a time) the boundary between generations.

It is our contention that something like the process of re-lexicalization and over-lexicalization produced the peculiar language used in the Gospel

---

[11] Halliday's first studies of anti-languages were among prison populations and gangs. Obviously our analogy here is rough and cannot be pushed too far.

of John. The creativity and originality of the Gospel's language maintained boundaries not only between the Johannine anti-society and the dominant Judean world, but also between John's group and competing Christian groups.[12] Moreover, like other boundary maintenance mechanisms adopted by groups seeking distinctiveness (e.g., taboos, behavioral requirements, dress, or food regulations) anti-language is high profile. It is out front and in your face.

Another important point has to do with secrecy and mystery. Members of anti-societies do not explain their peculiar talk to outsiders. Members do not teach outsiders how to use it. Outsiders may eventually catch on, but if they do, the anti-language users will up the ante by inventing new uses for yet more ordinary words. They will over-lexicalize. Since anti-language is being used to distance its users from all others, the gap between Johannine group members and outsiders is not going to be narrowed by group members openly teaching people anywhere and everywhere how to speak Johannine. That teaching will be reserved only for those who are becoming part of their group.

A third and final point we wish to emphasize before turning to the Nicodemus story is the importance of anti-language in forming identity. Anti-language is an identity marker *par excellence*. As sociolinguists Howard Giles, Anthony Mulac, James Bradac, and Patricia Johnson point out, "When one of an individual's social group memberships is construed as situationally salient, he or she will attempt to differentiate from relevant outgroup individuals on dimensions that are valued as core aspects of their group identity."[13] That is, in situations where group membership could be construed as important by a Johannine disciple, one would expect some distinctive Johannine identity marker to be on high profile. These sociolinguists then add, "Should *language* [emphasis added] be a salient dimension of that group membership, as it so often is for ethnic groups, then differentiation by means of language or nonverbal divergence will ensue (on one of the following dimensions: language, dialect, slang, phonology, discourse structures, isolated words and phrases, posture, and so on) in order to achieve a positive psycholinguistic distinctiveness."[14] Language is exactly what is used by the Johannine group to achieve distance from the Judean world and from other Christians. It is also what members of the Johannine group used to signal an identity and thereby gain solidarity and reassurance from each other.

[12] Space does not permit a discussion here of what sociolinguists call language "convergence" and "divergence." Language divergence is an important means by which anti-societies maintain their separate group identity. For a discussion of the matter, see Malina, "John's," 169–72.

[13] Giles, et al., "Speech Accommodation Theory," 29.

[14] Ibid., 29.

Interestingly we also have a rough analogy for this in contemporary religious circles. Fundamentalist Christians in the United States, wishing to draw boundary lines between themselves and the dominant secular society, use language in just this distinctive way. Their conversation is sprinkled with "Jesus-speak": "Praise Jesus!" Hallelujah!" "The Lord spoke to me . . ." "Glory to Jesus!" Such terms are not part of the vocabulary of mainstream America. But they appear immediately when fundamentalists want (1) to identify themselves to each other or (2) to reassure each other that they are in the presence of like-minded friends. The language serves as an identity marker. Among some fundamentalist groups this way of talking has recently come to be called "spiritual Hebrew." Thus when a new guest appears on an evangelical TV talk show, it is always just a matter of moments before the distinctive lingo begins to appear. The display is obligatory. The audience thereby knows immediately that the speaker is one they can really trust. As Howard Giles and John Wieman point out, this kind of language is always a key factor in tenuous interpersonal relations.[15]

As an anti-society, then, the Johannine community had a language all its own. It is an anti-language, an original tongue. Any new member of the community had to learn the insider language in order to be part of the group. As persons did so, they assumed a new identity, an anti-society identity that could stand over against "this world" and "the Judeans." Their insider lingo effectively displayed the group's opposition to the values of the dominant society. Johannine anti-language may also have been a form of resistance to competing groups of Christians whose style and language the Johannine group thought remained "of this world."

What's the Matter with Nicodemus?

As we noted above, scholars have spent considerable ink trying to figure out whether Nicodemus was a real believer. A number of scholars puzzling over the strange conversation between him and Jesus have chided Nicodemus for his incomprehension. Raymond Brown is typical. He claims to see " . . . the basic meaning of the interchange that the evangelist reports as having taken place between Jesus and Nicodemus, that is, the meaning that Nicodemus *should have been able to understand* [emphasis added] in the scene *as it is portrayed* [emphasis original]."[16] This is because, in Brown's mind, the Old Testament background "should have enabled Nicodemus to understand that Jesus was proclaiming the arrival of the eschatological time when men

---

[15] Giles and Wiemann, "Language, Social Comparison and Power," 351.

[16] Brown, *John*, 1:137.

would be God's children."[17] Thus Brown, like so many others, declares that Nicodemus was a timid, half-disciple who just didn't get it.

The list of interpreters attributing to Nicodemus one failing or another is a long one. Typical is Francis P. Cotterell, who accuses Nicodemus of a "woodenly uncooperative" attitude.[18] To Don Williford, Nicodemus is a sincere inquirer with "limited belief," a "representative of an old order that is passing away."[19] For James Bell, Nicodemus is a man troubled by unanswered intellectual questions.[20] J. Bryan Born claims Nicodemus is a person of "insufficient faith."[21] Terence Donaldson thinks Nicodemus is a figure of ambiguity in a Gospel of certainty.[22] One way or another Nicodemus is seen to be inadequate.

Perhaps Nicodemus is lacking in some way. But given what has been said about anti-language and how it functions, Nicodemus's experience with Jesus was more likely exactly like the experience of any outsider, whether an inquirer or not, who encountered a Johannine type for the first time. As an outsider, Nicodemus got hit immediately with anti-language. Like any other unsuspecting person from the mainstream society, Nicodemus assumed he was hearing ordinary language when in fact he was not. He was hearing Jesus speak "Johannine."

So Nicodemus became confused. Of course anti-language can indeed be confusing; in fact anti-language is *intended* to be so. Thus if Nicodemus had been able to understand Jesus's rejoinder, Jesus's language would have *failed in its primary function*. It would not have drawn an immediate boundary or marked a distinct identity. But pointedly the story itself tells us the language functioned precisely the way it was supposed to: it left Nicodemus confused (John 3:9–10). He did not get it. The story thus describes exactly the way any outsider (Nicodemus is identified as ἄνθρωπος ἐκ τῶν φαρισαίων.) would initially react when encountering the purposely obscurantist language of the Johannine community.

Of course it may well be that Nicodemus was timid or inadequate or any of the other things so often ascribed to him by readers who go beyond the text. In the end he may not have been a full or adequate believer. But his *initial* reaction to Jesus is exactly what one would expect from someone encountering for the first time a person speaking Johannine: confusion.

---

[17] Ibid., 137.

[18] Cotterell, "Nicodemus Conversation," 240.

[19] Williford, "*gennêthênai anôthen*," 453.

[20] Bell, "Intellectual's Quest," 237.

[21] Born, "Literary Features," 7.

[22] Donaldson, "Nicodemus," 121–24.

It is important to be precise here about what exactly Nicodemus assumes in v. 4. He assumes an ordinary meaning for ἄνωθεν, a meaning derived from the word's usage in mainstream society. Nicodemus expects an ordinary meaning because he does not (yet?) speak Johannine. He does not fail because he cannot see the "higher" meaning in Jesus's words, as Brown puts it. He does not fall short because he fails to appreciate "the radical difference between the flesh and the spirit," at least not as Brown uses those terms.[23] Like most scholars, Brown uses the terms *flesh* and *spirit* for what they mean in ordinary language. Ironically, such ordinary language use is precisely Nicodemus's mistake! One might say that Brown and Nicodemus are on the same page.

Nor is what is going on here to be termed "irony" in the usual sense. As Halliday points out, anti-language is not a *literary* technique. It is a social phenomenon. Johannine language is not so much ironic to the core as it is anti-language to the core. Our task is thus not so much to find the code (meaning) of Johannine language, as would be the case if it were irony, as it is to appreciate the distancing the language was designed to create. To be sure, Johannine language often has meanings of which the characters in the story are not aware. To *us* that looks like irony. To *us* it looks like literary technique. But anti-language is not technique. It is life. It is intended to obscure and confuse, not to tease the hearer-reader into thinking at (higher) levels where the language can be decoded.

The problem is that we who read Johannine language today are not part of an alienated social group. Because we do not speak or relate well to anti-language, we are unlikely to sense its presence. Instead we project our own literary repertoire onto the writings of a group whose social experience (and thus whose language) is alien to our own.

Above all, the Nicodemus story is not an example of the so-called revelatory language in the Gospel of John. It is an example of the obscurantist language in the Gospel of John. Through the years a debate has emerged over the content of the Johannine language. Rudolph Bultmann, who knew nothing of anti-language, argued that it was the fact (*das Das*) of Jesus's revelation that mattered, not its content (*ihr Was*).[24] Later Wayne Meeks, who knew nothing about anti-language either, made the point that it is the function of Johannine language that matters most.[25] Gail O'Day picked up on this and then argued that it is critical to see *how* Johannine language functions in

---

[23] Brown, *John*, 1:138.

[24] Bultmann, *Theology of the New Testament*, 2:66.

[25] Meeks, "Man from Heaven," 44–72. As he puts it on page 69, the narrative in John *"functions for the reader in the same way that the epiphany of its hero functions within its narratives and dialogues"* [italics original].

order to understand how it goes about *revealing* the Johannine Jesus.[26] Her view is that the language functions as irony, as language with a double meaning, and that by that method the narrative leads the reader to see the "higher" meaning in what is said. Irony, she suggests, is used for the purpose of revelation. Mode (irony) serves the function of content (*Was*). It reveals.[27]

However, Norman Petersen, one of the first to understand the nature of Johannine anti-language, saw that treating anti-language as irony assumes the language in John, given the right decoding of its second-level meaning, is finally and fully comprehensible. In that manner it can be revelatory. But as Petersen argues, this is to misunderstand. Anti-language is not intended to be decoded or to reveal; anti-language is intended to create distance.

At one level both Meeks and O'Day are right that the function of the Johannine language is the key to understanding the text. But at least in the Nicodemus episode, the function of the language is not to reveal but to obscure. The language is intended to display distinctiveness, distance, and boundaries. This distance is not literary technique but social experience. It is not irony, but anti-language.

Conclusion

To insiders of course the anti-language did have a meaning. But in John's narrative it did not yet have a meaning to Nicodemus. In this initial encounter he is still an outsider. He does not understand. Whether he ever does understand and become a believer is something we will leave to others to determine. We simply point out that in the initial encounter he is appropriately confused. By contrast we may note that in the story of the Samaritan woman, we do get to see someone being taught to speak Johannine. The woman is in the process of becoming an insider (no ambiguity here), so she gradually learns the lingo. As she does, she assumes a new identity and insiders (readers) could begin to trust her (or those of whom she is a representative) as one of their own.

Of course all that might be true for Nicodemus as well, even though the author gives us no glimpse of further steps he may have taken. All we see is his first encounter and his initial confusion. Therein we learn what it is like to encounter for the first time members of an anti-society and their strange way of talking. Prepare to be confused. Prepare to feel distance. Understand that a flag of distinction is being waved.

Clearly what all this means for the end of the episode is that Jesus is not "explaining" his strange way of speaking in John 3:11–21. He is not

---

[26] She writes ("Narrative Mode," 662): "Any study of Johannine revelation that ignores the form, style, and mode of Johannine revelatory language will always miss the mark."

[27] Ibid., 664.

"clarifying" or "revealing." There is misunderstanding (3:10), but it is not followed by explanation. Jesus simply goes on speaking Johannine. Note that the passage is heavily loaded with the special vocabulary of Johannine anti-language:

> Truly, truly, I say to you, we speak of what we *know*, and *bear witness* to what we have *seen*; but you do not *receive* our *testimony*. If I have told you *earthly things* and you do *not believe*, how can you *believe* if I tell you *heavenly things?* No one has *ascended* into heaven but he who *descended* from heaven, the Son of man. And as Moses *lifted up* the serpent in the wilderness, so must the Son of man be *lifted up*, that whoever *believes in him* may have *eternal life*. For God so *loved* the *world* that he gave his only Son, that whoever *believes* in him should not perish but have *eternal life*. For God *sent* the Son into the *world*, not to *condemn* the world, but that the *world* might be saved through him. He who *believes* in him is *not condemned;* he who *does not believe* is *condemned* already, because he *has not believed* in the name of the only Son of God. And this is the judgment, that the *light* has come into the *world*, and men loved *darkness* rather than *light*, because their deeds were evil. For every one who does evil *hates the light*, and does not *come to the light*, lest his deeds should be exposed. But he who does what is *true comes to the light*, that it may be clearly *seen* that his deeds have been wrought in God (3:11–21, italics added).

The typical Johannine over-lexicalization is obvious.[28] Note also the strongly oppositional terms here that make it unmistakable that boundaries are the point of the episode (3:18–21). It is *us* and *them*. That is what boundaries are about. And they are drawn immediately when outsider first encounters insider. In the end this is what the Nicodemus story comes to.

So, pointedly, there is no indication in the story that after the extended speech of Jesus in 3:12–21, Nicodemus finally "got it." We do not read about a glimmer of recognition or about Nicodemus's hesitant attempt to use the Johannine language himself. At the end of the story all we really know about Nicodemus is that when he first encountered Jesus, and Jesus began speaking Johannine, the anti-language worked.

---

[28] For a more complete description of the italicized terms as Johannine anti-language, see Malina and Rohrbaugh, *Gospel of John*.

Epilogue

W E STARTED out with the simple fact that the Bible is not a Western book. This means that American readers reading a Mediterranean document are unavoidably engaged in a cross-cultural conversation with the writers.

From what has been said so far, this cross-cultural communication might seem a daunting (perhaps even an impossible) task. Yet the fact that successful cross-cultural communication is possible is demonstrated every day by the fact that it actually happens in the contemporary world. People can and do communicate successfully with those from other cultures. What is always necessary for success, however, is that conversation partners from dissimilar cultures undertake two important tasks: One is to learn as much as possible about the culture of the other. That is fundamental. Without the willingness to undertake such learning, cross-cultural communication will inevitably remain problematic. The other task is to recognize the peculiarities of one's own culture and one's own style of communication so as not to project them onto the conversation unawares.

We shall comment a bit more on these two imperatives in a moment, but first we must acknowledge a severe limitation. Since one of the conversation partners (in this case the New Testament writers) cannot engage in either task, honesty compels us to acknowledge that the cultural gap between ourselves and the Bible can never be completely overcome. There will always be much about the unwritten part of biblical texts that we will never know. But that very limitation makes all the more urgent that we do everything we can to overcome the culture gap at our end of the conversation. If we do not, the Bible will inevitably become an echo chamber in which we simply hear our own voices coming back.

Unfortunately, undertaking sustained and detailed cultural inquiry has not been the norm with either professional scholars or those who use the Bible in American churches. Many, if not the vast majority, are simply oblivious to the problem. As Western biblical scholars, we are only now, and very slowly, becoming aware of the ethnocentrism and cultural anachronism that plagues our work. To some degree the slow change is a result of the efforts of social science critics over the last two decades, who have begun to uncover and articulate the cultural world of the Bible. But perhaps to a greater degree it has been the growing internationalization of biblical scholarship that has finally forced recognition that not everyone reads the Bible the way Americans do. There is nothing like a contemporary cross-cultural discussion of biblical texts to challenge the received wisdom of the Western scholarly or religious worlds.

The problem in American churches has its own special dimensions. As we noted in thinking about the identity of Jesus (chapter 5), discovering a Jesus quite unlike the American ideal would be deeply traumatic to most American Christians. We prefer a Jesus who confirms our own self-image and expectations. As a result of these preferences, our incentive to recognize the ethnocentric way we treat the Bible is very, very low.

The same is true on a larger scale with American values. For example, the capitalist obsession with wealth and acquisition that dominates our culture is regularly legitimated by the use of the Bible in the American church. "Success" theologies of one sort or another are commonplace—with no apparent recognition that they are in fundamental conflict with the limited-good worldview of Jesus. Sadly, American churchgoers (we are not alone here) have developed a near-total inability to distinguish Scripture from culture in a way that allows the Scripture to be heard for what it actually is. Yet in spite of our fondest hopes, the Bible is not and never will be a warrant for the baptism of American cultural values.

One of the more important perceptions in American churches, building perhaps on the Protestant notion that the Holy Spirit is the ultimate interpreter of Scripture for every person (yes, one more example of the extreme individualism of Western culture and theology), is the idea that reading the Bible to discover "what it means to me" is a responsible way to engage the conversation. It is not. It disrespects the cultural otherness of the writers and offers an open invitation for self-projection. It is simply a strategy for using the Bible as a platform to articulate perceptions of one's own creation. Neither cultural knowledge of the other, nor understanding of the peculiarities of American perception, is ever allowed its legitimate place. The fact that this way of treating the Bible is widely encouraged in American Christianity is simply and profoundly irresponsible. In the most basic sort of way it implies something that is not true: that the Bible can be understood without taking the cultural gap seriously.

Cross-Cultural Reading of the Bible

The cottage industry (cited in chapter one) aimed at assisting people who must communicate across cultures (e.g., diplomats, businesspeople, exchange students) recognizes the two imperatives cited above. The first is the necessity of learning all one can about the cultural other. Those in the field of sociolinguistics see this as the *sine qua non* of cross-cultural communication. Perhaps we can say then that the studies undertaken in this collection are intended as a contribution toward that goal. But neither they nor the dozens of other such studies now being produced by social-science-oriented New Testament scholars are sufficient. There is a generation and more of learning here to do. And while it is a task in which American scholars must play their part, it is also one that will increasingly benefit from the internationalization of our discipline.

The other imperative (i.e., learning about the peculiarities of the American style of communication) has unfortunately attracted almost no attention from the scholarly guild to date. The modest attempt of chapter one to address this issue is my own first effort at doing so and admittedly has a long way to go. Unfortunately, however, I know of no other attempt by an American biblical scholar to tackle this issue, in spite of the fact that an enormous literature in this field of communication and cultural analysis has emerged from sociolinguists. The book by Edward C. Stewart and Milton J. Bennett (*American Cultural Patterns: A Cross-Cultural Perspective*, Yarmouth, ME: Intercultural Press, 1991) is a gold mine of such information, and a valuable place to start for anyone interested in learning how American communication differs from communication in the rest of the world. Few of us have any idea how peculiar and uncommon American habits of mind really are. Of course the volume cited above is just that—a start; similar literature in that field is voluminous, even if unknown to scholars of the New Testament. Here too there is a generation and more of learning to do.

Finally it is worthwhile reasserting an old commonplace in New Testament study. Exegesis, in this case *culturally informed* exegesis, must precede any attempt to translate New Testament writings into something relevant today. A simple illustration that we used early on in our discussion of cross-cultural encounters will suffice to make this point.

We noted that ignorance of the evil eye combined with the persistent habit of projecting backwards our modern understandings of things such as light and vision led to this unfortunate translation of Matthew 6:22-23 (NRSV):

> The eye is the lamp of the body. So, if your eye is healthy, your whole
> body will be full of light; but if your eye is unhealthy, your whole

> body will be full of darkness. If then the light in you is darkness, how
> great is the darkness!

Read without cultural knowledge of the other (i.e., of Matthew), an American
reader would assume here that Jesus is addressing eye problems. Taken meta-
phorically (as seems obvious), Jesus suggests that we don't see clearly enough,
that we are unable to take in the light of God.

However sanguine a theological thought that might be, it misses completely the point Jesus is making. The problem he is addressing is not what
we can or cannot take in. The problem Jesus is addressing is what we do or
do not give out. In the ancient view, light originated in the heart. It was then
projected out through the eyes and illuminated or damaged whatever it hit.
The problem therefore is not with our eyes but with what originates in our
hearts. We have heart problems, so to speak, not eye problems. Light is understood to be the carrier that projects greed and envy (the core of evil-eye
belief) out from the heart, through the eyes, from whence it damages those
it hits. The problem then is not what we take in; the problem is what we give
out.

The translation above is therefore completely misleading. Moreover, it is
difficult to know what to say to those who encourage Americans to pick up a
text like this in order to determine "what it means to me." That such a discov-
ery of meaning is attempted *before* and *apart from* the hard work of engaging
the cultural "otherness" of the writer is frankly appalling. Whatever such an
exercise might be, it cannot be called "reading." It is much closer to gazing in
a mirror and pronouncing the result a gospel insight. Considerate conversation partners do not treat each other that way, and yet the astonishing fact
remains that we think this kind of interaction acceptable when reading the
Bible. It is time for biblical scholars with any interest or stake in the use of
the Bible in the church to say flatly and often that this kind of "reading" is
not acceptable.

Fortunately the day is rapidly approaching when this kind of ethnocentric (and egocentric) biblical interpretation will be increasingly challenged by
Christians from non-Western cultures. They simply will no longer read the
Bible in the same way we have read it in the cultures of the modern West. In
my opinion, that day cannot come soon enough.

Abbreviations

AAASP	American Anthropological Association Special Publications
AB	Anchor Bible
Abr.	*De Abrahamo* (Philo)
Acts Paul	*Acts of Paul*
Ag. Ap.	*Against Apion* (Josephus)
AmAnth	*American Anthropologist*
Ant.	*Jewish Antiquities* (Josephus)
AJS	*American Journal of Sociology*
AJOS	*American Journal of Oriental Studies*
AQ	*Anthropological Quarterly*
ARA	*Annual Review of Anthropology*
ASR	*American Sociological Review*
Aug.	*Augustus* from *Lives of the Caesars* (Suetonius)
b.	Babylonian Talmud (*Bavili*)
BA	*Biblical Archeaologist*
BDF	Friedrich Blass, Albert Debrunner, and Robert W. Funk. *A Greek Grammar of the New Testament and Other Early Christian Literature*
BETL	Biblioteca ephemeridum theologicarum lovaniensium
Bib	*Biblica*
Bijd	*Bijdragen*
BJRL	*Bulletin of the John Rylands University Library of Manchester*
B. Qam.	*Baba Qamma*
BR	*Biblical Research*
BRev	*Bible Review*
BTB	*Biblical Theology Bulletin*
CAnth	*Current Anthropology*
Cato Min.	*Cato Minor* (Plutarch)
CBQ	*Catholic Biblical Quarterly*
CQ	*Covenant Quarterly*

CRSA	*Canadian Review of Social Anthropology*
CSSA	Cambridge Studies in Social Anthropology
Det.	*Quad detritus potiori insidari soleat* (Philo)
Deus	*Quod Deus sit immutabilis* (Philo)
Disc.	*Discourses* (Dio Chysostom)
Ep.	*Epistles* (Diogenes Cynicus)
ESV	English Standard Version
EQ	*Evangelical Quarterly*
ExpTim	*Expository Times*
GBS	Guides to Biblical Scholarship
Gos. Thom.	Gospel of Thomas
GRBS	*Greek, Roman, and Byzantine Studies*
H. E.	*History of the Church* (Eusebius)
HR	*Human Relations*
HTS	*Hervormde Teologiese Studies*
HSCP	*Harvard Studies in Classical Philology*
IBD	*Interpreter's Dictionary of the Bible.* 4 vols. Edited by George A. Buttrick, et al. Nashville: Abingdon, 1962.
ICC	International Critical Commentary
IMJ	*The Israel Museum Journal*
Inst. Orat.	*Institutio Oratoria* (Quintillian)
Int	*Interpretation*
j.	Jerusalem Talmud (*Yerushalmi*)
JAR	*Journal of Anthropological Research*
JASP	*Journal of Abnormal and Social Psychology*
JBL	*Journal of Biblical Literature*
JC	*Journal of Communication*
JCCP	*Journal of Cross-Cultural Psychology*
JCCR	*Journal of Cross-Cultural Research*
JETS	*Journal of the Evangelical Theological Society*
JJS	*Journal of Jewish Studies*
JMS	*Journal of Mediterranean Studies*
JNTS	*Journal of New Testament Studies*
JPA	*Journal of Psychological Anthropology*
JRitSt	*Journal of Ritual Studies*
JRA	*Journal of Roman Archeaology*
JRS	*Journal of Roman Studies*
JSNT	*Journal for the Study of the New Testament*
JSOT	*Journal for the Study of the Old Testament*
Jud	*Judaica*
JUH	*Journal of Urban History*

J. W.	*Jewish War* (Josephus)
KJV	King James Version
LCL	Loeb Classical Library
Leg.	*Legum allegoriae* (Philo)
Life	*The Life* (Josephus)
m.	Mishnah
M.Rab.Lam.	*Midrash Rabbah Lamentations*
Migr.	*De migratione Abrahami* (Philo)
NAV	New Amplified Version
Ned.	*Nedarim*
Nic. Eth.	*Nicomachean Ethics* (Aristotle)
NIGTC	New International Greek Testament Commentary
NIV	New International Version
NJB	New Jerusalem Bible
NTS	*New Testament Studies*
NovT	*Novum Testamentum*
NRSV	New Revised Standard Version
OBT	Overtures to Biblical Theology
Opif.	*De Opificio Mundi* (Philo)
PG	Patrologia graeca, edited by Jean-Paul Migne, 162 vols. Paris 1857–1886
Phys.	*Physiognomica* (works by Polemo and by Pseudo-Aristotle)
Post.	*De Posteritate Caini* (Philo)
Poxy	Papyrus Oxrhynchus
PRS	*Perspectives in Religious Studies*
PSB	*Princeton Seminary Bulletin*
Pseudolog.	*Pseudologista* (Lucian)
Quaest. Conv.	*Quaestiones Convivales* (Plutarch)
RelS	*Religious Studies*
REV	Revised English Version
RevExp	*Review and Expositor*
Rhet.	*Rhetoric* (Aristotle)
RLSI	*Research, Language, and Social Interaction*
RQ	*Restoration Quarterly*
RSB	*Religious Studies Bulletin*
RSV	Revised Standard Version
RTR	*Reformed Theology Review*
Sanh.	*Sanhedrin*
SBEC	Studies in the Bible and Early Christianity
SBLDS	Society of Biblical Literature Dissertation Series

SBLSBS	Society of Biblical Literature Sources for Biblical Study
SIDIC	*Journal of the Service International de documentation judeo-chrétienne*
SJT	*Scottish Journal of Theology*
SNTSMS	Society of New Testament Studies Monograph Series
SNTSU	Studien zum Neuen Testament und seiner Umwelt
SSR	*Sociology and Social Research*
ST	*Studia Theologica*
Str-B	Strack, Hermann L., and Paul Billerbeck. *Kommentar zum Neuen Testament aus Talmud und Midrasch.* 6 vols. Munich: Beck, 1956.
TAPA	*Transactions and Proceedings of the American Philological Association*
TAPS	*Transactions of the American Philosophical Society*
THKNT	Theologischer Handkommentar zum Neuen Testament
ThTo	*Theology Today*
Tehar.	*Teharoth*
TR	*Theological Review*
TZ	*Theologische Zeitschrift*
UAnth	*Urban Anthropology*
VE	*Vox Evangelica*
Virt.	*De virtutibus* (Philo)
WSIF	*Women's Studies International Forum*
WSIQ	*Women's Studies International Quarterly*
WUNT	Wissenschaftliche Untersuchungen zum Neuen Testament
WW	*Word and World*
YCS	*Yale Classical Studies*
ZNW	*Zeitschrift für die neuentestamentliche Wissenschaft und die Kunde der älteren Kirche*
ZS	*Zeitschrift für Soziologie*
ZTK	*Zeitschrift fur Theologie und Kirche*

Bibliography

Abel, E. L. "The Genealogies of *Jesus ho Christos*." *NTS* 20 (1974–1975) 203–10

Abu-Hilal, Ahmad. "Arab and North-American Social Attitudes: Some Cross Cultural Comparisons." *Mankind* 22 (1982) 193–207.

Abrahams, Roger D. "A Performance-Centered Approach to Gossip." *Man* 5 (1970) 290–301.

Adkins, A. W. H. *Merit and Responsibility: A Study in Greek Values*. Oxford: Oxford University Press, 1960.

Albertz, Rainer. "Die 'Antrittspredigt' Jesu im Lukasevangelium auf ihrem alttestamentlichen Hintergrund." *ZNW* 74 (1983) 182–206.

Alexander, L. C. A. "Luke's Preface in the Context of Greek Preface-Writing." *NovT* 28 (1986) 48–74

———. *The Preface to Luke's Gospel*. SNTSMS 79. Cambridge: Cambridge University Press, 1993.

———. "The Preface to Acts and the Historians." In *History, Literature and Society in the Book of Acts*, edited by Ben Witherington III, 73–103. Cambridge: Cambridge University Press, 1996.

Almaney, A. J., and A. J. Alwan. *Communicating With the Arabs: A Handbook for the Business Executive*. Prospect Heights, IL: Waveland, 1982.

Anderson, Hugh. "Broadening Horizons: The Rejection of Nazareth Pericope of Luke 4:16-30 in Light of Recent Critical Trends." *Int* 18 (1964) 259–75.

Anderson, Peter A., et al. "Nonverbal Communication Across Cultures." In *Cross-Cultural and Intercultural Communication*, edited by William B. Gudykunst, 73–90. Thousand Oaks, CA: Sage, 2003.

Arno, Andrew. "Fijian Gossip as Adjudication: A Communication Model of Informal Social Control." *JAR* 36 (1980) 343–360.

Arterbury, Andrew E. "The Ancient Custom of Hospitality, The Greek Novels, and Acts 10:1—11:18." *PRS* 29 (2004) 53–72.

———. *Entertaining Angels: Early Christian Hospitality in Its Mediterranean Setting*. New Testament Monographs 8. Sheffield: Sheffield Phoenix, 2005.

Asante, Molefi Kete and William B. Gudykunst, editors. *Handbook of International and Intercultural Communication*. Newbury Park, CA: Sage, 1989.

Ashton, John. *Understanding the Fourth Gospel*. Oxford: Clarendon Press, 1991.

Aune, David E. "A Note on Jesus' Messianic Consciousness and 11QMelchizidek." *EQ* 45 (1973) 161–65.

———. "Greco-Roman Biography." In *Greco-Roman Literature and the New Testament: Selected Forms and Genres,* edited by David E. Aune, 107–26. SBLSBS 21. Atlanta: Scholars, 1988.

Aus, Roger D. "Luke 15:11–32 and R Eliezer Ben Hyrcanus's Rise to Fame." *JBL* 104 (1985) 443–69.

Austin, Michael R. "The Hypocritical Son [Lk 15:11-32]." *EQ* 57 (1985) 307–15.

Axtell, Roger E., editor. *Dos and Taboos Around the World.* 3d ed. New York: Wiley, 1993.

Bailey, F. G., editor. *Gifts and Poisons: the Politics of Reputation.* Pavilion Series: Social Anthropology. Oxford: Blackwell, 1971.

Bailey, Kenneth E. *Poet and Peasant: A Literary-Cultural Approach to the Parables in Luke.* Grand Rapids: Eerdmans, 1976.

———. *Through Peasant Eyes: More Lucan Parables, Their Culture and Style.* Grand Rapids: Eerdmans, 1980.

———. "Early Arabic New Testaments of Mt Sinai and the Task of Exegesis (with special focus on Sinai Ar 72 and Luke 15) [Arabic text]." *TR* 12 (1991) 45–62.

Barna, Laray M. "Stumbling Blocks in Intercultural Communication." In *Intercultural Communication: A Reader.* 7th ed. Edited by Richard E. Porter and Larry A. Samovar, 337–46. Belmont, CA: Wadsworth, 1994.

Barnard, Leslie W. "To Allegorize or not to Allegorize?" *ST* 36 (1982) 1–10.

Bash, Anthony. "A Psychodynamic Approach to the Interpretation of 2 Corinthians 10–13." *JNTS* (2001) 51–67.

Bassler, Jouette M. "Mixed Signals: Nicodemus in the Fourth Gospel." *JBL* 108 (1989) 635–46.

Beare, Francis Wright. *The Gospel according to Matthew: A Commentary.* Oxford: Blackwell, 1981.

Beasley-Murray, George R. "John 3:3–5: Baptism, Spirit and the Kingdom." *ExpTim* 97 (1986) 167–70.

Beckerlegge, Gwilym. "Jesus' Authority and the Problem of His Self-Consciousness." *HeyJ* 19 (1978) 365–82.

Bell, James F. "An Intellectual's Quest for Christ." *PSB* 1 (1978) 236–40.

Bennett, Milton J., editor. *Basic Concepts of Intercultural Communication: Selected Readings.* Yarmouth, ME: Intercultural, 1998.

Berger, Peter L., et al. *The Homeless Mind: Modernization and Consciousness.* New York: Vintage, 1974.

Bernstein, Basil B. *Class, Codes and Control.* Vol. 1, *Theoretical Studies Towards a Sociology of Language.* Primary Socialization, Language, and Education 4. London: Routledge and Kegan Paul, 1971.

Betz, Otto. "Die Frage nach dem messianischen Bewusstsein Jesu." *NovT* 6 (1963) 20–48.

Black, Matthew. "The Parables as Allegory." *BJRL* 42 (1960) 273–87.

Blass, Friedrich, and Albert Debrunner. *A Greek Grammar of the New Testament and Other Early Christian Literature.* Translated by Robert W. Funk. Chicago: University of Chicago Press, 1961.

Blanton, Richard E. "Anthropological Study of Cities." *ARA* 5 (1976) 249–64.

Blumenthal, Albert. "The Nature of Gossip." *SSR* 22 (1937) 31–37.

Boehm, Christopher. *Blood Revenge: The Anthropology of Feuding in Montenegro and Other Tribal Societies.* Lawrence: University Press of Kansas, 1984.

Born, J. Bryan. "Literary Features in the Gospel of John." *Direction* 17 (1988) 3–17.

Bornkamm, Günther. *Jesus of Nazareth.* Translated by Irene and Fraser McLuskey and James M. Robinson. New York: Harper, 1960.

Botha, P. J. J. "Mark's Story as Oral Literature: Rethinking the Transmission of Some Traditions about Jesus." *HTS* 47 (1991) 304–31.

Bott, Elizabeth. *Family and Social Network: Roles, Norms, and External Relationships in Ordinary Urban Families.* London: Tavistock, 1957.

Brandes, Stanley H. "Reflections on Honor and Shame in the Mediterranean." In *Honor and Shame and the Unity of the Mediterranean,* edited by David D. Gilmore, 121–34. AAASP 22. Washington, DC: American Anthropological Association, 1987.

Braudel, Fernand. *The Mediterranean and the Mediterranean World in the Age of Phillip II.* Vol. 1. New York: Harper and Row, 1972.

Bregman, Lucy. "Baptism as Death and Birth: A Psychological Interpretation of Its Imagery." *JRitSt* 11 (1987) 27–42.

Broshi, Magen. "The Diet of Palestine in the Roman Period—Introductory Notes." *IMJ* 5 (1989) 41–56.

Brown, Raymond E. "How Much Did Jesus Know?—A Survey of the Biblical Evidence." *CBQ* 29 (1967) 315–45.

———. *The Gospel according to John.* 2 vols. AB 29–29a. Garden City, NY: Doubleday,1966–70.

———. *The Birth of the Messiah: A Commentary on the Infancy Narratives in Matthew and Luke.* Garden City, NY: Doubleday, 1975.

———. *The Community of the Beloved Disciple.* Mahwah, NJ: Paulist, 1979.

———. "Did Jesus Know He was God?" *BTB* 15 (1985) 74–79.

Brunt, Peter. "Josephus on Social Conflicts in Roman Judea." *Klio* 59 (1977) 149–53.

Bultmann, Rudolf. "Die Frage nach dem messianischen Bewusstsein Jesu und das Petrusbekenntnis." *ZNW* 19 (1919) 165–75.

———. *Theology of the New Testament.* 2 vols. Translated by Kendrick Grobel. New York: Scribner, 1951–1955.

———. *Jesus and the Word.* Translated by Louise P. Smith, and Erminie H. Lantero. New York: Scribner, 1958.

———. *The History of the Synoptic Tradition.* Translated by John Marsh. New York: Harper and Row, 1963.

Burridge, Richard A. *What Are the Gospels?: A Comparison with Greco-Roman Biography.* SNTSMS 70. Cambridge: Cambridge University Press, 1992.

Busse, Ulrich. *Das Nazareth-Manifest: Eine Einführung in das lukanische Jesusbild nach Lk 4:16-30.* Stuttgarter Bibelstudien 91. Stuttgart: Katholisches Bibelwerk, 1978.

Caird, G. B. *The Gospel of St. Luke.* Pelican Gospel Commentaries. New York: Seabury, 1968.

Campbell, John K. *Honor, Family and Patronage: A Study of Institutions and Moral Values in a Greek Mountain Community.* Oxford: Clarendon, 1964.

Cantwell, Laurence. "The Quest for the Historical Nicodemus." *RelS* 16 (1980) 481–86.

Carlston, Charles E. "A Positive Criterion of Authenticity?" *BR* 7 (1962) 33–44.

———. "Reminiscence and Redaction in Luke 15:11-32." *JBL* 94 (1975) 368–90.

Carney, Thomas F. *The Shape of the Past: Models and Antiquity.* Lawrence, KS: Coronado, 1975.

Childe, V. Gordon. "The Urban Revolution." *Town Planning Review* 12 (1950) 3–17.

———. "Civilizations, Cities and Towns." *Antiquity* 31 (1957) 36–38.

Chilton, Bruce D. "Jesus ben David: Reflections on the *Davidssohnfrage*." *JSNT* 14 (1982) 88–112.

Cicourel, Aaron V. "Text and Discourse." *ARA* 14 (1985) 159–85.

Collier, Mary Jane. "Cultural Identity and Intercultural Communication." In *Intercultural Communication: A Reader.* 7th ed. Edited by Richard E. Porter and Larry A. Samovar, 36–45. Belmont, CA: Wadsworth, 1994.

Collis, John. "Central Place Theory is Dead: Long Live the Central Place." In *Central Places, Archaeology and History,* edited by Eric Grant, 37–39. Sheffield: Department of Archaeology and Prehistory, University of Sheffield, 1986.

Condon, John C., and Fathi S. Yousef. *An Introduction to Intercultural Communication.* New York: Macmillan, 1985.

Conn, Harvie M. "Lucan Perspectives and the City." *Missiology* 13 (1985) 409–28.

Corlett, Tom. "This Brother of Yours." *ExpTim* 100 (1989) 216.

Cotterell, Francis P. "The Nicodemus Conversation: A Fresh Appraisal." *ExpTim* 96 (1985) 237–42.

Cotterell, Peter. "Sociolinguistics and Biblical Interpretation." *VE* 16 (1986) 61–76.

Cox, Bruce A. "What is Hopi Gossip About? Information Management and Hopi Factions." *Man* 5 (1970) 88–98.

Crawshaw, Ralph. "Gossip Wears a Thousand Masks." *Prism* 2 (1974) 45–47.

Creed, John Martin. *The Gospel according to St. Luke: The Greek Text with Introduction, Notes, and Indices.* London: Macmillan, 1930.

Crockett, Larrimore C. "Luke 4:25-27 and Jewish-Gentile Relations in Luke-Acts." *JBL* 88 (1969) 177–83.

Crossan, John Dominic. *In Parables: The Challenge of the Historical Jesus.* New York: Harper, 1973.

———. *The Historical Jesus: The Life of a Mediterranean Jewish Peasant.* San Francisco: HarperSanFrancisco, 1991.

———. *Jesus: A Revolutionary Biography.* San Francisco: HarperSanFrancisco, 1994.

Culpepper, R. Alan. *Anatomy of the Fourth Gospel: A Study in Literary Design.* Foundations and Facets: New Testament. Philadelphia: Fortress, 1983.

Danker, Fredrick W. *Jesus and the New Age: A Commentary on the Third Gospel.* Rev. ed. Philadelphia: Fortress, 1988.

———, et al., editors. *A Greek–English Lexicon of the New Testament and Other Early Christian Literature.* 3d ed. Chicago: University of Chicago Press, 2000.

Davis, John. "Family and State in the Mediterranean." In *Honor and Shame and the Unity of the Mediterranean,* edited by David D. Gilmore, 22–34. AAASP 22. Washington, DC: American Anthropological Association, 1987.

de Jonge, Marinus. *Jesus, Stranger from Heaven and Son of God: Jesus Christ and the Christians in Johannine Perspective.* Edited and translated by John E. Steely. SBLSBS 11. Missoula, MT: Scholars, 1977.

Delany, Carol. "Seeds of Honor, Fields of Shame." In *Honor and Shame and the Unity of the Mediterranean,* edited by David D. Gilmore, 35–48. AAASP 22. Washington, DC: American Anthropological Association, 1987.

Derrett, J. Duncan M. "Law in the New Testament: The Parable of the Prodigal Son." *NTS* 14 (1967) 56–74.

———. "Correcting Nicodemus (John 3:2, 21)." *ExpTim* 112 (2001) 126.

Diaz, May N., and Jack M. Potter. "Introduction: The Economic Relations in Peasant Society." In *Peasant Society: A Reader,* edited by Jack M. Potter, et al., 50–56. Boston: Little, Brown, 1967.

———. "Introduction: The Social Life of Peasants." In *Peasant Society: A Reader,* edited by Jack M. Potter, et al., 154–68. Boston: Little, Brown, 1967.

Dinkler, Erich. "Peter's Confession and the 'Satan' Saying: The Problem of Jesus' Messiahship." In *The Future of Our Religious Past: Essays in Honour of Rudolf Bultmann,* edited by James M. Robinson. Translated by Charles E. Carlston and Robert P. Scharlemann, 169–202. New York: Harper & Row, 1971.

Doble, Peter. "The Temptations." *ExpTim* 72 (1960–1961) 91–93.

Dodd, C. H. *The Parables of the Kingdom.* Rev. ed. New York: Scribner, 1961.

Dominian, Jack. *One Like Us: A Psychological Interpretation of Jesus.* London: Darton, Longman & Todd, 1998.

Donaldson, Terence L. "Nicodemus: A Figure of Ambiguity in a Gospel of Certainty." *Consensus* 24 (1998) 121–24.

Dorn, Pamela. "Gender and Personhood: Turkish Jewish Proverbs and the Politics of Reputation." *WSIF* 9 (1986) 295–301.

Drury, John. *Tradition and Design in Luke's Gospel: A Study in Early Christian Historiography.* Atlanta: John Knox, 1976.

du Boulay, Juliet. *A Portrait of a Greek Mountain Village.* Oxford Monographs on Social Anthropology. Oxford: Clarendon, 1974.

———. "Lies, Mockery and Family Integrity." In *Mediterranean Family Structures*, edited by Jean G. Péristiany. CSSA 13. Cambridge: Cambridge University Press, 1976.

Duke, Paul D. *Irony in the Fourth Gospel.* Atlanta: John Knox, 1985.

Duling, Dennis C. *The New Testament: History, Literature and Social Context.* 4th ed. Belmont, CA: Wadsworth, 2003

———, and Norman Perrin. *The New Testament: Proclamation and Parenesis, Myth and History.* 3d ed. New York: Harcourt Brace, 1994.

Elliott, John H. *A Home for the Homeless: A Social-Scientific Criticism of I Peter, Its Situation and Strategy, with a New Introduction.* 1981. Reprinted, Eugene, OR: Wipf & Stock, 2005.

———. "Patronage and Clientism in Early Christian Society: A Short Reading Guide." *Forum* 3/4 (1987) 39–48.

———. "The Fear of the Leer: The Evil Eye from the Bible to Li'l Abner." *Forum* 4/4 (1988) 42–71.

———. "Temple versus Household in Luke-Acts: A Contrast in Social Institutions." In *The Social World of Luke-Acts*, edited by Jerome H. Neyrey, 211–40. Peabody, MA: Hendrickson, 1991.

———. *What is Social-Scientific Criticism?* GBS. Minneapolis: Fortress, 1993.

Esler, Philip F. *Community and Gospel in Luke-Acts: The Social and Political Motivation for Lucan Theology.* SNTSMS 57. Cambridge: Cambridge University Press, 1987.

———, editor. *Modelling Early Christianity: Social-Scientific Studies of the New Testament in Its Context.* London: Routledge, 1995.

Evans, Elizabeth C. "Roman Descriptions of Personal Appearance in History and Biography." *HSCP* 46 (1935) 43–84.

———. "The Study of Physiognomy in the Second Century A.D." *TAPA* 72 (1941) 96–108.

———. *Physiognomics in the Ancient World.* TAPS 59 no. 5. Philadelphia: American Philosophical Society, 1969.

Festinger, Leon. "A Theory of Social Comparison Processes." *HR* 7 (1954) 117–140.

Fiensy, David A. *The Social History of Palestine in the Herodian Period: The Land is Mine.* SBEC 20. Lewiston, NY: Mellen, 1991.

Finkel, Asher. "Jesus' Preaching in the Synagogue on the Sabbath (Luke 4:16-28)." *SIDIC* 17 (1984) 4–10.

Finley, Moses I. *The Ancient Economy.* Sather Classical Lectures 48. Berkeley: University of California Press, 1973.

———. "The Ancient City: From Fustel do Coulanges to Max Weber and Beyond." *Comparative Studies in Society and History* 19 (1977) 305–27.

Firth, Raymond. "Rumor in a Primitive Society." *JASP* 53 (1950) 122–32.

Fitzmyer, Joseph A. *The Gospel according to Luke.* 2 vols. AB 28–28a. New York: Doubleday, 1981–1985.

Flusser, David. "Die Versuchung Jesu und ihr jüdischer Hintergrund." *Jud* 45 (1989) 110–28.

Ford, Stephen. *The Evil Tongue Tryed and Found Guilty, or, The Hainousness and Exceeding Sinfulness of Defaming and Back-biting Opened and Declared.* 1672. Microfilm, Ann Arbor, MI: University Microfilms International, 1982.

Foster, George M. "Peasant Society and the Image of Limited Good." *AmAnth* 67 (1965) 293–315.

———. "Introduction: What is a Peasant?" In *Peasant Society: A Reader,* edited by Jack M. Potter, et al., 2–14. Boston: Little, Brown, 1967.

———. "Peasant Society and the Image of Limited Good." In *Peasant Society: A Reader,* edited by Jack M. Potter et al., 300–323. Boston: Little, Brown, 1967.

Fowler, Roger. *Literature as Social Discourse: The Practice of Linguistic Criticism.* Bloomington: Indiana University Press, 1981.

———, et al. *Language and Control.* London: Routledge and Kegan Paul, 1979.

Freyne, Seán. *Galilee from Alexander the Great to Hadrian: 323 B.C.E. to 135 C.E.* University of Notre Dame Center for the Study of Judaism and Christianity in Antiquity 5. Wilmington, DE: Glazier, 1980

Frick, Frank S. *The City in Ancient Israel.* SBLDS 36. Missoula, MT: Scholars, 1977.

Friedrich, Paul. "Sanity and the Myth of Honor: The Problem of Achilles." *JPA* (1977) 281–305.

Fuchs, Albert. "Versuchung Jesu." *Studien zum Neuen Testament und seiner Umwelt* 9 (1984) 95–159.

Funk, Robert W., Roy W. Hoover, and the Jesus Seminar. *The Five Gospels: The Search for the Authentic Words of Jesus.* New York: Macmillan, 1993.

Funk, Robert W., et al. *The Parables of Jesus (Red Letter Edition): A Report of the Jesus Seminar.* Jesus Seminar Series. Sonoma, CA: Polebridge, 1988.

Fustel de Colanges, Numa Denys. *The Ancient City.* Translated by Willard Small. Garden City, NY: Doubleday 1956.

Gamson, William A. "The Social Psychology of Collective Action." In *Frontiers in Social Movement Theory,* edited by Aldon D. Morris and Carol McClurg Mueller, 53–76. New Haven: Yale University Press, 1992.

Gardner, Jane F., and Thomas E. J. Wiedemann. *The Roman Household: A Sourcebook.* London: Routledge, 1991.

Garnsey, Peter. *Social Status and Legal Privilege in the Roman Empire.* Oxford: Clarendon, 1970.

Gellner, Ernest, and John Waterbury, editors. *Patrons and Clients in Mediterranean Societies.* London: Duckworth, 1977.

Gerhardsson, Birger. *The Testing of God's Son (Matt 4:1-11 and par.): An Analysis of an Early Christian Midrash.* Coniectanea Biblica, New Testament Series 2. Lund, Sweden: Gleerup, 1966.

Giblin, Charles H. "Structural and Theological Considerations on Luke 15." *CBQ* 24 (1962) 15–31.

Gibbons, Debbie. "Nicodemus: Character Development, Irony and Repetition in the Fourth Gospel." *Proceedings: Eastern Great Lakes and Midwest Biblical Societies* 11 (1991) 116–28.

Giles, Howard, et al. "Speech Accommodation Theory: The First Decade and Beyond." In *Communication Yearbook* 10. Edited by Margaret L. McLaughlin, 13–48. Beverly Hills, CA: Sage, 1987.

Giles, Howard and Klaus R. Scherer, editors. *Social Markers in Speech.* European Studies in Social Psychology. Cambridge: Cambridge University Press, 1979.

Giles, Howard, and John M. Wiemann. "Language, Social Comparison and Power." In *Handbook of Communication Science*, edited by Charles R. Berger and Steven H. Chaffee, 350–84. Beverly Hills, CA: Sage, 1987.

Gilmore, David D. "Varieties of Gossip in a Spanish Rural Community." *Ethnology* 17 (1978) 89–99.

———. "Anthropology of the Mediterranean Area." *ARA* 11 (1982) 175–205.

———. *Aggression and Community: Paradoxes of Andalusian Culture*. New Haven: Yale University Press, 1987.

———. *Honor and Shame and the Unity of the Mediterranean*. AAASP 22. Washington, DC: American Anthropological Association, 1987.

Glaser, Barney G, and Anselm L. Strauss. "Awareness Contexts and Social Interaction." In *Symbolic Interaction: A Reader in Social Psychology*, edited by Jerome G. Manis and Bernard N. Meltzer. Boston: Allyn & Bacon, 1967.

Gluckman, Max. "Gossip and Scandal." *CAnth* 4 (1963) 307–16.

———. "Psychological, Sociological and Anthropological Explanations of Witchcraft and Gossip." *Man* 3 (1968) 20–34.

Gnilka, Joachim. *Jesus of Nazareth: Message and History*. Translated by Siegfried S. Schatzmann. Peabody, MA: Hendrickson, 1997.

Goitein, S. D. *A Mediterranean Society: The Jewish Communities of the Arab World as Portrayed in the Documents of the Cairo Geniza*. Vol. 5, *The Individual*. Berkeley: University of California Press, 1988.

Goldschmidt, Walter. "An Ethnography of Encounters: A Methodology for Enquiry into the Relationship between the Individual and Society." *CAnth* 13 (1972) 59–78.

Goldsmith, Daena. "Gossip from the Native's Point of View." *RLSI* 23 (1989) 163–93.

Goodman, Martin. "The First Jewish Revolt: Social Conflict and the Problem of Debt." *JJS* 33 (1982) 417–27.

Gordon, Cyrus H. "Paternity at Two Levels." *JBL* (1977) 96: 101.

Goulder, Michael D. "Nicodemus." *SJT* 44 (1991) 153–68.

Gramsci, Antonio. *Selections from the Prison Notebooks of Antonio Gramsci*. Edited and translated by Quintin Hoare and Geoffrey Nowell Smith. New York: International, 1972.

Grant, Elihu. *The People of Palestine: The Life, Manners and Customs of the Village*. 1907. Reprinted, Eugene, OR: Wipf and Stock, 2005.

Greenwald, Anthony G., and Anthony R. Pratkanis. "The Self." In *The Handbook of Social Cognition*. Vol. 3. Edited by Robert. S. Wyler and Thomas. K. Srull, 129–78. Hillsdale, NJ: Erlbaum, 1984.

Gregory, James R. "Image of Limited Good, or Expectation of Reciprocity?" *CAnth* 16 (1975) 73–92.

Grese, William C. "'Unless One Is Born Again': The Use Of a Heavenly Journey in John 3." *JBL* 107 (1988) 677–93.

Grundmann, Walter. *Das Evangelium nach Lukas*. THKNT 3. Berlin: Evangelische Verlagsanstalt, 1971.

Gundry, Robert H., and Russell W. Howell. "The Sense and Syntax of John 3:14–17 with Special Reference to the Use of OYTOS...OSTE in John 3-16." *NovT* 41 (1999) 24–39.

Gudykunst, William B. *Cross-Cultural and Intercultural Communication*. Thousand Oaks, CA: Sage, 2003.

Gumperz, John J., editor. *Language and Social Identity*. Cambridge: Cambridge University Press, 1982.

Guss, David M. "The Enculturation of Makiritare Women." *Ethnology* 21 (1982) 259–69.

Hall, Edward T. *Beyond Culture*. New York: Anchor, 1976.

———. "Context and Meaning." In *Intercultural Communication: A Reader.* 7th ed. Edited by Richard E. Porter and Larry A. Samovar, 60–70. Belmont, CA: Wadsworth, 1994.

———, and Mildred Reed Hall. *Understanding Cultural Differences.* Yarmouth, ME: Intercultural, 1990.

Halliday, M. A. K. *Learning How to Mean: Explorations in the Functions of Language.* Explorations in Language Study. Baltimore: University Park, 1975.

———. "Anti-languages." *AmAnth* 78 (1976) 570–84.

———. *Language as Social Semiotic: The Social Interpretation of Language and Meaning.* London: Arnold, 1978.

Hamm, Dennis. "Luke 19:8 Once Again: Does Zacchaeus Defend or Resolve?" *JBL* 107 (1988) 431–37.

Hammond, Mason. *The City in the Ancient World.* Harvard Studies in Urban History. Cambridge: Harvard University Press, 1972.

Handelman, Don. "Gossip in Encounters: The Transmission of Information in a Bounded Social Setting." *Man* 8 (1973) 210–227.

Hannerz, Ulf. "Gossip, Networks and Culture in a Black American Ghetto." *Ethnos* 32 (1967) 35–60.

Hanson, Ann E. "Ancient Illiteracy." In *Literacy in the Roman World,* edited by J. H. Humphrey, 159–98. JRA Supplementary Series 3. Ann Arbor, MI: JRA, 1991.

Hanson, K. C. "The Herodians and Mediterranean Kinship, Part I: Genealogy and Descent." *BTB* 19 (1989) 75–84.

———. "The Herodians and Mediterranean Kingship, Part II: Marriage and Divorce." *BTB* 19 (1989) 142–51.

———. "The Herodians and Mediterranean Kingship, Part III: Economics." *BTB* 20 (1989) 10–21.

———, and Douglas E. Oakman. *Palestine in the Time of Jesus: Social Structures and Social Conflicts, with CD-ROM.* Minneapolis: Fortress, 2002.

Harms, L. S. *Intercultural Communication.* New York: Harper & Row, 1973.

Harper, George. "Village Administration in the Roman Province of Syria." *YCS* 1 (1928) 105–68.

Harris, William V. *Ancient Literacy.* Cambridge: Harvard University Press, 1991.

Hauser, Philip M. "Observations on the Urban-Folk and Urban-Rural Dichotomies as Forms of Western Ethnocentrism." In *The Study of Urbanization,* edited by Philip M. Hauser and Leo F. Schnore, 503–17. New York: Wiley, 1965.

———, and Leo F. Schnore, editors. *The Study of Urbanization.* New York: Wiley, 1965.

Haviland, John Beard. "Gossip as Competition in Zinacantan." *JC* 27 (1977) 186–91.

———. *Gossip, Reputation and Knowledge in Zinacantan.* Chicago: University of Chicago Press, 1977.

Hengel, Martin. "Entstehungzeit und Situation des Markusevangeliums." In *Markus-Philologie: Historische, literargeschichtliche und stilistische Untersuchungen zum zweiten Evangelium,* edited by Hubert Cancik, 1–45. WUNT 33. Tübingen: Mohr/Siebeck, 1984.

Schneemelcher, Wilhelm and Robert M. Wilson, editors. *New Testament Apocrypha.* 2 vols. Rev. ed. Louisville: Westminster John Knox, 1991.

Herzfeld, Michael. "Honor and Shame: Problems in the Comparative Analysis of Moran Systems." *Man* 15 (1980) 339–50.

Hill, David. "The Rejection of Jesus at Nazareth (Luke iv 16-30)." *NovT* 13 (1971) 161–80.

Hobbie, F. Wellford. "Luke 19:1-10." *Int* 31 (1977) 285–90.

Hobbs, T. Raymond. "Hospitality in the First Testament and the 'Teleological Fallacy.'" *JSOT* 95 (2001) 3–30.

Hodge, Robert, and Gunther Kress. *Social Semiotics*. Ithaca, NY: Cornell University Press, 1988.

Hofius, Otfried. "Alttestamentliche Motive im Gleichnis vom verlorenen Sohn." *NTS* 24 (1978) 240–48.

Holub, Robert C. *Reception Theory: A Critical Introduction*. New Accents. London: Methuen, 1984.

Hood, Rodney T. "The Genealogies of Jesus." In *Early Christian Origins: Studies in Honor of Harold R. Willoughby*, edited by Allen P. Wikgren, 1–15. Chicago: Quadrangle, 1961.

Hooker, Morna D. *The Gospel According to Saint Mark*. Peabody, MA: Hendrickson, 1993.

Hoopes, David S., editor. *Readings in Intercultural Communication*. Vol. 1, *Intercultural Communication Workshop*. Pittsburgh: Intercultural Communications Network, 1975.

Horsfall, Nicholas. "Statistics or States of Mind?" In *Literacy in the Roman World*, edited by J. H. Humphrey, 59–76. JRA Supplementary Series 3. Ann Arbor, MI: JRA, 1991.

Horsley, Richard A. *Jesus and the Spiral of Violence: Popular Jewish Resistance in Roman Palestine*. San Francisco: Harper and Row, 1987.

———. *Sociology and the Jesus Movement*. New York: Crossroad, 1989.

———, and John S. Hanson. *Bandits, Prophets, and Messiahs*. 1985. Reprinted, Harrisburg, PA: Trinity, 1999.

Hui, Harry C., and Harry C. Triandis. "Individualism-Collectivism: A Study of Cross-Cultural Researchers." *JCCP* 17 (1989) 225–48.

Humphrey, J. H., editor. *Literacy in the Roman World*. JRA Supplementary Series 3. Ann Arbor, MI: JRA, 1991.

Humphries, S. C. *Anthropology and the Greeks*. International Library of Anthropology. London: Routledge & Kegan Paul, 1978.

Hunt, Arthur S., and C. C. Edgar, translators. *Select Papyri: Non-Literary Papyri. Public Documents*. LCL 282. Cambridge: Harvard University Press, 1977–1992.

Hurtado, Larry W. *Mark*. New International Biblical Commentary 2. Peabody, MA: Hendrickson, 1989.

Hymes, Dell H. *Foundations of Sociolinguistics: An Ethnographical Approach*. Philadelphia: University of Pennsylvania Press, 1974.

Jameson, Fredric. *The Political Unconscious: Narrative as a Socially Symbolic Act*. London: Meuthen, 1981.

Jauss, Hans Robert. "Literary History as a Challenge to Literary Theory." In *New Directions in Literary History*, edited by Ralph Cohen, 127–64. Baltimore: Johns Hopkins University Press, 1974.

Jeremias, Joachim. "Zum Gleichnis von verlorenen Sohn, Lk 15:11-32." *TZ* 5 (1949) 228–31.

———. *The Parables of Jesus*. Rev. ed. Translated by S. H. Hooke. New York: Scribner, 1963.

———. *Jerusalem in the Time of Jesus: An Investigation into Economic and Social Conditions in the New Testament Period*. Translated by F. H. Cave and C. H. Cave. Philadelphia: Fortress, 1969.

———. "Tradition und Redaktion in Lukas 15." *ZNW* 62 (1971) 172–89.

Jones, A. H. M. "The Urbanization of Palestine." *JRS* 21 (1931) 78–85.

———. *The Cities of the Eastern Roman Provinces*. 2d ed, revised by Michael Avi-Yona, et al. Oxford: Clarendon, 1971.

Jones, Deborah. "Gossip: Notes on Women's Oral Culture." *WSIQ* 3 (1980) 193–98.

Karris, Robert J. "Poor and Rich: The Lukan *Sitz im Leben*." In *Perspectives on Luke-Acts*, edited by Charles H. Talbert, 114—25. Perspectives in Religious Studies: Special Studies Series 5. Danville, VA: Association of Baptist Professors, 1978.

Kee, Howard C. "The Linguistic Background of Shame in the New Testament." In_On Language, Culture and Religion, edited by Matthew Black and William A. Smalley, 133–48. The Hague: Mouton, 1974.

Kennedy, George A. A History of Rhetoric. Vol. 1, The Art of Persuasion in Greece. Princeton: Princeton University Press, 1963.

———. A History of Rhetoric. Vol. 2, The Art of Rhetoric in the Roman World. Princeton: Princeton University Press, 1972.

———. New Testament Interpretation Through Rhetorical Criticism. Studies in Religion. Chapel Hill: University of North Carolina Press, 1984.

Keppler, Angela. "Der Verlauf von Klatschgesprachen." ZS 16 (1987) 288–302.

Kilgallen, John J. "Provocation in Lk 4:23-24." Bib 70 (1989) 511.

Kim, Chan-Hie, "Papyrus Invitation." JBL 94 (1975) 391–402.

King, J. S. "Nicodemus and the Pharisees." ExpTim 98 (1986) 45.

Kodell, Jerome. "Luke's Gospel in a Nutshell (4:16-30)." BTB 13 (1983) 16–18.

Koenig, John. New Testament Hospitality: Partnership with Strangers as Promise and Mission. 1985. Reprinted, Eugene, OR: Wipf & Stock, 2006.

Koester, Craig R. Symbolism in the Fourth Gospel: Meaning, Mystery, Community. 2d. ed. Minneapolis: Fortress, 2003.

Koester, Helmut. Introduction to the New Testament. 2 vols. Foundations and Facets: New Testament. Philadelphia: Fortress, 1982.

———. Cities of Paul, Images and Interpretations: from the Harvard New Testament and Archaeology Project. Minneapolis: Fortress, 2004. CD-ROM.

Koet, B. J. "'Today this Scripture Has Been Fulfilled in Your Ear.' Jesus' Explanation of Scripture in Luke 4:16-30." Bijd 47 (1986) 368–94.

Kozar, Joseph Vlcek. "Absent Joy: An Investigation of the Narrative Pattern of Repetition and Variation in the Parables of Luke 15." TJT 8 (1992) 85–94.

Kraft, Charles H. Christianity in Culture: A Study in Dynamic Biblical Theologizing in Cross-Cultural Perspective. Maryknoll, NY: Orbis, 1979.

Kress, Gunther R. "Textual Matters: The Social Effectiveness of Style." In Functions of Style, edited by David Birch and Michael O'Toole, 39–59. Open Linguistics Series. London: Pinter, 1987.

Kuper, Adam. "Lineage Theory: A Critical Retrospect." ARA 11 (1982) 71–95.

Kysar, Robert. John's Story of Jesus. Philadelphia: Fortress, 1984.

———. John: The Maverick Gospel. Rev. ed. Louisville: Westminster John Knox, 1993.

Lambrecht, Jan. Once More Astonished: The Parables of Jesus. New York: Crossroad, 1983.

Lampard, Eric E. "Historical Aspects of Urbanization." In The Study of Urbanization, edited by Philip M. Hauser and Leo F. Schnore, 519–54. New York: Wiley, 1965.

Lampl, Paul. Cities and Planning in the Ancient Near East. New York: George Braziller, 1968.

Lapidus, Ira M. "Cities and Societies: A Comparative Study of the Emergence of Urban Civilization in Mesopotamia and Greece." JUH 12 (1986) 257–92.

Leeds, Anthony. "Forms of Urban Integration: Social Urbanization in Comparative Perspective." UAnth 8 (1979) 227–47.

———. "Towns and Villages in Society: Hierarchies of Order and Cause." In Cities in a Larger Context, edited by Thomas W. Collins, 6–33. Southern Anthropological Society Proceedings 14. Athens: University of Georgia Press, 1980.

Leiner, Martin. Psychologie und Exegese: Grundlagen einer textpsychologischen Exegese des Neuen Testaments. Gutersloh, Germany: Kaiser, 1995.

Leivestad, Ragnar. Jesus in His Own Perspective: An Examination of His Sayings, Actions and Eschatological Titles. Translated by David E. Aune. Minneapolis: Augsburg, 1987.

Lenski, Gerhard. *Power and Privilege: A Theory of Social Stratification.* McGraw-Hill Series in Sociology. New York: McGraw-Hill, 1966.

Lenski, Gerhard, and Jean Lenski. *Human Societies: An Introduction to Macrosociology.* New York: McGraw-Hill, 1974.

———. *Human Societies: An Introduction to Macrosociology. Human Societies: An Introduction to Macrosociology.* 5th ed. New York: McGraw-Hill, 1987.

Levison, Nahum. *The Parables: Their Background and Local Setting.* Edinburgh: T. & T. Clark, 1926.

Lewis, Oscar. "The Folk-Urban Ideal Types." In *The Study of Urbanization,* edited by Philip M. Hauser and Leo F. Schnore, 491–518. New York: Wiley, 1965.

Lieberman, Devorah A. "Ethnocognitivism, Problem Solving, and Hemisphericity." In *Intercultural Communication: A Reader.* 7th ed. Edited by Richard E. Porter and Larry A. Samovar, 178–93. Belmont, CA: Wadsworth, 1994.

Linnemann, Eta. *Jesus of the Parables: Introduction and Exposition.* Translated by John Sturdy. New York: Harper & Row, 1966.

Lloyd-Jones, Hugh. "Ehre und Schande in der griechishen Kultur." *Antike und Abendland* 33 (1987) 1–28.

Loewe, William P. "Towards an Interpretation of Luke 19:1-10." *CBQ* 36 (1974) 321–31.

Longenecker, Richard N. "'Son of Man' as a Self-Designation of Jesus." *JETS* 12 (1969) 151–58.

Malina, Bruce J. *The Gospel of John in Sociolinguistic Perspective.* 48th Colloquy of the Center Hermeneutical Studies, edited by Herman Waetjen. Berkeley, CA: Center for Hermeneutical Studies, 1985.

———. "The Received View: What it Cannot Do: III John and Hospitality." *Semeia* 35 (1986) 171–94. Reprinted in Malina 1996: 217–41.

———. "Wealth and Poverty in the New Testament and Its World." *Int* 41 (1987) 354–67.

———. "Patron and Client: The Analogy Behind Synoptic Theology." *Forum* 4 (1988) 2–32. Reprinted in Malina 1996: 143–75.

———. "Christ and Time: Swiss or Mediterranean?" *CBQ* 51 (1989) 1–31. Reprinted in Malina 1996: 179–216.

——— "Dealing with Biblical (Mediterranean) Characters: A Guide for U.S. Consumers." *BTB* 19 (1989) 127–41.

———. "Reading Theory Perspective: Reading Luke-Acts." In *The Social World of Luke-Acts: Models for Interpretation,* edited by Jerome Neyrey, 3–23. Peabody, MA: Hendrickson, 1991.

———. "Is There a Circum-Mediterranean Person? Looking for Stereotypes." *BTB* 22 (1992) 66–87.

———. "Hospitality." In *Biblical Social Values and Their Meaning: A Handbook,* edited by John J. Pilch and Bruce J. Malina, 104–07. Peabody MA: Hendrickson, 1993.

———. "Let a Man Deny Himself (Mark 8:34): A Social Psychological Model of Self- Denial." *BTB* 24 (1993) 106–19.

———. "John's: the Maverick Christian Group. Evidence From Sociolinguistics." *BTB* 24 (1994) 167–84

———. *The Social World of Jesus and the Gospels.* London: Routledge, 1996.

———. *The New Testament World: Insights from Cultural Anthropology.* 3d ed. Louisville: Westminster John Knox, 2001.

Malina, Bruce J., and Jerome H. Neyrey. *Calling Jesus Names: The Social Value of Labels in Matthew.* Social Facets. Sonoma, CA: Polebridge, 1988.

————."First-Century Personality: Dyadic, Not Individualistic." In *The Social World of Luke Acts: Models for Biblical Interpretation*. Edited by Jerome Neyrey, 67–96. Peabody, MA: Hendrickson, 1991.

————. "Honor and Shame in Luke-Acts: Pivotal Values of the Mediterranean World." In *The Social World of Luke-Acts: Models for Interpretation*, edited by Jerome H. Neyrey, 25–65. Peabody, MA: Hendrickson, 1991.

————. *Portraits of Paul: An Archaeology of Ancient Personality*. Louisville: Westminster John Knox, 1996.

Malina, Bruce J., and Richard L. Rohrbaugh. *Social Science Commentary on the Gospel of John*. Minneapolis: Fortress, 1998.

————. *Social Science Commentary on the Synoptic Gospels*. 2d ed. Minneapolis: Fortress, 2003

Marshall, I. Howard. *The Gospel of Luke: A Commentary on the Greek Text*. NIGTC. Grand Rapids: Eerdmans, 1978.

Marshall, Peter. "A Metaphor of Social Shame: *thriambeuein* in 2 Corinthians 2:14." *NovT* 25 (1983) 302–17.

Martyn, J. Louis. *The Gospel of John in Christian History: Essays for Interpreters*. 1978. Reprinted, Eugene, OR: Wipf & Stock, 2004.

Mason, Steve. *Josepus and the New Testament*. Peabody, MA: Hendrickson, 1992.

McCabe, Robert V. "The Meaning of 'Born of Water and Spirit' in John 3:5." *Detroit Baptist Seminary Journal* 4 (1999) 85–107.

McVann, Mark. "Rituals of Status-Transformation in Luke-Acts: The Case of Jesus the Prophet." In *The Social World of Luke-Acts: Models for Interpretation*. ed. Jerome H. Neyrey, 333–60. Peabody, MA: Hendrickson, 1991.

————. "Family-Centeredness." In *Biblical Social Values and Their Meaning*, edited by John J. Pilch and Bruce J. Malina, 70–73. Peabody, MA: Hendrickson, 1993.

Meeks, Wayne A. "The Man from Heaven in Johannine Sectarianism." *JBL* 91 (1972) 44–72.

Meyer, Ben F. "Jesus' Ministry and Self-Understanding." In *Studying the Historical Jesus: Evaluations of Current Research*, edited by Bruce D. Chilton and Craig A. Evans, 337–52. New Testament Tools and Studies 19. Leiden: Brill, 1994.

Meyer, Paul W. "The Problem of the Messianic Self-Consciousness of Jesus." *NovT* 4 (1960) 122–38.

Meyers, Eric M. "The Challenge of Hellenism for Early Judaism and Christianity." *BA* 55 (1992) 84–91.

Miller, Gerald R. "Persuasion." In *Handbook of Communication Science*, edited by Charles R. Berger and Steven H. Chaffee, 446–83. Beverly Hills, CA: Sage, 1987.

Minear, Paul. "Luke's Use of the Birth Stories." In *Studies in Luke-Acts*, edited by Leander E. Keck and J. Louis Martyn, 111–30. Nashville: Abingdon, 1966.

Miner, Horace. "The Folk-Urban Continuum." *ARS* 17 (1952) 529–37.

Monshouwer, Dirk. "The Reading of the Prophet in the Synagogue at Nazareth." *Bib* 72 (1991) 90–99.

Moxnes, Halvor. *The Economy of the Kingdom*. OBT. Philadelphia: Fortress, 1988.

————. "Patron-Client Relations and the New Community in Luke-Acts." In *The Social World of Luke-Acts: Models for Interpretation*, edited by Jerome H. Neyrey, 241–68. Peabody, MA: Hendrickson.

Mumford, Lewis. *The City in History: Its Origins, Its Transformations, and Its Prospects*. New York: Harcourt, Brace, and World, 1961.

Munro, Winsome. "The Pharisee and the Samaritan in John: Polar or Parallel?" *CBQ* 57 (1995) 710–28.

Murphy-O'Connor, Jerome. "The Corinth that Saint Paul Saw." *BA* 47 (1984) 147–59.

Myers, Ched. *Binding the Strong Man: A Political Reading of Mark's Story of Jesus.* Maryknoll, NY: Orbis, 1988.

Neyrey, Jerome H. "The Idea of Purity in Mark's Gospel." In *Social-Scientific Criticism of the New Testament and Its Social World*, edited by John H. Elliott, 91–128. Semeia 35. Decatur, GA: Scholars, 1986.

———. "Ceremonies in Luke-Acts: The Case of Meals and Table Fellowship." In *The Social World of Luke-Acts: Models for Interpretation*, edited by Jerome H. Neyrey, 361–87. Peabody, MA: Hendrickson, 1991.

———, editor. *The Social World of Luke-Acts: Models for Interpretation.* Peabody, MA: Hendrickson, 1991.

———. "Equivocation." In *Biblical Social Values and Their Meaning: A Handbook*, edited by John J. Pilch and Bruce J. Malina, 59–63. Peabody, MA: Hendrickson, 1993.

Nicol, George G. "Nicodemus." *ExpTim* 103 (1991) 80–81.

Niles, F. Sushila. "Individualism–Collectivism Revisited." *JCCR* 32 (1998) 315–41.

Nydell, Margaret K. *Understanding Arabs: A Guide for Westerners.* Yarmouth, ME: Intercultural, 1987.

Oakman, Douglas E. *Jesus and the Economic Questions of His Day.* SBEC 8. Lewiston, NY: Mellen, 1986.

———. "The Countryside in Luke-Acts." In *The Social World of Luke-Acts: Models for Interpretation*, edited by Jerome Neyrey, 152–64. Peabody, MA: Hendrickson, 1991.

O'Day, Gail R. "Narrative Mode and Theological Claim: A Study in the Fourth Gospel." *JBL* 105 (1986) 657–68.

———. *Revelation in the Fourth Gospel: Narrative Mode and Theological Claim.* Philadelphia: Fortress, 1986.

——— "New Birth as a New People: Spirituality and Community in the Fourth Gospel." *WW* 8 (1988) 53–61.

Oesterly, W. O. E. *The Gospels in the Light of their Jewish Background.* London: SPCK, 1936.

O'Fearghail, Fergus. "Rejection at Nazareth: Lk 4:22." *ZNW* 75 (1985) 60–72.

O'Hanlon, Joseph. "The Story of Zacchaeus and the Lukan Ethic." *JSNT* 12 (1981) 2–26.

O'Rourke, John J. "Some Notes on Luke 15:11-32." *NTS* 18 (1972) 431–33.

Orton, David E. *The Understanding Scribe: Matthew and the Apocalyptic Ideal.* JSNTSS 25. Sheffield: JSOT Press, 1989.

Osborn, Carroll D. "Some Exegetical Observations on John 3:5-8." *RQ* 31 (1989) 129–38.

Osborn, Robert T. "The Father and His Two Sons: A Parable of Liberation." *Dialogue* 19 (1980) 204–09.

O'Toole, Robert F. "The Literary Form of Luke 19:1-10," *JBL* (1991) 107–16.

Paine, Robert. "What is Gossip? An Alternative Hypothesis." *Man* 2 (1967) 278–85.

———. "Gossip and Transaction." *Man* 3 (1968) 305–08.

———. "Informal Communication and Information Management." *CRSA* 7 (1970) 172–88.

Pannenberg, Wolfhart. *Jesus: God and Man.* Translated by Lewis L. Wilkins and Duane A. Priebe. Philadelphia: Westminster, 1968.

Parsons, Mikeal. "'Short in Stature': Luke's Physical Description of Zacchaeus." *NTS* 47 (2001) 50–57.

Patai, Raphael. *The Arab Mind.* New York: Scribner, 1983.

Pazdan, Mary M. "Nicodemus and the Samaritan Woman: Contrasting Models of Discipleship." *BTB* 17 (1987) 145–48.

Péristiany, Jean G. "Introduction." In *Mediterranean Family Structures*, edited by Jean G. Péristiany, 1–26. CSSA 13. Cambridge: Cambridge University Press, 1976.

————, editor. *Honor and Shame: The Values of Mediterranean Society*. The Nature of Human Society Series. Chicago: University of Chicago Press, 1966.

————, editor. *Mediterranean Family Structures*. CSSA 13. Cambridge: Cambridge University Press, 1976.

————, and Julian Pitt-Rivers, editors. *Honor and Grace in Anthropology*. CSSA 76. Cambridge: Cambridge University Press, 1992.

Perlman, Chaim, and Lucie Olbrecht-Tyteca. *The New Rhetoric: A Treatise on Argumentation*. Translated by John Wilkinson and Purcell Weaver. Notre Dame: University of Notre Dame Press, 1969.

Pesch, Rudolf. "Zur Exegese Gottes durch Jesus von Nazaret: eine Auslegung des Gleichnisses vom Vater und den beiden Söhnen (Lk 15:11-32)." In *Jesus: Ort der Erfahrung Gottes*, edited by Bernhard Casper, 140–89. Freiburg: Herder, 1976.

Petersen, Norman R. *The Gospel of John and the Sociology of Light: Language and Characterization in the Fourth Gospel*. Valley Forge, PA: Trinity, 1993.

Pilch, John J. "Healing in Mark: A Social Science Analysis." *BTB* 15 (1985) 142–50.

————. "Understanding Biblical Healing: Selecting the Appropriate Model." *BTB* 18 (1988) 60–66.

————. "Sickness and Healing in Luke-Acts." In *The Social World of Luke-Acts: Models for Interpretation*, edited by Jerome Neyrey, 181–209. Peabody, MA: Hendrickson, 1991.

————, and Bruce J. Malina, editors. *Biblical Social Values and Their Meaning: A Handbook*. Peabody, MA: Hendrickson, 1993.

————. "Secrecy in the Mediterranean World: An Anthropological Perspective." *BTB* 24 (1994) 151–57.

————. "Psychological and Psychoanalytical Approaches to Interpreting the Bible in Social-Scientific Context. *BTB* 27 (1997) 112–16.

Pitt-Rivers, Julian. *The Fate of Shechem: Or the Politics of Sex: Essays in the Anthropology of the Mediterranean*. CSSA 19. Cambridge: Cambridge University Press, 1977.

————. "Postscript: The Place of Grace in Anthropology." In *Honor and Grace in Anthropology*, edited by Jean G. Peristiany and Julian Pitt-Rivers, 215–46. CSSA 76. Cambridge: Cambridge University Press, 1992.

Plummer, Alfred. *A Critical and Exegetical Commentary on the Gospel according to St. Luke*. ICC. Edinburgh: T. & T. Clark, 1908.

Pöhlmann, Wolfgang. "Die Abschichtung des Verlorenen Sohnes (Lk 15:12f) und die erzählte Welt der Parabel." *ZNW* 70 (1979) 194–213.

Pokorny, Petr. "The Temptation Stories and Their Intention." *NTS* 20 (1973) 115–27.

Porter, Richard E. and Larry A. Samovar, editors. *Intercultural Communication: A Reader*. 7th ed. Belmont, CA: Wadsworth, 1994.

Räisänen, Heikki. "The Prodigal Gentile and His Jewish Christian Brother." In *The Four Gospels 1992: Festschrift Frans Neirynck*, edited by Frans van Segbroek, et al, 2: 37–60. 3 vols. BETL 100. Leuven: Leuven University Press, 1992.

Rasmussen, Susan J. "Modes of Persuasion: Gossip, Song and Divination in Tuareg Conflict Resolution." *AQ* 64 (1991) 30–46.

Redfield, Robert. "The Folk Society." *ARS* 52 (1947) 296–97.

————. *Peasant Society and Culture: An Anthropological Approach to Civilization*. Chicago: University of Chicago Press, 1956.

————, and Milton Singer. "The Cultural Role of Cities." In *Peasants and Peasant Societies: Selected Readings*, edited by Teodor Shanin, 337–65. Penguin Modern Sociology Readings. Baltimore: Penguin, 1971.

Reichardt, Michael. *Psychologische Erklärung der paulinischen Damaskusvision? ein Beitrag zum interdisziplinären Gespräch zwischen Exegese und Psychologie seit dem 18. Jahrhundert.* Stuttgart: Katholisches Bibelwerk, 1999.

Reicke, Bo. "Jesus in Nazareth—Lk 4:16-30." In *Das Wort und die Wörter: Festscrift G. Friedrich zum 65. Geburstag,* edited by H. Balz, and S. Schulz, 51–53. Stuttgart: Kohlhammer, 1973.

Resenhofft, Wilhelm. "Jesu Gleichnis von Talenten, erganzt durch die Lukas-Fassung." *NTS* 26 (1980) 318–31.

Rhoads, David. "Social Criticism: Crossing Boundaries." In *New Approaches in Biblical Studies,* edited by Janice C. Anderson and Stephen D. Moore, 135–61. Minneapolis: Fortress, 1992.

Richard, Earl. "Expressions of Double Meaning and Their Function in the Gospel of John." *NTS* 31 (1985) 96–112.

Robbins, Vernon K. *Jesus the Teacher: A Socio-Rhetorical Interpretation of Mark.* Philadelphia: Fortress, 1984.

———. "The Social Location of the Implied Author of Luke-Acts." In *The Social World of Luke Acts: Models for Biblical Interpretation,* edited by Jerome H. Neyrey, 305–32. Peabody, MA: Hendrickson, 1991.

Roberts, C. H. "Books in the Graeco-Roman World and in the New Testament." In *Cambridge History of the Bible.* Vol. 1, *From the Beginnings to Jerome,* edited by P. R. Ackroyd and C. F. Evans. 48–66. Cambridge: Cambridge University Press, 1970.

Rodgers, Margaret. "Luke 4:16-30—A Call for a Jubilee Year?" *RTR* 40 (1981) 72–82.

Rodin, Paul. *Primitive Man as Philosopher.* New York: Appleton, 1927.

Rohrbaugh, Richard L. "Legitimating Sonship: A Test of Honour: A Social Scientific Study of Luke 4:1-30." In *Modelling Early Christianity: Social-Scientific Studies of the New Testament in Its Context,* edited by Philip. F. Esler, 183–97. London: Routledge, 1991.

———. "The Preindustrial City in Luke-Acts: Urban Social Relations." In *The Social World of Luke-Acts: Models for Interpretation,* edited by Jerome H. Neyrey, 125–50. Peabody, MA: Hendrickson, 1991.

———. "The Social Location of the Markan Audience." *BTB* 23 (1993) 114–27.

———. "Psychological and Psychoanalytical Approaches to Interpreting the Bible in Social-Scientific Context." *BTB* 27 (1997) 112–16.

———. "Gossip in the New Testament." In *Social Scientific Models for Interpreting the Bible: Essays by The Context Group in Honor of Bruce J. Malina,* edited by John J. Pilch, 239–59. Leiden: Brill, 2000.

Roll, Eric. *A History of Economic Thought.* 4th ed. London: Faber, 1973.

Rosenfeld, Lawrence B., and Jean M. Civikly. *With Words Unspoken: The Nonverbal Experience.* New York: Holt, Rinehart & Winston, 1976.

Rosnow, Ralph, and Gary A. Fine. *Rumor and Gossip: The Social Psychology of Hearsay.* New York: Elsevier, 1976.

Rostovtzeff, Michael I. *Social and Economic History of the Roman Empire.* 2d ed. Revised by P. M. Fraser. 2 vols. Oxford: Clarendon, 1957.

Rush, Ormond "Reception Hermeneutics and the 'Development' of Doctrine." *Pacifica* 6 (1993) 125–40.

Rysman, Alexander. "How the 'Gossip' Became a Woman." *JC* 27 (1977) 176–80.

Sabourin, Leopold. "About Jesus' Self-Understanding." *RSB* 3 (1983) 129–34.

Sack, R. David, *Human Territoriality: Its Theory and History.* Cambridge Studies in Historical Geography 7. Cambridge: Cambridge University Press, 1986.

Said, Ibrahim. *Sharh Bisharat Luqa.* Beirut: Near East Council of Churches, 1970.

Saldarini, Anthony J. "The Social Class of the Pharisees in Mark." In *The Social World of Formative Christianity and Judaism: Essays in Tribute to Howard Clark Kee*, edited by Jacob Neusner et al., 69–77. Philadelphia: Fortress, 1988.

Salom, A. P. "Was Zacchaeus Really Reforming?" *ExpTim* 78 (1965) 87.

Sanders, H. A. "The Genealogies of Jesus." *JBL* 32 (1913) 184–93.

Sanders, Jack T. "Tradition and Redaction in Luke 15:11-32." *NTS* 15 (1969) 433–38.

Sanford, John A. *Mystical Christianity: A Psychological Commentary on the Gospel of John*. New York: Crossroad, 1993.

Saville-Troika, Muriel. *The Ethnography of Communication: An Introduction*. Language in Society 3. Oxford: Blackwell, 1982.

Schiller, Herbert I. *Communication and Cultural Domination*. White Plains, NY: M. E. Sharpe, 1976.

Schneiders, Sandra M. "Born Anew." *ThTo* 44 (1987) 189–96.

Schoenborn, Ulrich. "'Im Wechsel der Worte das Wort' Oder: Dialog und Offenbarung in Johannes 3." In *Bezwingende Vorsprung des Gute: Exegetische und theologische Werkstattberichte F. S. Wolfgang Harnisch*, edited by Ulrich Schoenborn, et al., 108–25. Münster: Lit, 1994.

Schottroff, Luise. "Das Gleichnis vom verlorenen Sohn." *ZTK* 68 (1971) 27–52.

Schottroff, Luise, and Wolfgang Stegemann. *Jesus and the Hope of the Poor*. Translated by Matthew J. O'Connell. Maryknoll, NY: Orbis, 1986.

Schweizer, Eduard. *The Good News according to Mark*. Translated by Donald H. Madvig. Richmond, VA: John Knox, 1970.

Scott, Bernard Brandon. *Hear Then the Parable: A Commentary on the Parables of Jesus*. Minneapolis: Fortress, 1989.

Seethaler, Paula-Angelika. "Eine Kleine Bermerkung zu den Stannbäumen Jesu nach Matthäus und Lukas." *BZ* 16 (1972) 256–57.

Segbroeck, Frans van, et al., editors. *The Four Gospels 1992: Festschrift Frans Neirynck*, 3 vols. BETL 100. Leuven: Leuven University Press, 1992.

Sellew, Philip. "Interior Monologue as a Narrative Device in the Parables of Luke." *JBL* 111 (1992) 239–53.

Shweder, Richard A., and Edmund J. Bourne. "Does the Concept of Person Vary Cross-Culturally?" In *Cultural Conceptions of Mental Health and Therapy*, edited by Anthony J. Marsella and Geoffrey M. White, 97–137. Culture, Illness, and Healing 4. Boston: Reidel, 1982.

Sjoberg, Gideon. *The Preindustrial City, Past and Present*. Glencoe, Ill.: Free, 1960.

Smith, M. G. "Complexity, Size and Urbanization." In *Man, Settlement and Urbanism*, edited by Peter J. Ucko et al., 567–74. London: Duckworth, 1972.

Snodgrass, Klyne R. "That Which is Born of *Pneuma* is *Pneuma*: Rebirth and Spirit in John 3:5-6." *CQ* 49 (1991) 13–29.

Snyder, Gradon F. "The Social Context of the Ironic Dialogues in the Gospel of John." In *Putting Body & Soul Together: Essays in Honor of Robin Scroggs*, edited by Virginia Wiles and Alexandra Brown, 3–23. Valley Forge, PA: Trinity, 1997.

Stark, Rodney. "Antioch as the Social Situation for Matthew's Gospel." In *Social History of the Matthean Community: Cross-Disciplinary Approaches to an Open Question*, edited by David L. Balch, 189–210. Minneapolis: Fortress, 1991.

Ste. Croix, G. E. M. de. *The Class Struggle in the Ancient Greek World: From the Archaic Age to the Arab Conquests*. Ithaca, NY: Cornell University Press, 1981.

Stegemann, Ekkehard, and Wolfgang Stegemann. *The Jesus Movement: A Social History of Its First Century*. Translated by O. C. Dean Jr. Minneapolis: Fortress, 1999.

Stegemann, Wolfgang, et al., editors. *The Social Setting of Jesus and the Gospels*. Minneapolis: Fortress, 2002.

Stegner, William R. "The Temptation Narrative: A Study in the Use of Scripture by Early Jewish Christians." *BR* 35 (1990) 5–17.

Stephan, Cookie White, and Walter G. Stephan. "Cognition and Affect in Cross-Cultural Relations." In *Cross-Cultural and Intercultural Communication*, edited by William B. Gudykunst, 73–90. 2003. Thousand Oaks, CA: Sage, 2003.

Stewart, Edward C., and Milton J. Bennett. *American Cultural Patterns: A Cross-Cultural Perspective*. Rev. ed. Yarmouth, ME: Intercultural, 1991.

Stibbe, Mark W. G. *John*. Readings: A New Biblical Commentary. Sheffield: JSOT Press 1993.

Stillwell, Richard, editor. *The Princeton Encyclopedia of Classical Sites*. Princeton: Princeton University Press, 1976.

Stine, Philip C. "Sociolinguistics and Bible Translation." In *Issues in Bible Translation*, edited by Philip C. Stine, 146–72. United Bible Societies Monograph Series 3. New York: United Bible Societies, 1988.

Strack, Hermann L., and Paul Billerbeck. *Kommentar zum Neuen Testament aus Talmud und Midrasch*. Vol. 2. Munich: Beck, 1956.

Suls, Jerry M. "Gossip as Social Comparison." *JC* 27 (1977) 164–68.

Swanston, Hamish. "The Lucan Temptation Narrative." *JTS* 17 (1966) 71.

Talbert, Charles H. *Reading Luke: A Literary and Theological Commentary on the Third Gospel*. New York: Crossroad, 1982.

Tannehill, Robert L. *The Narrative Unity of Luke-Acts: A Literary Interpretation*. Foundations and Facets. Philadelphia: Fortress, 1986.

———. "The Story of Zacchaeus as Rhetoric: Luke 19:1–10." *Semeia* 64 (1994) 201–12.

Taussig, Michael T. *The Devil and Commodity Fetishism in South America*. Chapel Hill: University of North Carolina Press, 1980.

Taylor, A. B. "Decision in the Desert: The Temptation of Jesus in the Light of Deuteronomy." *Int* 14 (1960) 300–309.

Theissen, Gerd. "Lokal - und Sozialkolorit in der Geschichte von der syrophönikischen Frau (Mk 7:24–30)." *ZNW* 75 (1984) 202–25.

———. *Psychological Aspects of Pauline Theology*. Philadelphia: Fortress, 1987.

———. *The Gospels in Context: Social and Political History in the Synoptic Tradition*. Translated by Linda M. Maloney. Minneapolis: Fortress, 1991.

———. "Gruppenmessianismus: Überlegungen zum Ursprung der Kirche im Jüngerkreis Jesu." *JBT* 7 (1992) 101–23.

———, and Annette Merz. *The Historical Jesus: A Comprehensive Guide*. Translated by John Bowden. Minneapolis: Fortress, 1998.

Tcherikover, Victor. *Hellenistic Civilization and the Jews*. New York: Atheneum, 1970.

Thieme, Karl. "Augustinus und der 'Ältere Bruder': Zur patristischen Auslegung von Lk 15:25–32" In *Universitas; Dienst an Wahrheit: Albert Stohr*, 2 vols., edited by Ludwig Lenhart, 1:79–85. Mainz: Matthais-Gruenewald, 1960.

Throckmorton, Burton H. Jr. "Genealogy (Christ)." In *IBD* 2:365–66.

Tiede, David L. "Proclaiming the Righteous Reign of Jesus: Luke 4 and the Justice of God." *WW* 7 (1987) 83– 90.

Ting-Toomey, Stella. *Communicating Across Cultures*. New York: Guilford, 1999.

Todd, Emmanuel. *The Explanation of Ideology: Family Structures and Social Systems*. Translated by David Garrioch. Family, Sexuality, and Social Relations in Past Times. Oxford: Blackwell, 1985.

Tolbert, Mary Ann. *Perspectives on the Parables: An Approach to Multiple Interpretations.* Philadelphia: Fortress, 1979.

Triandis, Harry C. "Cross-Cultural Studies in Individualism and Collectivism." In *Cross-Cultural Perspectives*, edited by John J. Berman, 41–133. Nebraska Symposium on Motivation 37. Lincoln: University of Nebraska Press, 1989.

———. *Individualism and Collectivism.* San Francisco: Westview, 1995.

———, et al. "An Etic-Emic Analysis of Individualism and Collectivism." *JCCP* 24 (1992) 366–83.

Trible, Phyllis. *Texts of Terror.* OBT. Philadelphia: Fortress, 1984.

Trigger, Bruce. "Determinants of Urban Growth in Preindusrial Societies." In *Man, Settlement and Urbanism*, edited by Peter J. Ucko, et al., 575–99. London: Duckworth, 1972.

Ucko, Peter J., et al., editors. *Man, Settlement, and Urbanism.* London: Duckworth, 1972.

Urban, Greg. Review of *Language as Social Semiotic: The Social Interpretation of Language and Meaning*, by M. A. K. Halliday. *AmAnth* 83 (1971) 659–61.

Via, Dan O. *The Parables: Their Literary and Existential Dimension.* Philadelphia: Fortress, 1967.

Wallace-Hadrill, Andrew, editor. *Patronage in Ancient Society.* Leicester-Nottingham Studies in Ancient Societies 1. London: Routledge, 1989.

Watson, N. M. "Was Zacchaeus Really Reforming?" *ExpTim* 77 (1966) 282–85.

Weber, Max. *General Economic History.* Translated by Frank H. Knight. Adelphi Economic Series. New York: Greenberg, 1927.

Weinart, Francis D. "The Parable of the Throne-Claimant (Luke 19: 12, 14-15a, 27) Reconsidered." *CBQ* 39 (1977) 505–15.

Wheatley, Paul. "The Concept of Urbanism." In *Man, Settlement and Urbanism*, edited by Peter J. Ucko et al., 601–37. London: Duckworth, 1972.

White, L. Michael. "Crisis Management and Boundary Maintenance: The Social Location of the Matthean Community." In *Social History of the Matthean Community: Cross-Cultural Approaches to an Open Question*, edited by David L. Balch, 211–47. Minneapolis: Fortress, 1991.

White, R. C. "A Good Word for Zacchaeus? Exegetical Comment on Luke 19:1-10." *LTQ* 14 (1979) 89–96.

Whorf, Benjamin L. *Language, Thought and Reality.* New York: Riley, 1956.

Wikan, Unni. "Shame and Honour: A Contestable Pair." *Man* 19 (1990) 635–52.

Williamson, Lamar Jr. *Mark.* Interpretation. Atlanta: John Knox, 1983.

Williford, Don. "*gennêthênai anôthen*: A Radical Departure, A New Beginning." *RevExp* 96 (1999) 451–61.

Wilson, Peter J. "Filcher of Good Names." *Man* 9 (1974) 93–102.

Wilson, Robert R. "The Old Testament Genealogies in Recent Research." *JBL* 94 (1975) 168–89.

Wirth, Louis. "The Urban Society and Civilization." *AJS* 45 (1940) 743–55.

———. "Urbanism as a Way of Life." In *Urban Place and Process: Readings in the Anthropology of Cities*, edited by Irwin Press and M. Estellie Smith, 30–48. New York: Macmillan, 1980.

Wiseman, Richard L., editor. *Intercultural Communication Theory.* Thousand Oaks, CA: Sage, 1995.

Witherington, Ben III. "The Waters Of Birth: John 3:5 and I John 5:6-8." *NTS* 35 (1989) 155–60.

———. *The Christology of Jesus.* Minneapolis: Fortress, 1990.

———. "Jesus the Savior of the Least, the Last, and the Lost." *QR* 15 (1995) 195–211.

————. *John's Wisdom: A Commentary on the Fourth Gospel.* Louisville: Westminster John Knox, 1995.

Wright, Addison G. "The Widow's Mite: Praise or Lament? A Matter of Context." *CBQ* 44 (1982) 256–65.

Wright, N. T. "How Jesus Saw Himself." *BRev* 12 (1996) 22–29.

Yamauchi, Edwin M. *The Archaeology of New Testament Cities in Western Asia Minor.* Baker Studies in Biblical Archaeology. Grand Rapids: Baker, 1980.

Yavetz, Zvi. "Reflections on Titus and Josephus." *GRBS* 16 (1975) 431–32.

Yerkovich, Sally. "Gossiping as a Way of Speaking." *JC* 27 (1977) 192–97.

Zahn, T. *Die Evangelium des Lukas.* Kommentar zum Neuen Testament 3. Leipzing: Deichert, 1913.

Zerwick, Max. "Die Parabel vom Thronwärter." *Bib* 40 (1959) 654–74.

Zias, Joseph. "Death and Disease in Ancient Israel." *BA* 54 (1991) 146–59.

Zinovieff, Sofka. "Inside Out and Outside In: Gossip, Hospitality and the Greek Character." *JMS* 1 (1991) 120–34.